Reimagining Nabokov

Reimagining Nabokov

PEDAGOGIES FOR THE 21ST CENTURY

Eds. Sara Karpukhin
and José Vergara

Amherst College Press

Copyright © 2022 by José Vergara and Sara Karpukhin
Some rights reserved

This work is licensed under the Creative Commons Attribution-NonCommercial 4.0 International License. To view a copy of this license, visit http://creativecommons.org/licenses/by-nc/4.0/ or send a letter to Creative Commons, PO Box 1866, Mountain View, CA 94042, USA.

The complete manuscript of this work was subjected to a fully closed ("double-blind") review process. For more information, visit https://acpress.amherst.edu/peerreview/.

Published in the United States of America by
Amherst College Press

Library of Congress Control Number: 2022947526
DOI: http://doi.org/10.3998/mpub.12734178

ISBN 978-1-943208-50-0 (paper)
ISBN 978-1-943208-51-7 (OA)

To our teachers, Gennady Barabtarlo (1949–2019) and Alexander Dolinin, and to our students

Contents

Acknowledgments ix
Note on Transliteration and Translations xi
Foreword by Galya Diment xiii

Sara Karpukhin, Introduction 1

I. DIGITAL COLLABORATIONS
1 Teaching Nabokov in 3D by Yuri Leving 17
2 Good Readers, Good Writers: Collaborative Student Annotations for *Invitation to a Beheading* by José Vergara 39

II. MIXING CULTURES
3 Teaching *Poshlost'*: Texts and Contexts by Matthew Walker 55
4 Teaching Nabokov in a Virtual Time of Trouble by Tim Harte 75
5 Nabokov's Haunted Screen: The Exilic Uncanny in Weimar Film by Luke Parker 85

III. DISABILITY STUDIES AND QUEERINGS
6 Reading Disability in "A Guide to Berlin" by Roman Utkin 97
7 Nabokov, Creative Discussion, and Reparative Knowledge by Sara Karpukhin 109
8 Paranoid Reading, Reparative Reading, and Queering *The Real Life of Sebastian Knight* by Meghan Vicks 127

IV. PARATEXTS AND ARCHIVES

9 Patterns and Paratexts: Teaching Nabokov's Autobiography
by Robyn Jensen 149

10 Vulnerability, Discipline, Perseverance, Mercy:
On Teaching Nabokov's Short Stories by Olga Voronina 163

11 *The Original of Laura* and the Archival Nabokov
by Lisa Ryoko Wakamiya 179

Bibliography 189
Contributors 205

Acknowledgments

By its very nature, the process of piecing this volume together has led us to reflect on our own educations. First and foremost, we would like to thank Gennady Barabtarlo and Alexander Dolinin, whose tremendous impact on Nabokov studies cannot be overstated, much as their influence on our scholarship has been profound. We thank, too, David Bethea and Julian Connolly, whose presence and conversation guided and stimulated us early in our teaching and research. Together with Eric Naiman, they all prompted us to keep thinking about Nabokov the man and the author as well as about Nabokov's place in the history of Russian and American letters, his role(s) in the history of Slavic studies in the United States and in contemporary pedagogy.

We are immensely grateful to all the contributors to this volume: Yuri Leving, Matthew Walker, Tim Harte, Luke Parker, Roman Utkin, Meghan Vicks, Robyn Jensen, Olga Voronina, and Lisa Ryoko Wakamiya. We hope that readers will find just as much inspiration in their ideas and innovations as we have. A special note of gratitude goes to Galya Diment, who has championed this project from the start and who provided a rich, insightful foreword that looks at the past as much as into the future.

More broadly, we acknowledge our welcome debt to the varied, immense, and ever-growing global community of Nabokovians, inside and outside of academic institutions. In this community, we came across fellow readers whose passion for the writer's games of discovery stretched into a willingness to look beyond all prescribed or expected meanings. Importantly for our vision for this volume, this community taught us that Nabokov's readers can liberate themselves.

This entire project would not have been possible without one particular subset of that worldwide community, namely, the students in our Nabokov-related courses, especially the students in Sara Karpukhin's pilot course at the University of Notre Dame in 2016. Lesson plans rarely go exactly according to plan, and we're so appreciative to have seen what else might be reimagined in our teaching thanks to our students' enthusiasm, energy, and engagement with Nabokov's work.

Teaching, despite what might seem to be happening in the typical classroom, is rarely a solitary effort, and so we'd like to thank the many colleagues across several campuses who helped give shape to our thinking about teaching, both on Nabokov and in general, and provided other forms of support, whether technical or conceptual: Alison Cook-Sather, William C. Donahue, Karen Evans-Romaine, Sibelan Forrester, Alyssa Gillespie, Megan Kennedy, Melissa Miller, Nicole Monnier, Kirill Ospovat, Andrew Reynolds, Joel Schlosser, Irina Shevelenko, Roberto Vargas, and Mark Wallace. Lynn Glueck and John Zola of the Discussion Project at the School of Education at the University of Wisconsin-Madison helped redefine the pedagogical thinking of one of the editors in the summer of 2021, and Lynn then offered invaluable hands-on support as a mentor, interlocutor, and friend during the teaching of a Nabokov course in the fall semester of 2021.

It has been a true pleasure to work with Hannah Brooks-Motl at Amherst College Press, and we thank her for her support, vision, editorial acumen, and attention to detail. Thanks also go to Beth Bouloukus and the rest of the ACP production team. Our anonymous peer reviewers provided immensely helpful feedback that helped shape *Reimagining Nabokov* in generative ways.

As always, José Vergara is forever grateful to Jenny, Lucia, and Paz.

Note on Transliteration and Translations

A slightly modified Library of Congress (LC) transliteration system is used throughout the present book. For the sake of readability, names ending in –*ii* (Dostoevskii) are rendered with –*y* (Dostoevsky) within the main body; in the bibliography and in clear references to the bibliography, such names retain the LC transliteration. The same applies to the use of a single *i* (Lidia) in some female names rather than *ii* (Lidiia). One notable exception is the absence of straight apostrophes as soft sign markers (Gogol as opposed to Gogol'). Names of well-known figures appear in their familiar English-language variants (Alexander and Tolstoy instead of Aleksandr and Tolstoi).

Foreword

Galya Diment

I would like to start this foreword about the importance of the volume in front of you with a short account of my own personal experience of annually teaching Nabokov to 50–60 undergraduates at the University of Washington. Until recently, the course always featured *Lolita*, but then I caught myself increasingly wanting to skip it and instead teach thematic courses—such as "Nabokov and the Academic Novel" or "Nabokov and the Art of Self-Translation"—which for the past two years I have indeed been doing. This is because I have been finding it more and more challenging, given my own unease with some aspects of the novel, to respond to my students' collective discomfort with *Lolita* (which, they admit, is brilliant) because Nabokov often makes them sympathize with a pedophile and a rapist. Their heightened concern is being expressed at a time when we, as a society, are finally discussing openly the horror of sexual abuse, which some of my students have experienced firsthand. Another recently published book, *Teaching Nabokov's* Lolita *in the #MeToo Era*, edited by Elena Rakhimova-Sommers,[1] directly addresses this thorny issue of teaching Nabokov's most famous novel, but in my experience students' discomfort with what they perceive as Nabokov's questionable judgment is actually not limited to *Lolita* but extends to many of his other works. And this is where this volume—which is devoted to how to teach *all* of Nabokov, not just *Lolita*, to students today—becomes immensely helpful in addressing this particular pedagogical challenge. It presents a remarkable balance between confronting the negatives and accentuating the positives.

Let's start with the negatives. Our students are significantly different from those of previous generations, including my own. My cohort of literary scholars was often educated by American professors who espoused New Criticism, where literary and artistic values were all that mattered while cultural, social, and historical contexts were often beside the point. As Jane Gallop noted in the early 1980s, when I was still in graduate school, New Criticism was "appreciative, even worshipful" of the literary text through close and meticulous readings.[2] Having come as a young person from the Soviet Union, where the ugly official doctrine of Socialist Realism prescribed the opposite, and where the subversively nonpolitical Russian Formalism—which in many ways had helped to shape New Criticism—was virtually banned, I had no trouble eagerly embracing my professors' approach. And since Nabokov himself maintained that "A work of art has no importance whatever to society…no social purpose, no moral message…no general ideas to exploit"[3] as well as demanded—in his own lectures to Cornell students—very close (re)reading of texts, he and New Criticism seemed to be a match made in literary heaven.

Most of my current students, however, do not accept that such a purely aesthetic stand is either realistic or desirable in an artist, a critic, or a teacher. They live in a much more socially, culturally, and ethnically diverse environment than Nabokov and his characters inhabited, an environment where perceived prejudices against certain groups and segments of the population are, overall, much less tolerated than before. And let us face it, Nabokov had not only his share of strong opinions, he also had his share of strong prejudices, among them what my students perceive as obvious sexism, discernable racism, and unmistakable homophobia.

My students are of course not alone in seeing Nabokov as not being exactly complimentary to women's intellectual abilities and moral character. There are, as we all know, admirable women in Nabokov's works but, more often than not, they are objects of the protagonist's past loves, thus living more in his memory than in real life. Or they are smart and capable but just enough to be good helpmates (and typists) for extraordinary men, not unlike Nabokov's own wife, Véra. And even those "good women" are greatly outnumbered by rather despicable female creatures who are devious, disloyal and, often, plain evil. This regrettable tendency on Nabokov's part is more or less an accepted notion among literary critics and his fellow writers, so the question that faces them is usually not whether this prejudice exists but how to treat it. Some pull no punches. Thus Edna O'Brien, upon receiving the 2018 PEN Award for achievement in international literature—an award that is actually named after Nabokov—publicly regretted that "Mr Nabokov, genius that he was, was quite scathing of women."[4] Most Nabokov scholars, however, while avoiding directly praising his views on women or distorting them to make them sound better, tend instead to be very matter-of-fact about it, as Brian Boyd appears to be when he comments that Nabokov was "more comfortable with a woman as muse than a woman as writer."[5] The usual retort of many forgiving critics is that those were different times, and any attempt to blame authors for not having more progressive views than the majority of their contemporaries is a "woke" exercise in "cancel culture."[6]

And, yes, the times were different indeed. After the war, when Nabokov was teaching first at Wellesley, the women's college which he called, in a rather condescending manner, "Looks and Books,"[7] and then at Cornell, privileged young women who attended colleges were still assumed to be doing it mostly in order to net a suitable husband. Once they did supposedly accomplish this purpose, they were instructed to heed the advice of popular psychologists who warned female readers—based, supposedly, on "scientific surveys"—that "the women who earned enough to be financially independent of their husbands were not as happy as those more dependent on their husband's money" and that if a wife "does not expect her husband to be the head of the household," she is "likely a dominating person," which was, apparently, one of the worst things a woman could be.[8]

In *Lolita* Nabokov, through Humbert, made fun of such how-to manuals when it came to parental skills in handling daughters' boyfriends ("[S]top making the boys feel she's the daughter of an old ogre'"[9]), and yet, Nabokov, even in his late interviews, appeared to cling to at least some of the by then largely outdated notions of women's roles and abilities. "Bossy women strike him as irresistibly comic," one of his interviewers, Penelope Gilliatt, wrote in 1966.[10] The same year Nabokov declared to another interviewer, Alberto Ongaro, that he did "not believe the patriarchal structure of society has prevented women from developing in their own way...the reality is that women are biologically weaker than men."[11] A possible result of these beliefs is that Nabokov's exploration of women as multidimensional characters is indeed much weaker than that of men. As Rakhimova-Sommers accurately states in *Nabokov's Women: The Silent Sisterhood of Textual Nomads*, "The readers of the Nabokovian woman find themselves on a narratorial diet because entry into her emotional and physical 'I' is rarely granted and the nuances of her pain or pleasure are rarely discussed."[12]

But was he also a racist? This is a much more ambiguous territory. Upon arriving to the United States Nabokov was confronted by the most naked racism, which he, to his credit, immediately and vehemently rejected. In 1942, in a letter to Véra from South Carolina, where he was invited to give a lecture, Nabokov noted that the locals called their Black servants "darkies." It was, he told his Jewish wife, "an expression that jars me, reminding me distantly of the patriarchal 'Zhidok' [Yid] of western Russian landowners."[13] And yet he himself was not always above displaying more muted shades of this particular bias. In the 1950s and 1960s, as Nabokov was writing his three major American novels, *Lolita*, *Pnin*, and *Pale Fire*, he was inevitably thrust into heated and fluid cultural debates as to what the Black American population should call themselves. By that time the preferred term had become "colored," but Nabokov did not like it. He wanted them to be called "Negroes" instead. Why he felt this way is not totally clear, but we should probably pay attention to Kinbote, as unreliable as he may be, when, in *Pale Fire*, he tells us that Shade, "as a man of letters," objected to "colored" because it was "artistically misleading" and imprecise. It is also possible, of course, that to his ear "colored" did not sound that different from "darkies," since the term was likewise based on the pigment of one's skin. Consequently, in Nabokov's fiction, Black characters are, in fact, called "Negroes" much more often than "colored."[14] Kinbote further informs us that Shade did not appreciate that some Whites eagerly accepted the new term: "Many competent Negroes... considered it to be the only dignified word, emotionally neutral and ethically inoffensive: their endorsement obliged decent non-Negroes to follow their lead...the genteel adore endorsements."[15] While there is nothing wrong, of course, in Nabokov (and Shade) having his personal preferences, there is something quite condescending in claiming, as an outsider, that you know better what members of the Black community should call themselves.

Nabokov's 1942 comparison in a letter to Véra of the treatment of Black servants in the South and Jews in Russia comes to mind again with the question of just how far this parallel really went for him. We all know of course that by the time the Nabokovs arrived in the United States, the country had likewise witnessed fierce debates within American Jewish circles as to what they should call themselves—namely, "Jews," "Hebrews," or "Israelites." It was in many ways as thorny and vigorously debated an issue as that faced by the Black community. In one example from the early 1950s, as Nabokov was working on his early American novels, a prominent Jewish historian sternly warned his co-religionists in the pages of the *Jewish Quarterly Review* not to be flippant about the name change: "'What's in a name?' asked Juliet in Shakespeare's play. By this was meant that a name has no particular significance. This may apply to the name of an individual, but not to that of a nation....Such changes cannot be ascribed merely to chance or caprice. A nation must have a historical reason for changing its name."[16] Shade does have a preference in regard to Jews as well, but it is a rather minor one that involves using a noun rather than an adjective. Thus in the same annotation to Shade's poem in *Pale Fire*, Kinbote reveals that Shade prefers "is a Jew" to "is Jewish" and complains that "Left-Wingers" unjustifiably lump "two historical hells: diabolical persecution and the barbarous traditions of slavery,"[17] while Shade himself believes that the two are vastly different. For that reason alone, it is virtually impossible to imagine him, and through him Nabokov, insisting on—and using—"Israelites" or "Hebrews," which by then were deemed by many to be offensive to the population involved. It is also highly unlikely that either Shade or Nabokov would draw a distinction between "competent" Jews and the rest, thus implying that it was such a stand-alone group because most were not competent enough.

Nabokov, regretfully, also on occasion used directly racist language and images to describe Black characters, as when, in *Lolita*, Humbert Humbert refers to the old bellboy—who is first described as a "hunchbacked and hoary Negro in a uniform of sorts"—twice as "Uncle Tom" and once as "crayfish Tom."[18] We could of course choose to attribute this cultural insult solely to Humbert but that would probably be a bit too generous, even if convenient for reminding, and therefore assuring, one's shocked students that Humbert is, after all, an unreliable narrator.

And then there are his fictional homosexuals. As Lev Grossman points out in his 2000 *Salon* article about Sergey ("The Gay Nabokov"), "Nabokov was the archenemy of clich[é], a writer passionately committed to overturning tired literary conventions through careful observation of the real world, but his homosexual characters are as a rule egregiously stereotyped."[19] "Egregiously" is, unfortunately, not an exaggeration. While reading *Mary*, many of my students truly bristle at Nabokov's contemptuous depiction of giggling, cohabiting, and, therefore, obviously gay ballet dancers. Their disappointment becomes even more acute when they learn that Nabokov's own brother, who perished in a German concentration camp, as well as his two uncles, on maternal and paternal sides, were likewise homosexuals. Here, too, I am of course always keenly aware of how personal and painful such grotesquely stereotypical portrayal is to gay students in my class.

Some justify Nabokov's homophobia in *Mary* by how close he still was in 1926 to Uncle Ruka's (Vasily Rukavishnikov, his mother's brother) unwelcome caresses of his favorite nephew. But Nabokov's attitude toward homosexuality did not substantially change over the years. After all, *Mary* was one of the last two Russian novels to be translated into English (1970) and, as with his other Russian novels, Nabokov could have implemented some minor revisions to get rid of this overly clichéd representation of Kolin and Gornotsvetov. Nabokov, however, chose not to, even though by then he already knew the full circumstances of his brother's tragic fate as a gay man at the time of Nazi occupation.

While teaching at Cornell, Nabokov inevitably encountered gay faculty who were forced to hide their sexual preference, often not very convincingly. At the time they were easy subjects of humiliating caricaturization, which is precisely what Nabokov does with "prissy" Gaston Godin in *Lolita*. Professor Godin, who knows "all the small boys in our vicinity," is supposedly, like Humbert Humbert, a pedophile but because his amorous attention is directed toward adolescent boys rather than girls, he is immediately dismissed by his heterosexual counterpart as a ridiculous, one-dimensional, and insidious pervert.[20] Nabokov no doubt wanted us to appreciate a deep irony in this situation of one pedophile despising the other, and yet there is every indication that—to slightly paraphrase him—"there is a green lane in Paradise where Humbert is permitted to wander at dusk once a year; but Hell shall never parole" Godin.[21] Furthermore, reviving the crude stereotyping in *Mary*, but now applied to the other gender, Nabokov also makes Humbert poke fun at two female English professors, "tweedy and short-haired Miss Lester and fadedly feminine Miss Fabian,"[22] whose combined last names spell out "Les... bian" and who pretend to be just housemates.

And then there is, of course, Charles Kinbote in *Pale Fire*. As Stephen Bruhm wrote in "Queer, Queer Vladimir," "[T]he only thing more painful than the homophobia of *Pale Fire* is the license it has given critics to volley diatribes against the purported apposition between Kinbote's homosexuality and his madness, an apposition conveniently coalescing in the term 'narcissist'…so palpable and parodic."[23] As another critic, Jean Walton, observes in "Dissenting in an Age of Frenzied Heterosexualism: Kinbote's Transparent Closet in Nabokov's *Pale Fire*," back when Nabokov was writing his novel there, in most cases, was very little ambiguity as to what gay fictional characters stood for: "to read the presence of 'homosexuality' in a work of fiction as a figural or metaphorical index to something else is to engage, whether implicitly or explicitly, in avoidance tactics, and to collude with, rather than scrutinize, a prevailing heterocentric imperative."[24] Nabokov himself was undoubtedly aware that his contemporary readers would be hard pressed to see Kinbote as anything but his creator's disapproval of homosexuality. All this was of course happening at the time when the "Red Scare" was mightily competing with the "Lavender Scare," the belief that gays (here somewhat similarly to Jews as well) were not just perverted but disloyal while increasingly occupying too many positions of cultural and political power.[25]

This is, of course, not to suggest that we should "cancel" Nabokov. We also all know that among the writers of his generation, these biases are far from unique. Instead, the question pursued by many of us teaching Nabokov—and honestly engaged with by several articles in this volume, including by one of the editors—is how to present him to today's generation of students, who are much more attuned to the uncomfortable social issues his prose often poses.

There are other challenges in teaching Nabokov today that are not directly connected to his personal views. In my experience one of the issues that tends to alienate them in Nabokov is his "haughty" origins, of which, for my students' tastes, he was too proud and which they detect not just in his autobiographical writings but also in his fiction. Thus what they can easily forgive Tolstoy, they cannot always forgive Nabokov since he is a twentieth-century writer and students are predisposed to see him, unlike Tolstoy, as almost their contemporary. When I taught Nabokov side by side with Joseph Brodsky in the "The Art of Self Translation" course, the students kept telling me how much easier it was for them to relate to Brodsky's more humble beginnings than to Nabokov's nearly royal ones.

This is where accentuating the positive comes in: not just presenting him as deservedly one of the greatest twentieth-century writers—which previous Nabokov scholarship does so successfully—but also humanizing, updating, and retooling him for our students' particular sense and sensibility, as many articles in this volume do when discussing finding commonalities between what Nabokov talks about and depicts in his novels, short stories, and autobiographical writings and what our students are experiencing today. For even though Nabokov lectured his own students not to try to relate to characters or writers ("only children can be excused for identifying themselves with the characters in the book"),[26] we obviously cannot—and why should we?—instruct ours in a similarly stern manner not to do so. One of my most gratifying experiences in teaching Nabokov has been to see how many bilingual students in my Self-Translation class, most of them heritage speakers in a variety of languages, are thrilled to compare their experience to Nabokov's.

As to my teaching *Lolita* again, yes, I *am* going to teach the novel this academic year, now well armed with this volume as well as *Teaching Nabokov's* Lolita *in the #MeToo Era,* which preceded it. Both will be required readings for my course.

Notes

1 Elena Rakhimova-Sommers, ed., *Teaching Nabokov's* Lolita *in the #MeToo Era* (Lanham, MD: Lexington Books, 2021).
2 Jane Gallop, *Around 1981: Academic Feminist Literary Theory* (New York: Routledge, 1992), 7. My thanks to Eric Naiman for drawing my attention to this quote by using it in his article "Nabokov and #MeToo: Consent, Close Reading, and the Sexualized Workplace," in *Teaching Nabokov's* Lolita *in the #MeToo Era* (Lanham, MD: Lexington Books), 125–150.
3 Vladimir Nabokov, *Strong Opinions* (New York: Vintage, 1990), 33.
4 Martin Doyle, "Edna O'Brien: Lolita Author Nabokov Was 'Scathing of Women,'" *The Irish Times*, February 21, 2018. www.irishtimes.com/culture/books/edna-o-brien-lolita-author-nabokov-was-scathing-of-women-1.3399269. The prize, created in 2016 in partnership with the Vladimir Nabokov Literary Foundation, rewards "a living author whose body of work, either written in or translated into English, represents the highest level of achievement in fiction, nonfiction, poetry and/or drama, and is of enduring originality and consummate craftsmanship." See https://pen.org/pen-nabokov-award/.
5 Brian Boyd, *Vladimir Nabokov: The American Years* (Princeton, NJ: Princeton UP, 1991), 655.
6 See, for example, Eric Naiman's discussion of this attitude among some Nabokovians in "Nabokov and #MeToo," 140–141.
7 Vladimir Nabokov, *Think, Write, Speak: Uncollected Essays, Reviews, Interviews, and Letters to the Editor*, eds. Anastasia Tolstoy and Brian Boyd (New York: Knopf, 2019), 211.
8 Albert Edward Wiggam, *Let's Explore Your Mind* (New York: Pocket Books, 1946), 17, 38.
9 Vladimir Nabokov, *Lolita* (New York: Vintage, 1989), 185.
10 Penelope Gilliatt, "Vladimir Nabokov Interviewed by Penelope Gilliat," *Scraps from the Loft*, https://scrapsfromtheloft.com/2017/11/16/vladimir-nabokov-interviewed-by-penelope-gilliatt-1966/.

11 Nabokov, *Think, Write, Speak*, 346. When Ongaro pointed out that Nabokov had made Lolita stronger than Humbert Humbert, the writer replied: "She's stronger only because Humbert Humbert loves her. That's all." Ibid.
12 Elena Rakhimova-Sommers, *Nabokov's Women: The Silent Sisterhood of Textual Nomads* (Lanham, MD: Lexington Books, 2017), xv.
13 Vladimir Nabokov to Véra Nabokov, October 14, 1942. First published in English in "Russian Professor: The Author on Tour," *New Yorker*, June 13 and 20, 2011, 102–3. For other letters to Véra from the South, see Vladimir Nabokov, *Letters to Véra*, Brian Boyd and Olga Voronina, eds. (London: Penguin, 2014), 470–473.
14 See Galya Diment, "Masters and Servants: *Upstairs* and *Downstairs* in Nabokov," in Brian Boyd and Marijeta Bozovic, eds., *Nabokov Upside Down* (Evanston, IL: Northwestern UP, 2017), 131–142.
15 Vladimir Nabokov, *Pale Fire* (New York: Berkeley Books, 1982), 145–146.
16 Solomon Zeitlin, "The Names Hebrew, Jew, and Israel: A Historical Study," *Jewish Quarterly Review* 43, no. 4 (1953): 365.
17 Nabokov, *Pale Fire*, 217.
18 Nabokov, *Lolita*, 117, 118, 119, 122.
19 Lev Grossman, "The Gay Nabokov," *Salon*, May 17, 2000, www.salon.com/2000/05/17/nabokov_5/.
20 Nabokov, *Lolita*, 215, 181.
21 Vladimir Nabokov, *Despair* (New York: Vintage, 1989), xiii.
22 Nabokov, *Lolita*, 179.
23 Stephen Bruhm, "Queer, Queer, Vladimir," in *American Imago: Psychoanalysis and Culture* 53 (1996): 282.
24 Jean Walton, "Dissenting in an Age of Frenzied Heterosexualism: Kinbote's Transparent Closet in Nabokov's Pale Fire," *College Literature* 21, no. 2 (1994): 90.
25 See David K. Johnson, *The Cold War Persecution of Gays and Lesbians in the Federal Government* (Chicago: U of Chicago P, 2004).
26 Vladimir Nabokov, *Lectures on Literature*, ed. Fredson Bowers (San Diego: Harcourt, 1980), 150.

INTRODUCTION

Sara Karpukhin

Spring 2018 marked a momentous change in the academic reception of Vladimir Nabokov. Responding directly to the concerns raised in her undergraduate seminar after #MeToo had gone global in the fall of 2017, Anne Dwyer, a professor of Russian at Pomona College, published a short piece in *Inside Higher Ed* where she defended her decision to teach *Lolita*.[1] After the publication, a heated discussion broke out on the listserv for Nabokov enthusiasts, NABOKV-L, during which many college instructors admitted that, in the last ten years or so, *Lolita* had indeed become "difficult" to teach. Those with more experience in the classroom seemed to be the most up in arms about the reasons why this might be the case. The novel was controversial in itself, they felt, but there was also something about the zeitgeist that made it particularly problematic. One subscriber went so far as to write about "younger instructors raised on second-hand Foucault and Lacan" and "a new generation of 'woke' students who seemed alert to anything they might find offensive in literary texts."[2]

What spurred our interest in these conversations and eventually inspired this volume was the fact that *Lolita*'s current problematic pedagogical status was interpreted in terms of generational and political differences. The provocative tone (and the mention of French philosophers, the usual suspects of English-speaking academia) aside, the observations rang true, and rather than dismissing the sentiment behind this new wave of critique of *Lolita* as misguided, we wanted to look closer: after all, it was about us and our students.

Historically, Nabokov scholarship has developed under the influence of such interpretive traditions as Russian Formalism, European Structuralism, and Anglo-American New Criticism. In their various ways, they all treat literature as a realm of autonomous, self-sufficient meanings, to be elucidated through close reading. They also take literature's authority for granted: The question of whether a text is of value under given historical circumstances is always assumed to have a positive answer. These approaches seemed congenial for an author who experienced firsthand destructive political forces in Bolshevik Russia and Nazi Germany. For two formative decades in the beginning of his career, Nabokov wrote for a dwindling readership of Russian-speaking emigrants, outside the social structures of metropolitan Russia, on the margins of the societies where he lived. As an émigré, he experienced the lasting trauma of a historical defeat in Russian and Western European cultural contexts, both of which threatened to kill the defeated and to expunge them from the historical record. Under the circumstances, art, although responsive to the challenges of the day, *had* to provide the author with autonomous control and be a refuge from history and politics.

Upon his arrival in the United States, in his university lectures in the 1940s and '50s, Nabokov called the great novels he was teaching "fairy tales" to emphasize a "radical...degree of severance between reality and art,"[3] because, in his experience, the "average 'reality' perceived by the communal eye"[4] was inimical to art in so far as it was inimical to the individual artist. At the same time, it was the writer's anti-Communist (rather than antifascist or more generally anti-authoritarian) convictions that were destined to define his situation in postwar, Cold War America. Nabokov's European anti-Bolshevik liberal stance gradually merged with the American anti-Left conservative position[5] to the point that in 1957, in the wake of McCarthyist attacks on colleges, the author befriended an FBI agent assigned to Cornell and declared that he would be proud to have his son join the bureau in that role.[6] In 1965, in the second year of the American involvement in the Vietnam War and after *Lolita* had transformed him into a world-famous public figure, Nabokov sent a telegram to President Lyndon Johnson when the latter was undergoing a surgery wishing him a "speedy return to the admirable work you are accomplishing."[7]

Politics and prejudice were as inextricably linked in mid-twentieth-century America as they are now. But today's circumstances differ from those of Nabokov's time, and the difference allows us to speak instructively of Nabokov's attitudes, as understood by himself and the subsequent critical tradition. To take a salient example, after safely escaping with his Jewish Russian wife and son from Nazi-occupied Europe to the United States, Nabokov, an unwaveringly staunch opponent of anti-Semitism, whether casual or systemic, had to situate himself with regard to specifically American anti-Semitism.[8] While in personal, real-life encounters he did not shy away from showing anger at the slightest suspicion of prejudice, his great American fictions, *Lolita*, *Pnin*, and *Pale Fire*, all written and published between 1947 and 1962, presented a more complicated picture. In *Pnin*, the murder of Mira Belochkin and the shattering tragedy of the Holocaust, even though not witnessed personally, haunts the eponymous hero and leads him to an unforgiving rejection of Germany and German culture. But when a faculty member of an American liberal arts college where Pnin teaches tells an anti-Semitic joke, and a Jewish couple disinvite themselves from Pnin's housewarming party after learning that that faculty member will be present, the joke remains unreported by the narrator, and Pnin refrains from confronting the American anti-Semite directly.[9] In *Lolita*, John Farlow is about to make an anti-Semitic remark only to be stopped at the last minute by his wife, and the menace of American anti-Semitism, although ubiquitous, is unspoken by the villainous narrator, an undercurrent that never quite reaches the surface.[10] In fact, in both cases, it takes a trained commentator—or a trauma-versed reader—to notice what the silence is about and understand its full implications.

From today's vantage point, a similar evasiveness can be discerned in what Nabokov's great American novels had to say about the civil rights movement. While in private letters to his wife Nabokov described the injustices of segregation that he witnessed firsthand on his lecture tour in the South in the 1940s,[11] in *Pale Fire* (1962) the American poet John Shade memorably refuses to "lump together" anti-Semitism and racism, as "Left-Wingers" do.[12] Furthermore, while Shade acknowledges that African Americans prefer the word "colored" in reference to their community, he resists following their example because "poets do not like to be led."[13] *Pale Fire* was published on the eve of the Civil Rights Act of 1964, but the question of divisions and solidarity in the face of prejudice had been at the center of debates in Jewish and Black communities in the United States for a long time. In 1948, shortly before the formation of the State of Israel in May and before he left the United States for Paris in October, the Black author and critic James Baldwin published the famous essay "The Harlem Ghetto" in the February issue of the leading Jewish American periodical *Commentary*. In the essay, Baldwin argued that African Americans identified "almost wholly" with Jewish Americans due to their shared experience of hardship and exclusion, but at the same time "the American white Gentile has two legends serving him at once: he has divided these minorities and he rules....It seems unlikely that within this complicated structure any real and systematic cooperation can be achieved between Negroes and Jews....The structure of the American commonwealth has trapped both these minorities into attitudes of perpetual hostility....But just as a society must have a scapegoat, so hatred must have a symbol. Georgia has the Negro and Harlem has the Jew."[14]

Although Baldwin no longer considered himself a socialist at the time, the description of Black anti-Semitism as a self-perpetuating cycle of mutual mistrust may have given Shade the idea that racial sub-groups couldn't break out of it except by Leftist, and therefore wrong, means.[15] Perhaps more relevant, Shade's (and Nabokov's) position seems to run parallel with the editorial tone of *Commentary* itself, which in the course of 1950s and '60s, in response to the Cold War and the growing acceptance of the State of Israel by the American establishment, had shifted from its left-leaning origins toward embattled right conservatism.[16] The possible artistic or performative nature of Shade's statements in *Pale Fire* notwithstanding, with all the evidence considered, it appears that Nabokov's "apolitical," noncommittal, individualist art gravitated toward an anti-liberation conservative camp in the increasingly galvanized United States of the '60s, leaving subsequent generations of readers to unravel those complicated historical circumstances.[17] It is our hope that the essays gathered here will be invitations to take up this important and pressing work, particularly in relation to Nabokov and race.

The highest degree of political, sometimes radical activity at universities in the West came at a time when Nabokov had already retired as a tenured college professor—the first teach-ins during the Vietnam War, the student protests of 1968 in Europe from Paris to Prague, and the student strikes of 1970, the largest in American history. The following decades saw the political and intellectual advances of the civil rights movement, second- and third-wave feminisms, gay and trans rights activism, and AIDS activism as well as the establishment of the so-called New Left in academia. The theoretical and practical outputs of these movements became what is known today under the umbrella term of identity politics (confusingly, I think, because in each case it was not so much about identity as it was about liberation), whereas the anti-authoritarian radicalism of the Sixties New Left manifested itself, especially in Europe, in student occupations of universities and in the idea of counter-universities, or critical universities with alternative syllabi.[18]

This is one of the reasons why the current generation of college students, the most diverse in modern history, brings a heightened awareness of political issues to the classroom.[19] Their preoccupation with justice and equality is the heritage they have received from Martin Luther King Jr., Toni Morrison, Howard Zinn, Mark Fisher, bell hooks, and yes, Michel Foucault, to name a few. But their political commitments can also be attributed to advances in technology. The online stereotypes of the "social justice warrior" and the "snowflake" reduce this generation's ideas of justice to misplaced youthful enthusiasm, thin-skinned naïveté, and groundless protest stemming from a childlike obsession with social media trends, in much the same way as the word "woke" was ironized in the NABOKV-L post above, but the role of technology is no laughing matter.[20] Starting from the global financial crisis of 2008 and the miraculous year of 2011, when the "Arab Spring" unfolded at the same time as anti-austerity protests in Europe and Occupy Wall Street in the United States, young activists using social media have been a unique catalyst in political uprisings and organizing.[21] It was indeed in the last twenty years that technology has changed dramatically our notions of individual and communal, private and public, accessibility and reach. Even though the necessity to teach "digital natives" no longer causes a moral panic among educators the way it did in the 2000s and 2010s, few members of our profession today can afford to deny that technology is changing the way we all acquire and share knowledge. Today's classroom is a locus of a unique confluence of mutually amplifying politics and technology, a place for reimagining self and community on an unprecedented scale—with the virulence of the debates serving as an indicator of just how unprecedented. As a result, with some exceptions, students in literature courses today want to ask questions about race, gender, solidarity, power, resistance, and consciousness-raising, and teachers in these courses can't eschew such questions without running the risk of seeming insensitive or, worse, irrelevant.

It is a notoriously perilous task to generalize about a zeitgeist or a generation. Our subject would have probably been the first to raise an eyebrow at the "narrowness" of our historical vision. But among the moving forces behind this collection has been not only a desire for interpretive breadth and inclusivity but also a willingness to take epistemological risks. "Today," from this point of view, is a useful and necessary counterweight to the avowed timelessness of

Nabokov's art. And ultimately, for us, contemporaneity and timelessness are not a binary, and neither is meant to cancel out the other. In this volume, we have striven to create a historically continuous space where we can divide our attention between close reading and an awareness of different stakes for different readers.[22] Whether we admit that our choices are politically motivated or not, what starts political may end philosophical, and both a quest for justice and a bid for relevance may lead to broadened perception. We are mindful that what is dismissed as suspect radical politics and generation-specific ideology may be in fact epistemologies that allow Nabokov's previously least visible experiences in Russia, Europe, and the United States to be conceptually integrated into his image and his legacy without being repressed as humiliating or unseemly. It is a sort of epistemological joy that today's readers can see as historically contingent the watershed between the traumatized Nabokov and the successful Nabokov, can say that Nabokov's self-normativization in America came at a price. These attitudes then allow us to point out the silences of Nabokov's writing, from a place of responsibility and care, as teachable moments. In this sense, if the revisionism of today's perspective is a symptom of anything, it is as much a symptom of the energy and imagination of the young fighting for freedom (or a capitalist appropriation of this energy and imagination) as it is a symptom of the mature effort of a multigenerational system of cultural production and critique reaching for fuller and better self-knowledge. While the reader doesn't *have* to identify with the political and epistemological stances embodied in Nabokov's texts of any period, Nabokov's seemingly unwitting part in the day's "culture wars" is worthy of serious attention, and the culture's anti-authoritarian revisionist momentum can offer opportunities to have crucial conversations and to ask questions otherwise left unasked.

How does "an emphatically Eurocentric male writer of aristocratic background and demanding high cultural standards," as Nabokov's biographer Brian Boyd described him in a 2008 paper on *Lolita*, fare in the age of social media that gave rise to #MeToo and Black Lives Matter?[23] Is there anything edifying in the way that the sense of reality engendered by the Internet and its obsession with self-fashioning agrees or disagrees with what Martin Amis referred to as Nabokov's "Parnassian triumphalism" or Nabokov's insistence on the primacy of the creative imagination?[24] How does Nabokov's experience of exile resonate with international students in our classes? How does Nabokov's background strike first-generation college students? Was there anything queer about Nabokov's fervent attachment to Proust and postcolonial in his equally fervent attachment to Joyce? And are the contemporary charges against *Lolita* a "new form of a prissy bourgeois idealism," as another NABOKV-L contributor phrased it, or a legitimate page in the history of the book's reception?

In the unmediated and spontaneous setting of the classroom, questions such as these are as revolutionary as you want them to be. In the conversational context of a lecture, discussion, or seminar, where interpretation is up for grabs and the stakes are relatively low, established modes of reading can and should be tested against an influx of fresh ideas and a variety of lived experience. Pedagogy turns out to be an exceptionally powerful heuristic tool, with a special role to play in this constant renegotiation of values, where classroom dialogues are a source of new relevance for old texts, a testing site for ideas.

The essays in this collection, all of them from teachers of Nabokov, may not be radical in the same sense, but they are all informed by similar sensibilities. While they focus on Nabokov's high artistic achievement, they reflect the culture's anti-authoritarian impulse and embrace emergent methods of building relationships and communities, of gathering and sharing information. The creative uses of technology, translation, and new interpretive models as well as archival and editorial work all point toward the pedagogical ideal of shared agency and making students active stakeholders in the knowledge dispensed in the classroom. This ideal inspired the structure of the volume as well. The name of each section indicates what we think is a principal (but not the only) means by which the authors of the essays grouped in it set out toward this ideal: Digital Collaborations, Mixing Cultures, Disability Studies and Queerings, and Paratexts and Archives. The two opening chapters on the digital Nabokov complement the later queering reparative chapters in that both sets pay attention to textual "surface" and hyperlinked extratextual "depth." The breaking down of language and cultural barriers in Mixing Cultures reflects the foregrounding of previously underrepresented interpretive traditions in Disability Studies and Queerings. At the same time, the opening section on the virtual Nabokov is productively asymmetrical to the concluding chapters that offer creative ways to teach the less mediated Nabokov of the paratexts and archives. In each case, it is a live dialogue between student and teacher, author and reader, freedom and authority, old and new, where each side strives toward sharable discovery, whether sobering or joyful or both at once.

Yuri Leving offers a glimpse into his longitudinal project of creating website companions for *The Gift* and *Lolita* in collaboration with his students. The former novel, on which he has published a book companion, merited an app as well. Leving details the technological process of building interactive multimedia resources that are meant not to replace a complex literary work but to diversify and enrich its consumption. Students in his courses work on skills that go beyond the sphere of literary analysis and stretch as far as material culture, programming, web design, drawing, and marketing. He stresses that by involving students in collaborations he equalizes the classroom dynamic, not only between expert instructor and student but also between an all-knowing "manipulative" author such as Nabokov and his readers.

José Vergara uses technology to make possible collaborations among his students when he teaches *Invitation to a Beheading*. He creates a space for communal reading, a form of engagement with a text that he argues serves best this generation of readers. Through a collective Google Doc and the digital platform Scalar he helps students visualize connections and find textual patterns, effectively translating Nabokov's cognitive challenges from their native paper-and-ink format into a co-creative medium for annotations. Vergara makes it clear that it is the attention to the subjectivity of reader experience and interpretive positions that animates his approach. He sees his pedagogical goal in the shift in power dynamics between author and reader, instructor and student.

Shifting the focus from technology to translation, Matthew Walker relies on Nabokov's treatment of *poshlost'* in the 1944 critical study of *Nikolai Gogol* to teach the transcultural author as a fascinating case of conceptual self-translation from Russian to American English. He demonstrates how by paying close attention to the shimmering of the cultural, social, and historical nuances of a single key concept, the teacher can bring one Russian-language author (Nabokov) or two authors (Nabokov and Gogol) or an entire culture (Russian) closer to today's American audience, while reminding us of the human cost of ideological debates so freshly and excruciatingly evident in Russia's war in Ukraine. As often is the case in intercultural encounters, this approach sheds light on twenty-first-century American culture, too, for it allows us to ask questions of Nabokov and *poshlost'* that Nabokov himself would not have necessarily wanted to answer a half century ago.

Tim Harte addresses the uneasy question of how to teach a Nabokov course in the aftermath of a student strike mounted to urge his academic institution to respond actively to recent instances of racial injustice in the United States. A representative of the institution with considerable administrative power, Harte is attentive to the pedagogical implications of the shift in the balance of power between instructors and students that the strike practically effected. His perspective is valuable for this volume because the pressure for change in his case comes not from online conversations, so often suspected of performative shallowness, but from shared organized real-life actions on the part of the students.

Luke Parker shares his experience teaching Nabokov's Berlin narratives through the media of Weimar cinema, visualizing the concept of the uncanny in both. Literary texts in his course are in dialogue with black-and-white early European film as well as the digital platforms where today's students see it. The mixing of media languages and artistic representations across historical eras reflects for Parker the fruitfully estranged historical dimension of lived experience. "For today's students," he writes, "Nabokov both embodies a kind of generational attitude to an already mediated present—cinematic culture as *our* moment—and shows how, in his promotion of the irreducible uniqueness of the individual, to resist the idea of generational belonging altogether."

Opening the section on queer and disability studies, Roman Utkin focuses on the narrator of "A Guide to Berlin" and points out how the narrator's disability, added to the English version of the story, defamiliarizes the reading of the text and turns it into a "journey of self-discovery." Utkin adduces evidence that suggests an intimate connection between disability and knowledge. In reading the short story with his students through the lens of disability studies, he deconstructs the stereotypical literary use of disability as an othering device and associates it instead with one of Nabokov's most prized joys, the joy of creative transfiguration.

Sara Karpukhin talks about how the problematic outcomes of intergenerational and interlingual translation, from her native Russian to Nabokov's English to contemporary English, have prompted her to adopt Eve Kosofsky Sedgwick's concept of reparative epistemology when teaching *Pnin*, *Lolita*, and *Pale Fire*. Karpukhin's take on reparative epistemology foregrounds not just the difference or newness or relevance of a queer approach to the teaching and reading of Nabokov but also the rich potential of queer theory for enabling understanding across differences, whether generational, gender, or cultural.

Meghan Vicks uses Sedgwick's distinction between paranoid and reparative reading as an exciting new method of teaching and queering *The Real Life of Sebastian Knight*. Her students follow Nabokov's instructions on how to read him—only to imagine an alternative way of reading, or reading against the grain. Alternating between author-endorsed paranoid and author-resistant reparative modes, her students arrive at remarkable insights into the identity of the novel's eponymous hero. Significantly, Vicks teaches her students epistemological flexibility through challenging the authority of the author, and the queerness of the text emerges as an analytically satisfying consequence of the reader's and the student's liberation.

Moving on to literary production, Robyn Jensen describes teaching *Speak, Memory* through its paratexts, such as the illustrations and the index. She uses Nabokov's autobiography to introduce her social media–savvy students to methods of self-construal in literature. The centrality of the author-reader relationship and the means whereby texts become literature in her course indicate an interest in agency, which naturally informs Jensen's pedagogical stance and her attitude to the remapping of Nabokov's narrative. Her students transfer Nabokov's verbal and visual patterns into maps and images of their own, shifting media and engendering productively uncertain readings.

Olga Voronina teaches an array of Nabokov's Russian short stories in translation through the paratextual evidence of editorial correspondence and archival findings. Her students engage in close reading and get a glimpse of Nabokov's creative process, after which they undergo a similar apprenticeship in their own writing assignments, with edits and rewrites. While this approach is meant, first and foremost, to celebrate the author's mastery and to put his achievement on full display, in her course Voronina introduces students to a Nabokov who is at his most vulnerable, a Nabokov who is a student himself, relying on the assistance of others. She shows the achievement as the gradual outcome of significant collaborative effort, inspiring her students to think of literary excellence not so much in terms of power and status as in terms of continuous learning.

Last but certainly not least, Lisa Ryoko Wakamiya concentrates on archival and editorial work in her Nabokov seminar when teaching *The Original of Laura*, a rare and therefore all the more precious example of teaching an unpublished, unedited, in a word uncontrolled Nabokov text. She invites her students to take on the tasks of editorial research and preparation and to make their own decisions with respect to the writer's last unfinished project. The absence of the usual expected level of authorial control makes interpreting and evaluating *The Original of Laura* seem to be a risky proposition, but this is where the idea of the canon becomes transparent and open to disassembling. Students in Wakamiya's course participate in the contingent production of knowledge in the continual creation of the canon.

A representative snapshot of a moment in the history of an academic discipline, this collection is also forward-thinking and shows how, through positioning the instructor, the students, and the knowledge in a larger system of power relations, teaching Nabokov can be reimagined for the future. We hope that the reader will find here useful practical tips on how to approach the "problem" of Nabokov and, more generally, how to respond intellectually and morally to the often unpredictably fast change and reaction to change in the culture at large.

Notes

1 Anne Dwyer, "Why I Teach *Lolita*," last modified May 14, 2018, www.insidehighered.com/views/2018/05/14/teaching-lolita-still-appropriate-opinion.

2 The posts in the original exchange have been preserved in *The Nabokovian* under the heading "Teaching *Lolita* Today," www.thenabokovian.org/comment/71, last modified April 7, 2019.

3 John Updike, introduction to *Lectures on Literature*, by Vladimir Nabokov, ed. F. Bowers (San Diego: Harcourt Brace Jovanovich, 1980), xxv.

4 Vladimir Nabokov, *Pale Fire* (New York: Vintage, 1989), 130.

5 See Nataša Kovačević, *Narrating Post/Communism: Colonial Discourse and Europe's Borderline Civilization* (Milton, UK: Routledge, 2008), 21–24; Marijeta Bozovic, "The Transnational Vladimir Nabokov, Or, The Perils of Teaching Literature," in *Transnational Russian Studies*, ed. Andy Byford, Connor Doak, and Stephen Hutchings (Liverpool, UK: Liverpool UP, 2019), 127–140.

6 Brian Boyd, *Vladimir Nabokov: The American Years* (Princeton, NJ: Princeton UP, 1991), 311. Senator McCarthy is mentioned twice in *Pnin*, published shortly before this episode, and both times without judgment. For more context see chapter 9 in Andrea Pitzer, *The Secret History of Vladimir Nabokov* (New York: Pegasus Books, 2013).

7 Ibid., 503. Compare, too, Véra's wrath at student demonstrators at Cornell in 1969 in Stacy Schiff, *Véra (Mrs. Vladimir Nabokov)* (New York: Modern Library, 2000), 336.

8 For context see Maxim D. Shrayer, "Jewish Questions in Nabokov's Art and Life," in *Nabokov and His Fiction: New Perspectives*, ed. Julian W. Connolly (Cambridge: Cambridge UP, 1999), 73–91; Yuri Leving, "Nabokov's Jewish Family,"

Tablet, last modified December 17, 2012, www.tabletmag.com/jewish-arts-and-culture/books/119287/nabokov-jewishfamily. More recently, Leonid Livak, "Jewishness as Literary Device in Nabokov's Fiction," in *Nabokov in Context*, ed. David Bethea and Siggy Frank (Cambridge: Cambridge UP, 2018), 228–239; Gavriel Shapiro, "The Beneficial Role of Jews in Vladimir Nabokov's Life and Career," *Nabokov Online Journal* 18 (2019): 1–19.

9 Vladimir Nabokov, *Pnin* (New York: Vintage, 1990), 147, 160.

10 Vladimir Nabokov, *Annotated Lolita*, ed. Alfred Appel Jr. (New York: Vintage, 1991), 79; and Alfred Appel's annotations ibid., 372, 435–436.

11 See Galya Diment, "Masters and Servants: *Upstairs* and *Downstairs* in Nabokov," in *Nabokov Upside Down*, ed. Brian Boyd and Marijeta Bozovic (Evanston, IL: Northwestern UP, 2017), 131–142; see also Galya Diment's foreword to this volume.

12 Vladimir Nabokov, *Pale Fire* (New York: Vintage International, 1991), 216.

13 Ibid., 217.

14 James Baldwin, *The Price of the Ticket: Collected Nonfiction 1948–1985* (Boston: Beacon Press, 2021), 19, 21, 23.

15 As white anti-Semitism increased in the 1930s and '40s, so did Black anti-Semitism, despite the fact that the NAACP had been one of the two non-Jewish organizations in the United States that had spoken out against American anti-Semitism and the German persecution of the Jews between 1935 and 1945, and the National Urban League had called for a Black-Jewish coalition against bigotry as early as 1938. See Robert Michael, *A Concise History of American Anti-Semitism* (New York: Rowman and Littlefield, 2005), 202, 203. In 1967, James Baldwin, by then the foremost Black literary figure in the United States, revisited his original thesis in the *New York Times* op-ed "Negroes Are Anti-Semitic Because They're Anti-White."

16 See Benjamin Balint, *Running Commentary: The Contentious Magazine that Transformed the Jewish Left into the Neoconservative Right* (New York: Public Affairs, 2010).

17 Donald Barton Johnson, "Nabokov and the Sixties," in *Discourse and Ideology in Nabokov's Prose*, ed. David H. J. Larmour (London and New York: Routledge, 2002), 149–159. For more comprehensive descriptions of Nabokov's experience in America see Pitzer, *Secret History*; Robert Roper, *Nabokov in America: On the Road to Lolita* (New York: Bloomsbury, 2015).

18 Terence Renaud, *New Lefts: The Making of a Radical Tradition* (Princeton, NJ: Princeton UP, 2021), 246–247.

19 See, for instance, Hansi Lo Wang, "Generation Z Is the Most Racially and Ethnically Diverse Yet," last modified November 15, 2018, www.npr.org/2018/11/15/668106376/generation-z-is-the-most-racially-and-ethnically-diverse-yet.

20 The irony can be a reaction to the perceived insincerity of the image of aesthetically hip, fashionable protest and, by extension, the ongoing capitalist appropriation and commodification of counterculture. To advocate for dissent from a position of authority, even when dissent is reduced to difference as its least agented and

therefore most innocuous manifestation, means to expose oneself to the charge of disingenuousness. The status quo has used this double bind to either strip dissent of credibility and deny its reality by claiming that it exists solely as a marketing strategy — or to coopt dissent, control its narratives, and use its aesthetic to advertise the status quo itself. The truth is that the purity of motivation on which this argument seems to predicate the legitimacy of dissent, in academia or elsewhere, is unachievable and as such is something of a red herring. Teachers, for example, will always have some vested interest in the power structure that some of their teaching may be challenging. It does not affect the possibility of, and the need for, change. Conversely, the fact that teachers know that they are part of the system does not make irrelevant their obligation to examine their motives, find the extent of their individual agency within the system, and act accordingly. See Thomas Frank and Matt Weiland, eds., *Commodify Your Dissent: Salvos from The Baffler* (New York: W.W. Norton, 1997); Thomas Frank, *The Conquest of Cool: Business Culture, Counterculture, and the Rise of Hip Consumerism* (Chicago: U of Chicago P, 1998); Sarah Schulman, *The Gentrification of the Mind: Witness to a Lost Imagination* (Berkeley: U of California P, 2012).

21   Renaud, *New Lefts*, 288–289; Paul Mason, *Why It's Kicking Off Everywhere: New Global Revolutions* (London and New York: Verso, 2012), 292; see also, published in the last year alone, Steven Feldstein, *The Rise of Digital Repression: How Technology Is Reshaping Power, Politics, and Resistance* (New York: Oxford UP, 2021); Tetyana Lokot, *Beyond the Protest Square: Digital Media and Augmented Dissent* (London and New York: Rowman and Littlefield, 2021).

22   This volume undertakes to move beyond the pernicious dualism of "detached" timelessness and "fashionable" contemporaneity somewhat as the 2002 volume *Discourse and Ideology in Nabokov's Prose* proposed to move beyond the dualism of "collusion" or "collision," or "the text's testimony about the world and the reader's own witnessing of experience." David H. J. Larmour, "Introduction. Collusion and Collision," in *Discourse and Ideology in Nabokov's Prose*, ed. David H. J. Larmour (London and New York: Routledge, 2002), 4. Published twenty years ago, that collection is an important precursor to this volume. But whereas twenty years ago scholars felt the need to justify "collisions" as "an alternative way of celebrating [Nabokov's] endlessly fascinating texts" (ibid., 6), we want to acknowledge that the witnessed experience of today's readers can sometimes prevent the possibility, or at least the familiar ease, of such celebration.

23   Brian Boyd, "Literature, Pattern, *Lolita*: On Art, Literature, Science," in *Transitional Nabokov*, ed. Duncan White and Will Norman (Bern, Switzerland: Peter Lang, 2009), 32.

24   Martin Amis, *Experience: A Memoir* (New York: Vintage Books, 2001), 117.

PART I

DIGITAL COLLABORATIONS

Teaching Nabokov in 3D

Yuri Leving

At Beardsley Prep, what we stress are the three D's—Dramatics, Dance, and Dating.[1]

Taken as an epigraph, the tongue-in-cheek motto from the latest screen adaptation of Vladimir Nabokov's *Lolita* captures the supposed essence of American education some seventy years ago. Nabokov's America is long gone, and its pedagogical landscape has changed dramatically, especially with the introduction of the Internet and new media in the past two decades. In this chapter, I will address the problems of bridging the boundaries between academic classrooms and new technologies and share practical examples applicable to contemporary approaches to teaching Nabokov while using computer-generated imagery. Nabokov's three D's of artistic self-expression thus transform into a kind of 3D immersive practice similar to multidimensional experience that conveys depth perception to viewers by employing stereoscopy. Geolocation, virtual reality, linked data, data-driven analysis, and artificial intelligence are just some of the many opportunities for creating content, but recent scholars have been wondering whether these tools can work to produce a scholarly monograph or a new edition of classics.[2] We can slightly paraphrase this and ask: How can innovative technologies be utilized in studying and teaching literature in the twenty-first century? Nabokov the writer seems to offer a good opportunity for digital reading, and yet we must be careful not to be trapped by the false impression that "understanding is simple, singular, and clickable," as developed by some digital readers who, instead of seeing knowledge as complex, multiple, and difficult to excavate, stress entertainment over functionality.[3]

The editor of *Approaches to Teaching Nabokov's* Lolita argues that although Nabokov "did not care for teaching (it struck him as manifest neglect of his own writing), by now even the bricks in the Cornell University sidewalks must remember that Nabokov gave his first lecture in 1951 for Literature 311–312...and that the course would go on to become a student favorite by the time Nabokov left teaching, Cornell, Ithaca, and America."[4] On the other hand, Jürgen Pieters muses in a recently edited volume that if Nabokov had been teaching half a century later, his "dream about being replaced by a tape recorder or some other technological equipment would definitely have come true," which would subsequently encourage students "to work through the lectures individually before class, while in class the collective time of the classroom-moment would be dedicated to confronting Professor Nabokov with all sorts of queries of potential interest, both for the students and for their teacher."[5]

In a world that is rapidly moving toward an all-encompassing digital culture where touch-screen monitors are as accepted as paper editions, creating an interactive learning experience for the study of Nabokov's works pushes liberal arts programs toward experimentation with "amplified" editions.[6] Future publications of *Lolita, Pale Fire,* and *The Gift* equipped with interactive interfaces and accompanied by online study materials, multimedia presentations, and images are the primary focus of my current examination of Nabokov in the age of digital humanities.

Already a decade ago, Arlene Nicholas and John Lewis observed the benefits and limitations of e-textbooks in higher education as a radical alternative to the centuries-old standard of instruction, while registering some major shifts of faculty attitudes and usages of e-textbooks at small liberal arts colleges and larger universities.[7] Apple has sold more than 425 million iPads since the product's debut in 2010,[8] and the availability of e-textbooks is escalating along with the variety of electronic readers.[9]

In 2011, in an attempt to produce a pilot project based on Nabokov's novel *The Gift*, my research team and students in several consecutive classes started working on an integrated product with sound, video, and 3D models.[10] Our goal was to amalgamate an e-textbook with lecture notes on major chapters along with embedded textual and visual commentary, videos of scholarly presentations on related subjects, and options to take interactive exams. This project, titled *Studying Literature in a Digital Environment* (SLIDE), had as its aim the creation of an iLearn app, a text-based application that would include a database pertaining to a specific literary work, featuring interactive interface and study materials. The process was manifold, and it combined (1) code development for SLIDE; (2) content research and writing; (3) design and testing of the interface; (4) launch of the iLearn application for iPhone/iPad/Android devices; and (5) management, coordination, and distribution. More than an e-book and less than a computer game, this application was supposed to be a fun and interactive way of studying Nabokov's literary masterpiece. Furthermore, I was determined to make our scholarly app look aesthetically appealing and competitive with similar apps available in the Apple App Store or Google Play. While the app was not released in the commercially sustainable line of digital products—this was not the goal to begin with—we achieved our pedagogical goals of building knowledge and understanding how digital media are transforming cultural expression and modern education, in particular literary studies, through technological advancements.

The project was initially established in 2007 as a wiki, which allowed students to collaborate through the creation of an original scholarly compendium and showcase their work to peers as well as to interested readers worldwide. Fifteen years ago, such a public-facing aspect of a classroom project was still a novelty, and students felt excited to be able to considerably shorten

Figure 1. Icon developed for Gift App, by Andrey Bashkin from Yuri Leving's concept, 2009.

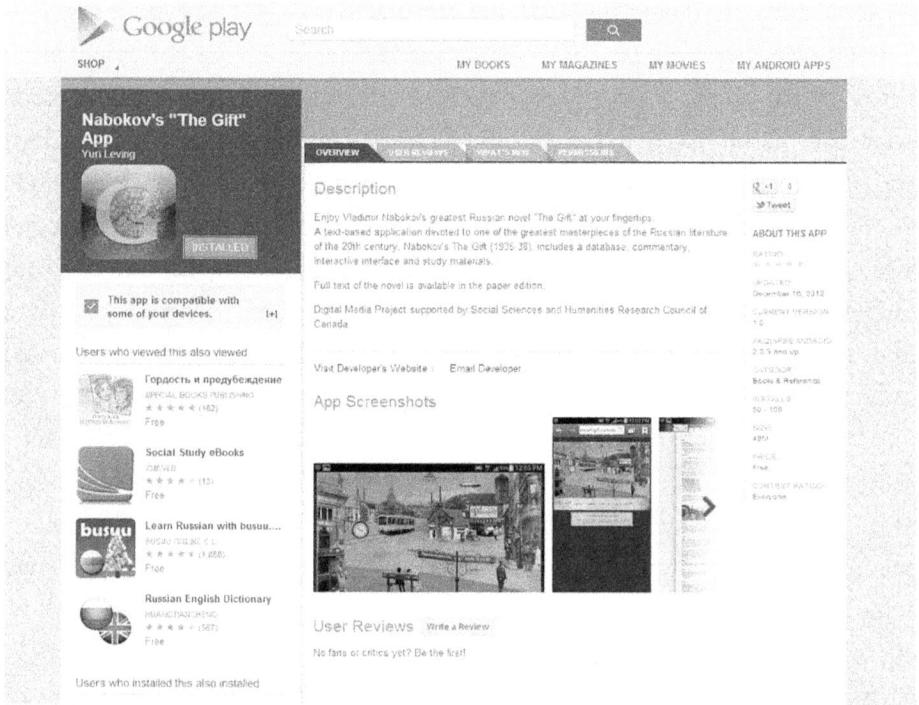

Figure 2. Screenshot of Gift App as available on Google Play (2012–2016).

the usually long path of making the fruits of their labor immediately available *urbi et orbi*. This collaborative input yielded a functioning computerized database devoted to *The Gift*, where commentary was organized both page by page and alphabetically (a clickable lineup led to extensive hypertext—various articles were interconnected and supplied an essential critical apparatus to Nabokov's novel). Basic pages were headed "Timeline in the Novel," "Motifs," "Criticism," and "*The Gift* Bibliography." Paintings, photographs, and other works of visual art were used on this site for identification and critical commentary. Images illustrative of a particular technique or school were complemented by jacket designs of various editions of *The Gift*, including archival photographic reproductions of the original journal publication in *Sovremennye zapiski* in 1937.

While dealing with external sources, we also learned about issues of copyright and proper citation. I used this as an opportunity to introduce undergraduate students to various types of media that they can incorporate into their work, the process of obtaining permissions, and the accepted volume of quotations in an Open Access scholarly project. Nabokov studies (at least in my experience) is a fortunate exception in modern humanities because the

Figure 3. Main page of Gift App loading, 2009.

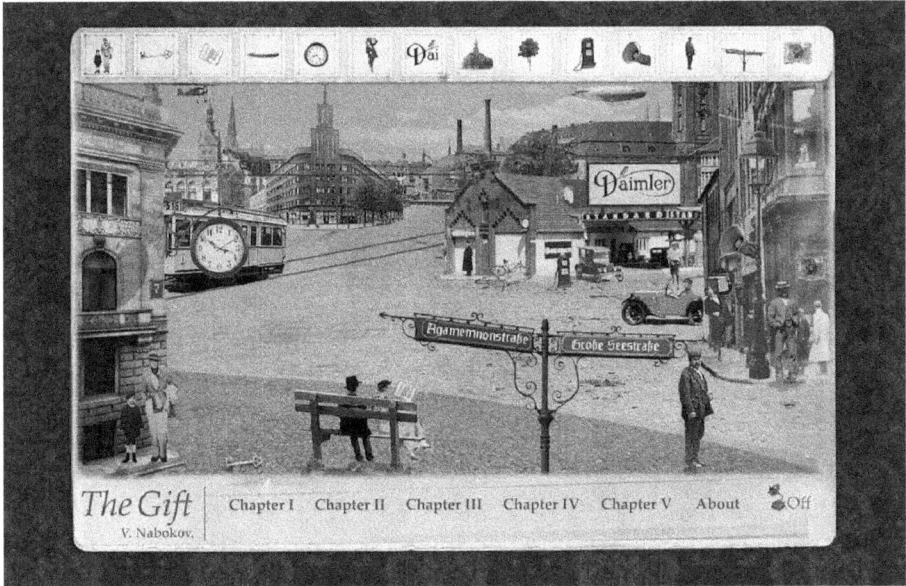

Figure 4. Main page of Gift App fully loaded, 2009.

current literary executors of Vladimir Nabokov's literary legacy are exceedingly cooperative with scholars, the practice championed by the late Dmitri Nabokov, whose expert and respectful handling of his father's creative legacy was exemplary and, to a large extent, helped shaped this field into a thriving academic industry.

In 2010–2011, the original Wiki page was abandoned, and a new website envisioned as an interactive digital companion to a literary guide *Keys to "The Gift"* was constructed (www.keystothegift.com).[11] The butterfly drawing by Nabokov greets the user who opens the website in a browser; as it takes a few moments to upload the Flash animation of the main page, the percentage, underneath the image that is being filled in with the colorful palette of

Nabokov's original sketch, is quickly showing the progress until it reaches the 100 percent mark.

The design idea for the website and app was prompted by Nabokov's novel itself. One of the key scenes in *The Gift* describes a mundane Berlin night, but disguised behind the deceptively laconic cityscape is a metatextual riddle:

> Behind the brightly painted pumps a radio was singing in a gas station, while above its pavilion vertical yellow letters stood against the light blue of the sky—the name of a car firm—and on the second letter, on the "*E*" (a pity that it was not on the first, on the "*B*"—would have made an alphabetic vignette) sat a live blackbird, with a yellow—for economy's sake—beak, singing louder than the radio.[12]

It is not accidental that in the Russian version the blackbird crowns the second letter "A," while the first letter turns out to be "D." The automobile brand remains the same in both versions of the text (Daimler-Benz), but the Russian version stresses an unpronounced title of the novel, DA—*Dar*.[13] Because one of the major motifs in the novel as well as of the artistic principles of Nabokov's prose is that of the "missing keys,"[14] symbolic keys were also used in the ultimate conceptual architecture of our website. It was decided to devise a non-existing place, located in Berlin, relying on a compound picture inspired by the passage from the novel cited above. Nabokov's places in Berlin are numerous and well documented. The author's own relocations have been reflected in Fyodor's wanderings in Berlin on the pages of *The Gift*. Between 1932 and 1937 the Nabokovs occupied two rooms on the third floor at Nestorstrasse 22; therefore, the image of that building is incorporated in the web page design. The silhouettes of the writer and his little son are discernable at the corner of the building bearing the number 7 (it is, of course, significant considering that Fyodor moves at the opening of the book into a house with this number in its address); the couple is standing beneath the street clock *always* showing ten minutes to four p.m. (yet another allusion to the first sentence of *The Gift*: "towards four in the afternoon on April the first..."). Other clues concealed in this complex image are left for the reader (and a viewer) to decode, although some of the game principles are specifically concentrated in a bar called "Clues." It contains various images in the form of clickable buttons hidden within the main page itself, each of those leading to a distinct category, which in a way pays respect to Nabokov's

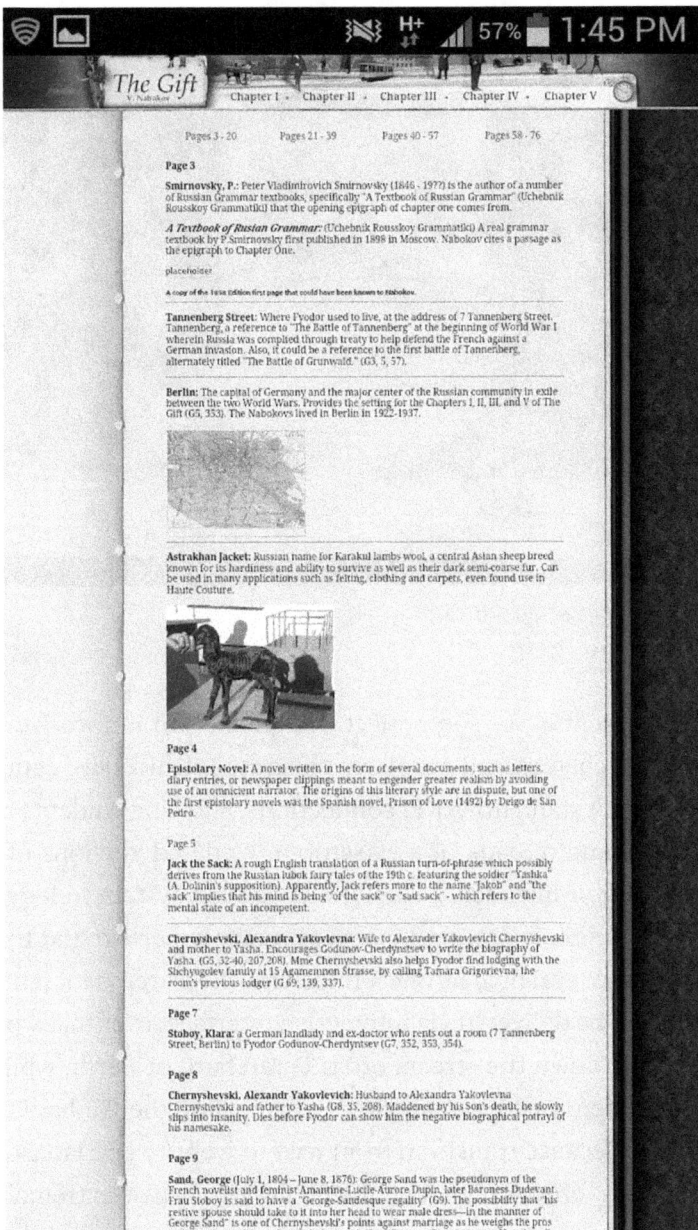

Figure 5. Sample commentary page in Gift App, 2009.

own teaching philosophy that favored attention to minute detail in prose composed by others ("What color was the bottle containing the arsenic with which Emma poisoned herself?").[15]

The advantages of running the website through an app is that a touch screen tablet responds to human gestures, thus enabling the next level of

Figure 6. Time and Chronology page in Gift App, 2009.

functionality, essential for the project designed as an innovative combination of game mechanics and scholarly apparatus. University campuses are now outfitted with standard Wi-Fi connections, allowing students to operate gadgets both in and outside of a classroom. Updated versions of The Gift app will include, for instance, a satellite navigation system to let users connect locations and their descriptions in a literary hypertext and to highlight them in an e-book available at one's fingertips. Research data pertaining to each chapter can be delivered via interactive interface, eventually prompting students to walk down the streets of St. Petersburg or Berlin while visiting specific places mentioned in Nabokov's novel using the Global Positioning System (GPS). Because transition from wiki to website and later to app was a lengthy process, often defined by the evolution (albeit extremely fast) of technology, students who were involved in the project at its early stages have not witnessed the transformative effect of the interactive interface, while for later generations of students it was equally impossible to appreciate the leap of the entire construct, and yet the quality pedagogy component was undoubtedly similar for all.

After developing an app dedicated to Nabokov's last Russian novel, I realized that *Lolita* and *Pale Fire* would be the obvious conceptual continuation of the project for digitizing Nabokov studies involving students. I invited my Nabokov class to participate in this ongoing research in lieu of their final projects. To this end, several creative teams have been formed, on *Lolita* and *Pale Fire,* respectively; here, I will focus on the former novel.

Each team was comprised of several students collaborating closely with peers sharing ideas about the future app using a virtual discussion board. Our strategy in building a new app included its overall concept (interface, imagery, graphics, and structural hierarchy), research, and accumulation of the bibliographic material to be processed and subsequently used in a database. (It is worth mentioning that no special skills in software engineering were required to complete these tasks.)

Similarly to the conceptualization process of The Gift app, we began with discussions of what the main screen should look like. Students noted that in *Lolita*, as readers, they deal with documents of varying stability: the (pseudo) confession, John Ray Jr.'s introduction, Lolita's class list, the diary excerpts, letters, etc. Visually and conceptually the *idea of documents* can be presented in elements such as postcards, roadmaps, and hotel brochures. These documents can relate to the road trip or form "Humbert's bookshelf" with excerpts from works by Shakespeare, Poe, Mérimée, Chateaubriand, Flaubert, and other authors providing additional information about intertextuality in *Lolita*. Similar structures will lead to ways of interaction with the app where documents could be organized in physical spaces such as a car's dashboard or a motel room space. Another possibility is to combine different elements through a specific motif, for instance that of evidence of a crime: records can be presented as exhibit items, both mirroring and questioning the way that Humbert puts his reader in the position of juror. The fingerprints in the FBI's "Wanted" order featuring a fictitious pedophile's portrait could be used to enter subcategories in the app's database. In this case, the question of unstable documents and concocted evidence could be a means to outlining important questions of authorship by the unstable narrator.

"Reading" Nabokov's novel in this unorthodox manner afforded students more conceptual freedom; considering various component parts allowed them to see how design and interface can interact with content and meaning. Furthermore, breaking down the narrative in an unconventional manner, different from that of traditional literary criticism, provides discussions with a sense of creativity and the allure of imagination in a truly Nabokovian understanding of a reader who, equipped with the magic lantern, would eagerly experiment with slides even if running the risk of turning them upside down.[16]

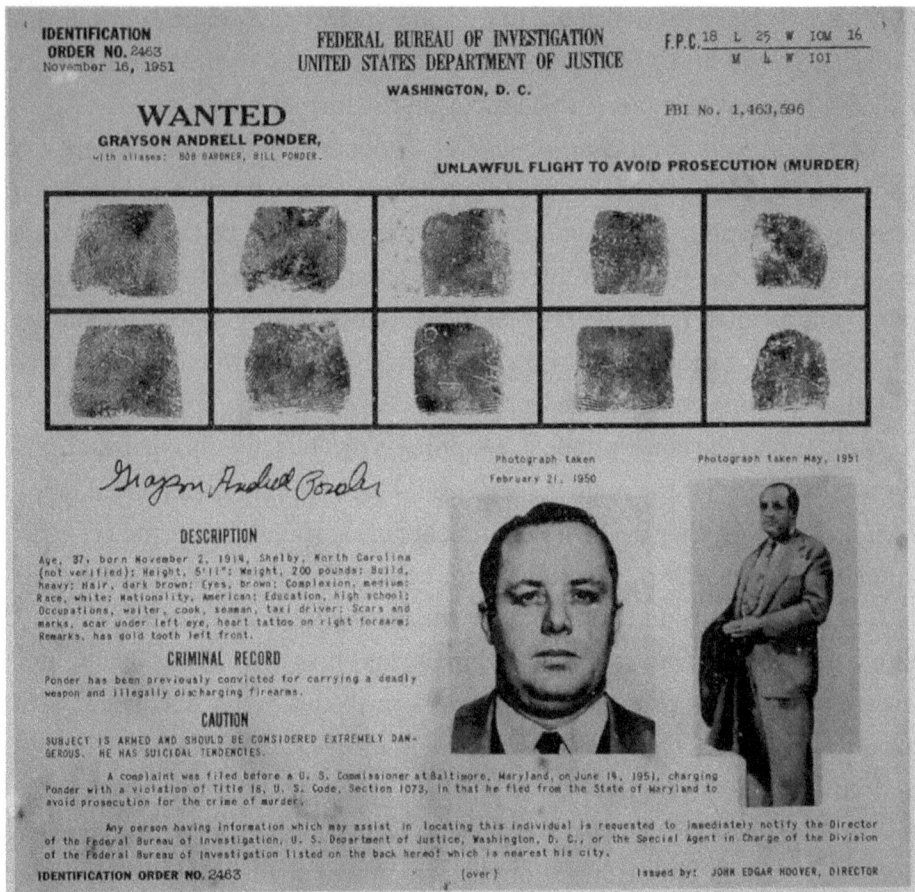

Figure 7. FBI identification order, dated November 16, 1951, used as visual prop in Lolita App, 2013.

Another idea for a home screen of the future app suggested by students is a 1940s writing desk. Because of the desk's relevance to both Nabokov and his character (a literary scholar), it could provide an easy visual organization and interesting background that can be continuously crowded with added objects. The desk image could incorporate drawers and a book hutch, exposing an assortment of "Easter egg"–type elements; when selected, a drawer would open a summary about Nabokov's life or offer dynamic explorations of thematic layers in *Lolita* and survey the tantalizing history of the novel's publication.

Some students argued that for the sake of consistency the main screen in the Lolita app should be designed in the style of a compound postcard analogous to the Berlin cityscape in The Gift app. The difference in this project naturally would be its components—instead of a "Europe of the 1930s"

Figure 8. Concept of Main Menu page in Lolita App, 2013.

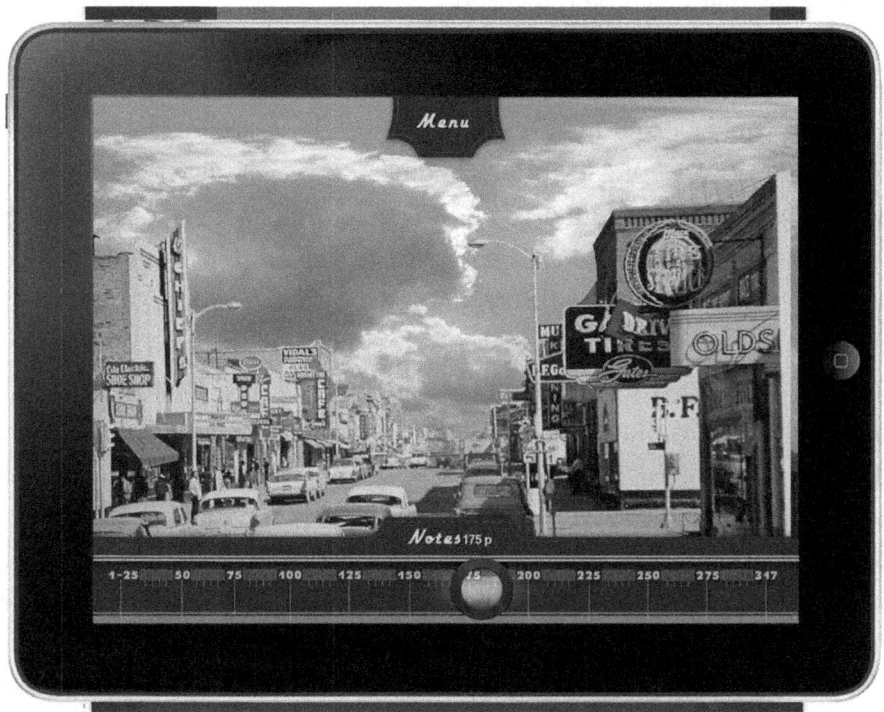

Figure 9. Page-by-page commentary in Lolita App, 2013.

theme, this new one should be based on the depiction of a generic midwestern street—featuring stylized shops, small cafés, motel entrances graced with vintage Coca-Cola signs, and typically long American automobiles rolling by. This somewhat mythologized contemporary lifestyle had been probed earlier by Norman Rockwell, who painstakingly collected and utilized props and costumes for his artwork that instantly became synonymous with the zeitgeist of postwar America. What Rockwell didn't have on hand, "he bought, borrowed, or rented—from a simple dime-store hairbrush or coffee cup to a roomful of chairs and tables from a New York City Automat."[17] Nabokov's writings are also deeply rooted in a historical context, requiring charts, maps, and accompanying illustrations that are particularly useful for understanding the material world of a given novel.[18] Material culture in *Lolita* represents an important slice of its characters' everyday lives, and Nabokov lovingly recreated in his prose contemporaneous reality from jukeboxes, radio sets, and automobiles of all brands to interiors of fast food restaurants and bars. Despite being located in the not-so-distant past, the visualization of this paraphernalia quickly sinking into oblivion requires a degree of familiarity with the visual vocabulary of America of the 1940s and 1950s.[19] In order to catalogue *Lolita*'s visual background, a team of students combed through the text in search of descriptions that could be translated into actual images (i.e., references to motels, specific clothes, print magazines, food items, and popular brands). Afterwards, students tracked down Nabokov's descriptions using search engines (mainly Google Images) for close matches pertaining to the world of *Lolita*. In the resulting log of our findings (we accumulated a substantial database with over three hundred images) one would find illustrations of the "tennis fashions" and the game's historical equipment;[20] pictures of Arizona from the 1940s;[21] and a milk bar produced in the same period.[22] They would also discover how the crime films were advertised;[23] what "malts" were[24] and what the malt maker looked like in the 1950s; what the "blanket parties"[25] meant and what "Wellingtons" referred to in the novel.[26]

Students thought it would be motivating to have a "signs and symbols" section of the app displayed on a sidebar of the home screen. The novel is filled with options that can be turned into clickable images: imagine, for instance, *Lolita holding an apple* (while moving the fruit out of her hand, or when the user touches it, a bite is taken out of its flesh); a *spiral* (encapsulating a frequently featured theme in Nabokov's works);[27] or the *Russian roulette* virtual simulator (Mr. McFate uses Humbert's revolver, and unexpected literary connections pop up in lieu of shots). Other possible dynamic illustrations are of Lolita and Humbert playing tennis (balls bounce back and forth against the four sides of the screen) or a game, "Shoot Quilty" (the goal is to "kill" the character with the limited amount of available munition while the target is constantly moving, and so forth). These humorous examples should not eclipse the didactic value and high-tech potential of digital humanities, especially as critics caution against what some call "the wholesale use of electronic texts in academic settings."[28]

The gamification and other digital-specific methods of engagement with a text should not be regarded as the end goal of the project but rather as an effective tool in pedagogical activity. This "playful" quality of the DIY assignments accompanied by classroom brainstorming sessions allowed students and myself (in the role of an instructor) a unique two-way communication where the former felt genuinely engaged and, what is more, typically observed and collectively gauged the progress of their output throughout the semester.

During our in-class discussions students suggested creating a family tree or a set of genograms—a kind of an ever-changing configuration reflecting the transformations that actually affect Humbert's family throughout the novel as well as the fantasies that he frequently indulges in (i.e., that he truly is

Figure 10. Imaginary Lolita family tree for Lolita App, by Brent Braaten from a concept by Brittany Kraus, 2013.

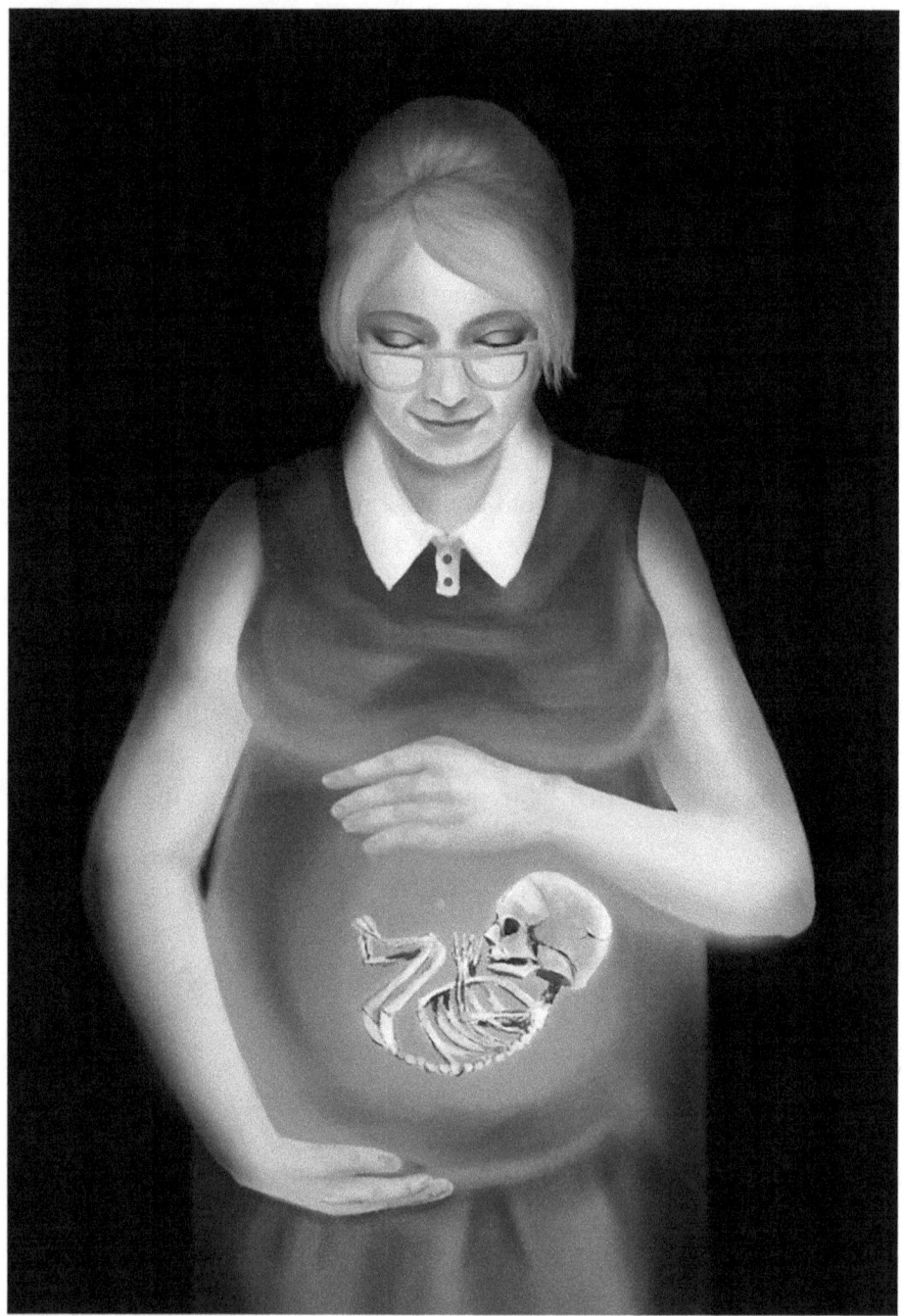

Figures 11–12 (continued)

Figures 11–12. Sketches for Lolita App, by Tess Hatfield, 2013.

Dolores Haze's father or that Charlotte and Dolores are sisters). An illustrated timeline for Nabokov's own life and, even more importantly, a timeline for the key events in *Lolita*, can also be depicted using graphic art.

To avoid copyright infringement, I commissioned original illustrations from those students who preferred to undertake creative assignments over dry research. Tess Hatfield's final semester submission consisted of six images of original artwork along with study sketches.[29] Executed in different techniques, her drawings were presented in class, as the student explained the ideas behind every image and guided us through her creative process.

The artist did some images of the series in a traditional technique, drawing others on an iPad using a stylus and then added computer graphics (for instance, the image of Humbert Humbert watching a movie with Charlotte and Lolita includes a shot from Stanley Kubrick's screen adaptation of *Lolita*, extracted with Photoshop and inserted in the background behind the trio; see figure 13).

Figure 13. Sketch for Lolita App, by Tess Hatfield, 2013.

In addition to illustrations, mini-games, and extra bonuses, the Lolita app will rely on effective interactive tools: a sidebar with underline, highlight, select, and copy options granting students limited editorial functions such as saving important passages, bookmarking pages, and highlighting selected quotes. Short quizzes located at the end of some chapters enhance the learning component of the application.

In the decades since its publication in 1955, Nabokov's *Lolita* has generated a tremendous body of criticism: monographs, scholarly articles, and book chapters. I'll briefly touch upon the methodology of collecting materials from published scholarship by participants working on the digital app. Students in this class were deployed on a mission of reviewing and scanning existing *Lolita* scholarship. A predetermined number of sources were assigned individually, and each student was tasked with identifying relevant excerpts that could be used as footnotes in the commentary in progress. It was important to condense the authors' original arguments to just a few sentences (with a bibliographic record provided in each case); the class project manager then conflated multiple notes into a master file while verifying the pagination following the 1992 Vintage edition of *Lolita*. The result of this

Figures 14–16. Screenshots from a short film made by students in Yuri Leving's Nabokov class, with Kaela McSharry as Charlotte Haze and George Aldous as Humbert Humbert, 2013.

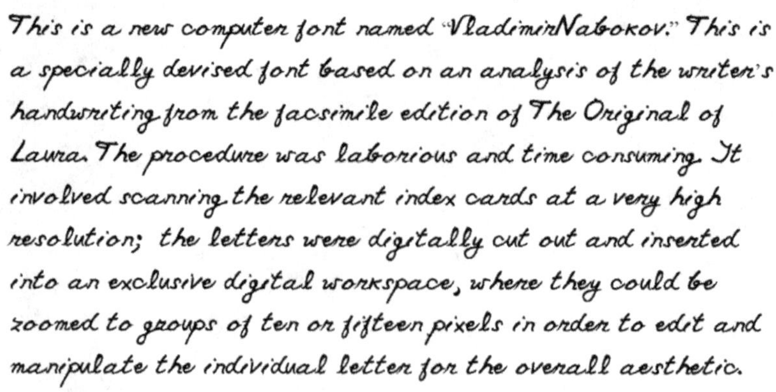

> *This is a new computer font named "VladimirNabokov." This is a specially devised font based on an analysis of the writer's handwriting from the facsimile edition of The Original of Laura. The procedure was laborious and time consuming. It involved scanning the relevant index cards at a very high resolution; the letters were digitally cut out and inserted into an exclusive digital workspace, where they could be zoomed to groups of ten or fifteen pixels in order to edit and manipulate the individual letter for the overall aesthetic.*

Figure 17. "VladimirNabokov" font, based on Vladimir Nabokov's handwriting, designed by Denis Kierans in Yuri Leving's Nabokov class, 2013.

collective research project conducted over a few semesters is a detailed commentary (totaling approximately three hundred pages) based on dozens of publications devoted to Nabokov's novel. This derivative but practical compilation will offer website users a functional searchable database covering years of cumulative scholarly achievement.

Finally, within the framework of the Lolita app project I invited students from my Russian cinema course to collaborate with their peers enrolled in the Nabokov course. Jointly they produced a multimedia piece (film students were responsible for technical aspects of video and sound production).[30] The screen adaptations of selected excerpts from *Lolita* will ultimately be integrated into the app based on the novel (a group of five students[31] filmed a key scene of Charlotte writing a letter to Humbert asking him to leave her house but desperately wanting him to stay: "This is a confession. I love you....").[32]

While thinking about the appropriate "packaging" of the future Lolita app, students have agreed that its design should be cryptic and allusive and contain hidden clues, patterns, and details. This sounds counterintuitive for an app that is supposed to be decoding things, but when elements are interactive and give the person accessing it some agency, it can make exploring the material less labor-intensive.

I will conclude with a final touch equally belonging to cognitive processes, technical skills, and playful aesthetics rooted in the tradition of Nietzsche's "gay science" (*Die fröhliche Wissenschaft*): one of my students, Denis Kierans, became fascinated with the Knopf 2009 edition of

The Original of Laura that reproduced index cards in Nabokov's own handwriting and decided to emulate and enhance some of its features as part of his final research project. Kierans created a new computer font named "VladimirNabokov" based on an analysis of the writer's script from the facsimile edition. The scrupulous procedure involved scanning relevant cards at a high resolution, then digitally cutting out the letters and inserting them into a digital workspace.[33]

The stereotyped image of traditional "bookish" humanists "cloistered in their ivory towers performing their scholarly activities such as reading, teaching, philosophizing, and publishing is now giving way to collaborative teamwork where humanists, technicians, librarians, information experts, students and artists engage with digital humanities scholarship."[34] As tangible proof and affirmation of the role of the Nabokovian reader, learners in classrooms perceive the process of interpretation as a kind of dynamic dialogue between a manipulating reader and the manipulative author.

When the co-editors of this volume asked me upon reading the first draft of this text to address the question of what lessons can be applied in other classrooms and what can the digital humanities approach to Nabokov provide our students and colleagues, I realized that the only valuable advice I could offer—putting on my Dr. Strangelove hat—is to stop worrying about the one and only correct construal of a work of art and love the "time-bomb" named *Nabokov*.

Notes

1. Stephen Schiff, *Lolita: The Book of the Film* (New York: Applause Books, 1998), 197. In Nabokov's original novel the phrase reads slightly differently: "Under the auspices of Beardsley School, dramatics, dances, and other natural activities are not technically sex play...." Vladimir Nabokov, *Lolita* (New York: Vintage Books, 1992), 196.
2. Paul Spence, "The Academic Book and Its Digital Dilemmas," *Convergence* 24, no. 5 (2018): 261.
3. Jim Casey, "Digital Shakespeare Is Neither Good Nor Bad, But Teaching Makes It So," *Humanities* 8, no. 2 (2019): 11.
4. Zoran Kuzmanovich, "Nabokov as Teacher," in *Approaches to Teaching Lolita*, ed. Zoran Kuzmanovich and Galya Diment (New York: Modern Language Association of America, 2010), 8–9.
5. Jürgen Pieters, "Afterword: (Flipping) Nabokov in the Classroom," in *Vladimir Nabokov's Lectures on Literature: Portraits of the Artist as a Reader and Teacher*, ed. Ben Dhooge and Jürgen Pieters (Leiden, Netherlands: Brill Rodopi, 2018), 219.

6 For discussion of the term "amplified," coined by the publishing giant Penguin Group to refer to e-books that are enhanced to "provide deeper, richer insight into an author's work" (Penguin Group USA), see Ryan James and Leon de Kock, "The Digital David and the Gutenberg Goliath: The Rise of the 'Enhanced' e-book," *English Academy Review* 30, no. 1 (2013): 108. As the researchers point out, "on a tablet, like the Apple iPad, a digital version of a text can be supplemented with media — audio clips, timelines, maps, contextual links and so on, all of which can be accessed by the reader as he or she reads the primary text."

7 Arlene J. Nicholas and John K. Lewis. "Learning Enhancement or Headache: Faculty and E-Textbooks," in *International Journal of Information Systems in the Service Sector* 5, no. 4 (2013): 63–71.

8 Daniel Nations, "How Many iPads Have Been Sold? After an Early Spike, the Market for New iPads Stabilized," last modified March 3, 2021, www.lifewire.com/how-many-ipads-sold-1994296.

9 It was noted at the time that "developers have barely begun to explore the features of the new platform." Dan Tonkery, "The iPad and Its Possible Impact on Publishers and Libraries," *Searcher* 18, no. 8 (2010): 39.

10 I am grateful to all participants of my undergraduate course devoted to Nabokov offered through the departments of English and Russian studies at Dalhousie University, Canada. The SLIDE project was funded by the grant from the Social Sciences and Humanities Research Council.

11 Yuri Leving, *Keys to "The Gift": A Guide to Vladimir Nabokov's Novel* (Boston: Academic Studies Press, 2011). The website is currently undergoing maintenance and upgrades, and it should be relaunched sometime in 2022.

12 Vladimir Nabokov, *The Gift* (New York: Vintage Books, 1991), 174.

13 Leving, *Keys*, 127. Nabokov considered using the affirmative "Da" (Yes) as a title for his novel.

14 As Julian Connolly writes, the protagonist Fyodor's "life has been marked by a series of losses — the loss of Russia and the loss of his father, as well as numerous minor annoyances, such as the loss of keys to his apartment." Symbolically, however, he keeps his keys to Russia through his linguistic bond and cultural legacy. Connolly, "The Major Russian Novels," in *The Cambridge Companion to Nabokov,* ed. Connolly (Cambridge: Cambridge UP, 2005), 144.

15 Ross Wetzsteon, "Nabokov as Teacher," in *Nabokov: Criticism, Reminiscences, Translations and Tributes*, ed. Alfred Appel Jr. and Charles Newman (Evanston, IL: Northwestern UP, 1970), 245.

16 I am alluding here to the opening lines of "An Evening of Russian Poetry," written in 1945 and first published in *The New Yorker*.

17 Ron Schick, *Norman Rockwell: Behind the Camera* (New York: Little, Brown, and Company, 2009), 23.

18 Leving, *Keys*, 333.

19 A variety of popular television series has revived interest in this period among twenty-first-century consumers. One successful period drama, *Mad Men* (Lionsgate Television, dir. Matthew Weiner), premiered on the cable network AMC in 2007.
20 Nabokov, *Lolita*, 162.
21 Ibid.
22 Ibid., 184.
23 Ibid., 170.
24 Ibid., 177.
25 Ibid., 177.
26 Ibid., 180.
27 As we click on the spiral, an image of Humbert as a child is presented, then his first love holding his hand, running through a beach. In this scene a seashell, which is naturally a spiral, can be seen in the foreground. Once the spiral goes full circle, Humbert is fleeing away from authorities, this time with Lolita.
28 Casey, "Digital Shakespeare," 3.
29 I found it hard to prescribe any exact number of images that would constitute the final project for an undergraduate course, not knowing the student-artist's pace but acknowledging the creative process in general. We agreed that this should be a reasonable input equivalent of a final research paper (20 percent of the total grade).
30 Responsibilities in this collective initiative were divided as follows: (1) selection, composition, and narrating of several dialogues or scenes staged and recorded as audio and video segments; (2–3) performing the excerpts in video; (4) filming/lighting aspects; (5) filming and composing soundtracks for the background.
31 Andrew Neville (camera, lights); Dillon Poberezhsky (original soundtrack, sound mixing); Kristie Smith (logistical support, selection of excerpts); featuring George Aldous as Humbert Humbert and Kaela McSharry as Charlotte Haze.
32 Nabokov, *Lolita*, 67.
33 In order to edit and manipulate the individual letters for the overall aesthetic, they had to be zoomed to groups of ten or fifteen pixels; sometimes no single letter properly represented the script as a whole; in these cases three or four examples were "averaged" to create a hybrid. All edited letters were exported from Photoshop as .tiff files and then imported into CorelDrawX4, which helped to smooth out the edges, leaving only a vector, a single curve. The font is available for a free download in Volume 5 (2011) of the *Nabokov Online Journal*.
34 Peng Qinglong, "Digital Humanities Approach to Comparative Literature: Opportunities and Challenges," *Comparative Literature Studies* 57, no. 4 (2020): 599.

Good Readers, Good Writers: Collaborative Student Annotations for *Invitation to a Beheading*

José Vergara

Introduction

A perennial question: Do our students complete the reading? Many instructors, I'd wager, would say no, that students would rather read 280 characters in their spare time than to get to know Tolstoy's dozens. Undoubtedly, aside from the present novelty of TikTok clips and Instagram stories, this has been a charge lobbied at every generation from A to Z. But is it true? Does it hold up today in any meaningful way, especially if, indeed, it is a *perennial* question?

For my part, I'm inclined to disagree, and following Nabokov's lead, I'd rather not generalize too much. The debate has already launched enough thinkpieces reflecting on alleged patterns in reading among young readers and even some gift guides targeting those same generations.[1] I linger on this stereotype of the average student, however, to situate my approach to teaching Nabokov, to consider the real issues that undergird it, and to propose at least one method to encourage an interactive form of reading in today's classroom. This method involves asking students to engage deeply with Nabokov's work by becoming annotators using Scalar, a digital publishing tool. In doing so, it likewise alters the terms of our shared work in the classroom—between student and instructor, between student and author—granting those we teach greater autonomy over their learning and inviting them to wield interpretative power often left to others. In this way, the annotations encourage better, more consistent reading, yes, but they also become a matter of shifting the power dynamics in the room and on the page. Students become the arbiters of significance and interpretation, to some extent, in this exercise.

Contexts

If students "aren't doing the reading," it's because there's a complex set of factors that are frequently elided in conversations about this issue. In fact, the vast scholarship on the subject suggests that often a combination of conflicting expectations, frequently unaddressed individual difficulties, and institutional exigencies lead to questions regarding student reading habits.[2] Pamela Howard and her colleagues, for instance, found "a paradox" in their study of student and faculty perceptions regarding the value of academic reading. While both groups agreed that a college education should make better readers of students, "data from this study indicate that practice and pedagogy related to academic reading do not align with this belief."[3] In some cases, it's the stark contrast between expert faculty readers, who "possess abundant knowledge about their content and understand the lexicon," and students, who wield less knowledge in particular domains, that may drive misunderstandings about how and why to read.[4] Researchers also cite the Dunning-Kruger effect, "which is characterized by an overestimation of competence based on the fact that individuals do not know what they do not know," as well as concerns among faculty over poor course evaluations for assigning "lots of reading."[5] Such matters, among others, can make reading a thorny subject for students and instructors alike. Furthermore, finding a functional praxis that helps resolve this tension and that allows students to begin reading according to disciplinary standards is no less complicated.

The Decoding the Disciplines model developed by Joan Middendorf and David Pace feels apposite here. Teachers often assume that reading across disciplines is the same and doesn't require special instruction even in courses that draw students from all over a campus, not just specific majors. That is, we often fall into the trap of thinking that because they can read, students may adapt to new lexicons and styles on their own without much trouble. Instead, the Decoding the Disciplines approach outlines why instruction should "match the specific conditions of each academic field."[6] It does so through a seven-step process: identifying bottlenecks to learning; asking how an expert does these things; considering how tasks can be explicitly modeled; providing practice and feedback; factoring motivation; reflecting on how well students are mastering tasks; and sharing the resulting knowledge. In Nabokov's case, students can often become overwhelmed by the density and allusiveness of his writing, and it's no surprise, as "students must be given a chance to perfect [reading] skills and to receive feedback that clarifies where they are and are not succeeding," to borrow Middendorf and Pace's words.[7] Although not an *exact* match for this pedagogical framework, my Scalar project achieved comparable goals by giving students a way "into" *Invitation to a Beheading* by providing a model for this work and by allowing students to regularly perform the kind of reading that experts do to make sense of texts such as Nabokov's novel (or, at least, one possible version of that work).

Along these lines, I had a conversation with a colleague not long ago in which we were clearly showing our age by waxing poetic about our relationship with books—their feel, their smell, their pull. They suggested that our reading was qualitatively (not to mention quantitatively) different than that of our students, who, in their and many others' view, require something else to become entranced by a novel, namely, a communal experience of reading a book together. While I find that students generally "do the reading" (even if there are, indeed, challenges), I firmly believe that this communal experience can be a beneficial frame to keep in mind when teaching how to read complex writers such as Nabokov. By community, I want to stress, I don't simply mean a group of bodies in the same room, whether virtual or physical. Rather, I have in mind work that is interactive and rooted in mutual, active exchange. It is also a process by which each contributor feels responsible for a portion of knowledge that can be shared to generate greater understanding among the collective.

Methods/Logistics

What my colleague said made me think of the annotations project I had recently completed while reading *Invitation to a Beheading* in a course on the twentieth-century Russian novel. To begin, I designed a website using the open-source publishing platform Scalar to have students share their work publicly. As its developers put it, Scalar "enables users to assemble media from multiple sources and juxtapose them with their own writing in a variety of ways, with minimal technical expertise required."[8] Likewise, this digital tool "gives authors tools to structure essay- and book-length works in ways that take advantage of the unique capabilities of digital writing, including nested, recursive, and nonlinear formats. The platform also supports collaborative authoring and reader commentary."[9] In other words, Scalar is a bit Nabokovian in design functionality, as it allows for nonlinear writing whereby readers can—and are even encouraged—to consider a digital book from multiple angles, finding and following paths that can be grouped thematically and via tags, for instance, rather than a single linear path forward. It embraces the concept of hypertext to reimagine the possible outcomes of scholarly work, and it can be used to cultivate communities of readers and writers.

I divided the site into sections based on the authors we read, from Mikhail Kuzmin to Evgeny Vodolazkin, and further subsections for each writing assignment: author biography; analysis of a short story or close reading of a passage from a novel; essay; and annotations.[10] If a way to harness students' minds and attention is a more clearly communal experience, then I can think of no better combination than Nabokov and annotations, particularly when paired with a flexible tool such as Scalar.

To prepare students to take on such a novel, multifaceted task, I asked the digital librarian, Roberto Vargas, at the institution where I was teaching at the time to visit my class at the beginning of the semester and introduce the platform. I took the opportunity to ask students to share what they consider annotations to be. Their responses varied: "a useful comment, an addition to a text to clarify, notes about the reading, reflections, additional facts, context, explanatory devices in a text, a note to elaborate on something that is mentioned or referenced in the text, any additional information added near text, further information, a word definition, a response to a particular part of text, a comment on the text, a note made about a certain portion of the text, something added to add to or comment on something in text, a short description to give more info/afterthought on a topic, and more detail." In general, such responses suggested that they understood annotations as something factual or contextual, rather than interpretive. With these ideas in hand, we could then talk about how they might come up with annotations as they read *Invitation* and the other novels. Later in the semester, we would return to this question, using the work on the Scalar project to consider how it had complicated our understanding of annotations. Naturally, such tools come with a learning curve, so it was important to scaffold the assignment properly. To that end, to close out this introductory session, students practiced building a page, placing text, and linking and importing media (photo, videos, and so on). During the semester, we also twice held open lab hours at which students could ask technical or conceptual questions.

To be sure, we didn't exactly set ourselves the goal of breaking scholarly ground through the practice of writing these annotations. Olga Skonechnaia's excellent notes on *The Nabokovian* website already exist.[11] Julian Connolly's *Nabokov's "Invitation to a Beheading": A Critical Companion*, Gavriel Shapiro's *Delicate Markers: Subtexts in Vladimir Nabokov's "Invitation to a Beheading,"* and, of course, the annotations in the Russian collected works are also terrific resources.[12] Nonetheless, the annotations produced by my students, while not as extensive (yet!), are open-access—an important and pedagogically useful concept that likewise challenges established academic structures.[13] For the most part, my students didn't make use of these previous commentaries either, opting instead to conduct their own research about various references in the novel. Furthermore, making use of the medium, they were able to incorporate materials not necessarily available in other commentaries (images, videos, and so on) that can expand readers' understanding of a work's subtexts, contexts, and allusions.

As with the rest of the novels we read, I carved *Invitation to a Beheading* up into page ranges based on the enrollment so that each student covered roughly the same amount of material from each book. When we reached those pages, students posted draft annotations, which included page numbers and references to characters, people, places, events, and items that a reader may not be familiar with, on a shared Google Doc on the respective days that students had been assigned. Of course, some books and pages generated more annotations than others. To ensure that we did not double up on annotations for a given text, students had to take a glance at the referents (e.g., a character or location) that their peers had already added. When a referent did reappear in their assigned section, they could simply add their commentary to the initial annotation and/or refer readers to earlier or later page(s).

After receiving my feedback and considering comments and ideas provided by other contributors on the Google Doc, students then expanded their annotations into a second-stage form on Scalar by midnight on the following Saturday each week. For the sake of consistency, the annotation pages had to follow the same preset style, unlike other sections of the website that permitted greater flexibility and personalization in design and formatting.

I requested that these annotations be no more than two paragraphs, but they could be significantly shorter depending on the topic. In this expanded iteration, the annotations included the page number, referent (word or phrase), the student's explanatory and/or interpretive annotation, and any relevant media. Where applicable, students were to add hyperlinks between pages on Scalar, demonstrating, first, the connections *within* individual novels and, second, how these works are also interrelated. I asked them to keep track of potential connections, with concrete examples, that they identified as the class progressed (either on a personal document or by commenting on the collective Google Docs). This process made it easier for them to identify ways to revise annotations and to link them to one another.

Results

What was most exciting to see was how students cross-referenced their pages to find those links organically. With Nabokov, these narrative connections can be difficult to spot, at the very least upon first reading. Rather than reveal them in a top-down, instructor-led fashion (whether exclusively or primarily), students can come to discover some for themselves, which is all the better to "Find What the Sailor Has Hidden," Nabokov's metaphor from his autobiography *Speak, Memory* for discovering hidden patterns not only in literature but also in life.[14] As they're already reading closely for details for their annotations, they're also more apt to feel out those links on their own as they make their way through the pages of *Invitation*. It's a reminder that puzzle-solving sometimes involves subjective decision-making; some literary puzzles, even Nabokov's, are less straightforward, more open-ended than other kinds. The work was in this way recursive, as by the time they revised their first-draft annotations, they had read more of the novel and could expand their analysis, make more connections, and relate their work to that of their peers.

The resulting annotations covered everything from the characters (their names, appearances, personalities) to historical contexts (conditions in the Soviet Union and Germany at the time of writing, Pushkin's life and death), from the French and Russian words that Nabokov weaves into the text to obscure items (the meerschaum pipe) and curious modifiers (lyrate). My students by and large resisted the temptation to turn into budding Kinbotes, but I was struck by certain annotations. For instance, one student described Cecilia C. on the website as an "extremely erratic and questionable woman."[15] In class, I used this and other annotations to hold another discussion, returning to what it means to perform such editorial work. By this point in the semester, some saw it as "reader's notes," which better reflected the subjective nature of annotating. In general, they had clearly become attuned to how the annotator's positionality, perspective, and preferences give shape to another reader's experience of a text, which nicely dovetailed with topics that *Invitation* raises: the nature of writing, the power of art, transparency and opacity. They wrestled with various related questions: How much context is necessary for a reader? What qualifies for an annotation? What should our sources be, and to what extent should we turn to the author's own statements for insights into the novel? Which aspects of *Invitation* should we elucidate? Which of them can or must we leave obscure?

Naturally, the annotation pages varied a great deal. Some grew into discursive explorations of themes and images with numerous entries, while others remained relatively more straightforward, factual, or technical. In terms of style, a couple students opted to use a more humorous tone, particularly when it came to image captions. There was also natural variation depending on the ranges assigned for *Invitation*; some sections are simply richer in allusions and references than others. Again, these circumstances, partly a matter of chance, opened possibilities when it comes to studying Nabokov not in a hierarchical manner but in one that allows for individual decisions and a mix of approaches. This doesn't mean other pedagogical models don't or can't do the same, but rather that this one foregrounds and fosters that style of learning to good benefit.

Particularly with a writer such as Nabokov, who wields immense authorial power, supercharged through a historical critical reception that emphasizes the author's tight narrative structures and control over his material, this approach can create a more inclusive, egalitarian classroom. First, students are granted greater agency in their learning, as they choose (to some extent) which words "matter" for the annotations. They become critics who unearth meaning from the text, taking apart the novel to unpack its structures, layers, and references and editors who curate their findings for a potentially wide audience. They can thus pursue their interests, following threads that grab them. Along these lines, one student wrote:

> As someone who is not Russian, not steeped in Russian culture, and not yet steeped in literature either, writing annotations for each of the books in our class was extremely helpful. Partially it just helped me to learn

some things about Russian culture and some landmarks in Russia. More interesting, though, was the web of references that the Scalar annotation project allowed me to see, both within novels and between them. An author references an obscure opera—suddenly, I am down a rabbit hole of investigating the final sequence of this opera which mirrors the end of the novel. Nabokov referenced Pushkin several times, whom I knew nothing of before this course, and learned about mainly through other authors' references. Mainly, the annotations helped to situate these often-confusing novels within time periods, cultures, and inspirations, and thereby made me feel less unmoored than I would have felt if thrown in headfirst to a world I only half-understood.

This is not to suggest that we, as instructors, abandon our position as the literary expert in the classroom. Instead, approaches such as this one permit us to collaborate, to co-create, to support students' individual learning strategies and preferences while still both highlighting what we deem most important about the texts to share with students and helping develop their critical interpretation and domain-specific reading skills. When it comes to Nabokov's dense *Invitation*, there's plenty to explore through this student-centric approach. My hope was that this process would allow students to gain a deeper understanding of and appreciation for these works and their contexts, and this collaborative project would serve as a valuable resource for others reading these writers and novels in future classes and beyond. Likewise, this assignment benefited students in numerous other ways. For instance, they explored the possibilities of curation and gained or developed skills in storytelling, project management, and the use of digital tools.

The Scalar project drew their attention to the details of the text, always crucial when it comes to reading Nabokov. The details. The repetitions. The texture and substance of the work. It's a commonplace of Nabokovian criticism to cite the author's imperative to "caress the details," but how to best do that with novice readers of this literature? These annotation projects offer one direct, effective means to do so.[16] On this note, when I asked my students to share their thoughts on the project, one responded: "The annotations were an engaging way to get me thinking about recurring motifs. It was very satisfying to see it all come together at the end, and it helped me understand some of the more complex themes at play." The assignment thus broke down the reading into small steps and an approach that felt more manageable and, indeed, shared.

Not only that, but it allowed students to do more of their own learning, even if only for their allotted page range. They took ownership over what they were reading. At the same time, the practice cultivated a useful broader practice of digging up information rather than skipping an unfamiliar word or potential allusion no matter the page:

> Reading and going through the annotations not only forced me to understand what I read (such as learning about operas or even simple terms like dachas), it also intrinsically prompted my mind to try to draw connections between various elements within the story that I've read while researching/writing the annotations. Because of this aspect, I felt much better prepared going into class and participating. Often when I read for pleasure and I happen to stumble across a word I'm unfamiliar with or a mention of a painting/book title/opera/pop-culture or any other references, I gloss over them, potentially losing out on much of the important literary elements that can enhance my reading experience (especially with texts like Nabokov's *Invitation to a Beheading*). Doing the annotations really helped me comprehend and gather my thoughts, forcing me to slow down my reading and analyze line by line to figure out potential connections.

The project's scaffolded structure thereby motivated students to read Nabokov in a productive manner that involves paying attention to the unfamiliar and revealed to them the benefits, both individual and communal, of doing so.

It's here, too, perhaps that we also see a shift away from an affirmation of Nabokov's authorial control and the instructor's ensuing position of authority when teaching him. This method makes excavators of the students, who prod and poke and peel back *Invitation*'s many discrete parts to see the wider picture. In this way, they're not dependent on the instructor for total clarity and meaning but rather take on this responsibility (a right, in other words) for themselves and share it with others, both within and without the class since their work is publicly available on the Scalar site.[17]

Furthermore, in yet another potential challenge to authorial power, this assignment grants these readers, often new to Nabokov studies, the freedom to deem something significant—or not. I realize that this is a precarious position, but it levels the playing field to an extent in positive ways. As I describe the goals of the project on the assignment guidelines for students, it may be tempting to view annotations as strictly "factual" definitions and descriptions. However, annotations, while offering context (historical, political, biographical, etc.), are also analytical and intended to clearly illuminate the connections between complex ideas, themes, metaphors, and symbols. A good annotation in some way explicates the importance of its referent to the novel, both as a whole and on a particular page. It might highlight the presence of a repeated motif. Annotations, in short, are subjective, interpretive, and dependent on what the editor (here: the student!) chooses to underscore. In this course, I stressed that my students also didn't need to write an annotation for every unfamiliar word as if for a dictionary. It seems to me that this methodology is a novel concept to most students, especially those who are *not* literature majors, as evidenced by their initial responses to my question regarding the nature of annotations. In short, the project encouraged fresh readings and creative explorations of the material, because it trusted the student-researchers and ensured close attention.

One of the greatest benefits of this project was certainly its community-building aspect. This aspect of the assignment was particularly important as I launched the Scalar project in our first semester of entirely remote learning during the COVID-19 pandemic. Since everyone was contributing to the same Google Docs and Scalar site, a sense of camaraderie naturally emerged amid the challenging era of "Zoom University." Students could learn from one another's work actively and regularly or, looking at things more cynically (for the sake of argument), feel compelled to generate solid work since it was all there for their peers to see.[18]

In a similar vein, I believe that the awareness that these annotations could potentially later be accessed by a wider readership in most cases motivated the students to generate their best work. It strikes me that so much of what students produce in our classes is essentially writing for the drawer. It appears on our desk or our content learning system, and from there, maybe one or two people read it, then unfortunately, it dies on the same platforms. Undergraduate work obviously requires different attention, particularly when it comes to research that will be made available online, but what is the point of all we do if not to put it in dialogue with other scholars and readers of these works? Here that sense of a much wider community of readers that can appeal to all readers of all generations who engage with the material in a meaningful way emerges.

Regardless of my students' motivations, the conversations we held regarding the novel bloomed thanks in part to this approach. They were generally focused on the nuances of the text, and we were still able to discuss key aspects of *Invitation*—the otherworld, the female characters, narrative tricks, and so on—that I consider critical, but students were consistently better equipped to contribute since they had each developed a minor expertise of sorts on their allotted page range—but usually even more. In a novel that features what one student playfully called a "mindscape bending" adventure, having these anchors and research practices helps tremendously. The students themselves recognized this, too:

> Writing annotations for various Russian works, including those by Nabokov, was a unique experience that not only was a fun course assignment, but also provided me with an opportunity to deeply engross myself in the texts. Some of the annotations were simple definitions, while others explored the significance of different parts of the novels, such as locations, names, artistic references, etc. I appreciated having this to look to when I was confused about a particular piece of the reading. The annotations overall provide a great library of information that can be used to understand the intricacies of the novels.

Perhaps the question should then not be, "Do our students read?" but rather, "How can we motivate deep reading of Nabokov, the kind of reading that carries over into discussions and writing and, most importantly, that will leave lasting impressions?" This community of annotators of *Invitation to a Beheading* didn't necessarily enter Nabokov's world on steady footing, but ultimately, they became assured readers of a highly complex work through a fruitful, dynamic interplay of individual research and communal exchange.

Notes

1 See, for instance, www.huffpost.com/entry/gifts-for-gen-z-gift-guide-genz_l_6 19ba6ede4b025be1adef78b, https://psmag.com/ideas/theres-a-crisis-of-reading-among-generation-z, https://princh.com/blog/which-generation-reads-the-most/#.YZ0_sPHMIQw, https://bookriot.com/how-does-generation-z-read/, or www.ypulse.com/article/2020/03/16/does-gen-z-read-books-answering-5-big-questions-about-the-generation/.

2   Consider Pamela J. Howard, Meg Gorzycki, Geoffrey Desa, and Diane D. Allen, "Academic Reading: Comparing Students' and Faculty Perceptions of Its Value, Practice, and Pedagogy," *Journal of College Reading and Learning* 48, no. 3 (2018), 199; Helen St. Clair-Thompson, Alison Graham, and Sara Marsham, "Exploring the Reading Practices of Undergraduate Students," *Education Inquiry* 9, no. 3 (2018) 284–298; Scott Carlson, "The Net Generation Goes to College," *Chronicle of Higher Education* (Oct. 7, 2005), www.chronicle.com/article/the-net-generation-goes-to-college/; Mary E. Hoeft, "Why University Students Don't Read: What Professors Can Do to Increase Compliance," *International Journal for the Scholarship of Teaching and Learning* 6, no. 2 (2012): 1–14; Sarah J. Hatteburg and Kody Steffy, "Increasing Reading Compliance of Undergraduates: An Evaluation of Compliance Methods," *Teaching Sociology* 41, no. 4 (2013): 346–352; Suhua Huang, Matthew Capps, Jeff Blacklock, and Mary Garza, "Reading Habits of College Students in the United States," *Reading Psychology* 35, no. 4 (2014): 437–467; Kouider Mokhtari, Carla A. Reichard, and Anne Gardner, "The Impact of Internet and Television Use on the Reading Habits and Practices of College Students," *Journal of Adolescent and Adult Literacy* 52, no. 7 (2009): 609–-619; Keith Starcher and Dennis Proffitt, "Encouraging Students to Read: What Professors Are (and Aren't) Doing about It," *International Journal of Teaching and Learning in Higher Education* 23, no. 3 (2011): 396–407; and Terry Tomasek, "Critical Reading: Using Reading Prompts to Promote Active Engagement with Text," *International Journal of Teaching and Learning in Higher Education* 21, no. 1 (2009): 127–132.

3   Howard et al., "Academic Reading," 199.

4   Ibid., 201.

5   Ibid., 201, 204.

6   Joan Middendorf and David Pace, "Decoding the Disciplines: A Model for Helping Students Learn Disciplinary Ways of Thinking," *New Directions for Teaching and Learning* 98 (2004): 1.

7   Ibid.

8   "About Scalar," *Scalar*, https://scalar.me/anvc/scalar/. Last accessed May 12, 2022.

9   Ibid.

10 For context, in this survey course, alongside *Invitation to a Beheading*, we also read Mikhail Kuzmin's *Wings*, Yury Olesha's *Envy*, Liudmila Chukovskaya's *Sofia Petrovna*, Anna Akhmatova's *Requiem*, portions of Alexander Solzhenitsyn's *Gulag Archipelago*, Sasha Sokolov's *Between Dog and Wolf*, Chingiz Aitmatov's *The Day Lasts More Than a Hundred Years*, Liudmila Ulitskaya's *Sonechka*, and Evgeny Vodolazkin's *The Aviator*.

11 Skonechnaia's annotations to *Invitation to a Beheading* are available, in English and in Russian, here: https://thenabokovian.org/annotations.

12 Julian W. Connolly, ed., *Nabokov's "Invitation to a Beheading": A Critical Companion* (Evanston, IL: Northwestern UP, 1997). Gavriel Shapiro, *Delicate Markers: Subtexts in Vladimir Nabokov's "Invitation to a Beheading"* (Frankfurt am Main: Peter Lang, 1998).

Vladimir Nabokov, *Sobranie sochineniia russkogo perioda v piati tomakh*, vol. 4 (Moskva: Simpozium, 2000).

13 The nature of the project means that students in future iterations of the course can expand and supplement the current notes.

14 Vladimir Nabokov, *Speak, Memory: An Autobiography Revisited* (New York: Vintage Books, 1989), 310.

15 Anonymous, "Vladimir Nabokov Annotations: Invitation to a Beheading 122–136)," *The 20th-Century Russian Novel: Revolution, Terror, Resistance*, https://ds-exhibits.swarthmore.edu/scalar/the-20th-century-russian-novel-/invitation-to-a-beheading-122-136?path=vladimir-nabokov-annotations.

16 Vladimir Nabokov, *Lectures on Literature*, ed. Fredson Bowers (San Diego: Harcourt Brace Jovanovich, 1980), xxiii.

17 Students were given the option to share their work with their names attached (first, last, or both) or submit the commentary anonymously or withhold their work entirely. Almost all students, in my case, opted for some version of the former.

18 As Middendorf and Pace write, "It is not sufficient to assume that the structures of learning created by this process will automatically motivate students. Conscious effort needs to be dedicated to making the students partners in the learning process. The nature of this process allows an instructor to present himself or herself as an ally who has devoted considerable energy to creating a course in which success is possible and who really wants students to do well." Middendorf and Pace, "Decoding the Disciplines," 8.

PART II

MIXING CULTURES

Teaching *Poshlost'*: Texts and Contexts

Matthew Walker

1

Being a "teacher of literature," I tend to focus on Vladimir Nabokov's strangeness and difficulty as a writer, but as a Russianist, it is always tempting to see things the other way around: in practical terms, Nabokov's close connection with American culture means that his work, however challenging, can potentially serve U.S. students as a more easily negotiated path into the broader field of Russian literature, a kind of gateway drug, if you will. After all, the usual obstacles of translation appear to have been hauled away, at least at first glance, and while other Russian writers might demand knowledge of unfamiliar ideological contexts in order to be understood "correctly," Nabokov, with his self-professed "vague old-fashioned liberalism," seems by contrast much nearer to American mores and manners.[1] On the other side of all the puzzles and puns, some students perceive a kindred spirit, and what is more, the author himself declared the same affinity: "It is in America that I found my best readers," Nabokov tells one interviewer in 1962, "minds that are closest to mine."[2]

Of course, 1962 is not 2022. Are we still Nabokov's "best readers"? After all, contexts and values change or, better, become contested, or they decay with time and have to be articulated anew. How much does that change, or render contestable, the way we should read a book—any book, but especially Nabokov's books? To what degree, for that matter, is the context in which they were written still properly accessible to us, to what degree does their material existence as writing already unmoor them from that context, from the values they would bear? Does a proper reading of a book have to reproduce or mimic the context of its original production in toto (think Nabokov's translation of Alexander Pushkin's *Onegin*) or is it folly to imagine we can do so (think *Pale Fire* or the translation machine in *Bend Sinister*). This is one problem we have to consider, one that Nabokov's works themselves seem to raise persistently.

Here is another: in reading Nabokov we find that there *are* in fact some particularly Russian cultural obsessions that need to be reckoned with, and one of the most important of these is no doubt the seemingly untranslatable concept of *poshlost'*, which Nabokov first glosses for his Anglophone audience in *Nikolai Gogol* (1944) as "not only the obviously trashy, but also the falsely important, the falsely beautiful, the falsely clever, the falsely attractive."[3] *Poshlost'* is both a regular theme in Nabokov's fiction and anathema to his aesthetics, one of the wellsprings of his art and its kryptonite, as it were; accordingly, in the monograph course I teach on his work I usually devote one or two lectures to elaborating the concept for my students, both in regard to how Nabokov seems to understand it and the way it operates more broadly in Russian culture. Nabokov is often credited with introducing *poshlost'* as a new word to the English language,[4] and at the peak of his post-*Lolita* celebrity discussion of the term became modish enough in the United States that a publication as middlebrow as *Time* magazine could run an article on it, hailing both the word's novelty and its necessity even as it clumsily mispronounced it as "push-lost."[5] That Nabokov introduced the word into English is true, though only to a point: the literary critic D. S. Mirsky mentions it in 1927, in a chapter on Gogol in his history of Russian literature (defining it as "self-satisfied inferiority"), but Nabokov brings it to a substantially larger auditorium and, of course, with considerably more artistic verve.[6] However, it is also the case that, unlike Russian words such as "intelligentsia," *poshlost'* has hardly ventured off on its own since. After all, for a word to belong to a language, it has to become to some degree common, and in English *poshlost'* still really belongs to Nabokov alone.

In Russian culture, however, the circumstances are rather different—the word circulates, it has a history. To begin giving students a sense of this, one obvious place to start is the dictionary. Kuznetsov's *Bol'shoi tolkovyi slovar' russkogo iazyka*, for instance, records three basic meanings for *poshlost'*, or rather the adjectival form *poshlyi*, from which the abstract noun derives:

1) Base, insignificant [*nichtozhnyi*] in relation to the spiritual or moral. *Poshlyi person, poshloe society, poshlaia milieu.* Expressing, revealing such qualities. *Poshlyi tone, poshlaia grin.*

2) Containing something indecent or obscene. *Poshlye anecdotes, photographs. Poshlyi magazine. Poshlaia joke, scene, appearance.*

3) Unoriginal, hackneyed, banal. *Poshlyi tune. Observing the rites of matchmaking seemed to him poshloe.* Tastelessly crude, vulgar. *Poshlye flowers. The fence is decorated with poshlye curlicues.*[7]

If we consider these senses separately, we see that there is nothing so ineffable about them that they resist translation into English in and of themselves. Rather, the main problem seems to be a lack of a single English word that encompasses all three at once, "banality, lack of spirituality, and sexual obscenity," as Svetlana Boym, for instance, catalogues them in her own more recent (and very useful) analysis of the concept.[8] Nabokov, writing in his monograph on Gogol a half century earlier, appears to be saying something similar, that "various aspects of the idea which Russians concisely express by the word *poshlost'* [...] are split among several English words."[9] Yet if we look back at the gloss of *poshlost'* in *Nikolai Gogol* I've cited above—that *poshlost'* is "not only the obviously trashy, but also the falsely important, the falsely beautiful, the falsely clever, the falsely attractive"—we should already sense that Nabokov is aiming for something more complicated than the standard dictionary definition, and that at the same time he is setting some parts of that definition to the side. What is the difference? Once students have the dictionary definition of *poshlost'* in hand, their task is to read Nabokov's definition closely and try to figure it out.

2

At this point, as an instructor, you actually have a choice between two texts in which Nabokov defines *poshlost'* that you can assign to your students, and each has its advantages and disadvantages for discussion. The first is the twelve pages of *Nikolai Gogol* that Nabokov devotes to unpacking the concept, while the second is shorter, "Philistines and Philistinism," an essay included in *Lectures on Russian Literature* that recycles bits and pieces from the definition in the Gogol book for a more general audience, namely his European literature survey at Cornell. The latter text, pedagogically speaking, is a simpler option in some respects, but if you opt for *Nikolai Gogol* instead, it at least warrants a few remarks. For one, "Philistines and Philistinism" slightly clarifies the gloss we started out with—here, *poshlost'* is "not only the obviously trashy, but *mainly* the falsely important," etc.[10] For another, the essay oddly enough seems considerably less bothered about the complexities of translating *poshlost'* into English, for toward its conclusion we find Nabokov renders the word succinctly and without any suggestion of remainder as "smug philistinism," with "philistine" defined at the outset as "a full-grown person whose interests are of a material and commonplace nature, and whose mentality is formed of the stock ideas and conventional ideals of his or her group or time."[11] Lastly, if your course is primarily focused on *Lolita*, Nabokov's least Russian novel, then "Philistines and Philistinism" is a logical supplementary reading if you want to explain, with less of an extended detour into Russian culture, what Nabokov means in his afterword when he writes, "Nothing is more exhilarating than philistine vulgarity."[12]

The word *philistine* of course comes with its own complicated genealogy. Most famously deployed in Matthew Arnold's *Culture and Anarchy* (1868–1869), wherein Arnold implores Victorian England to see beyond its fetishization of the mere "machinery" of material culture in favor of its spiritual or aesthetic realization as "sweetness and light," the term is quite explicit about drawing a line between those who would ostensibly "have" culture and those who would not. In the eighteenth and nineteenth centuries students in German university towns used *Philister* as a derogatory term for uneducated local citizens, that is, non-students or "townies," in the jargon of North American liberal arts colleges, and before that in ancient Israel it had a meaning similar to what *barbarian* implied for the Greeks.[13] Today we might deem both of these historical uses elitist or exclusionary, but it is important to note that Nabokov, for his part, unlike Arnold, takes pains to deny that philistinism as a mode of being necessarily has anything to do with a particular body politic or political economy. "Philistinism is international," Nabokov writes, "It is found in all nations and in all classes. An English duke can be as much of a philistine as an American Shriner or a French bureaucrat or a Soviet citizen."[14] Whether or not we want to take Nabokov at his word here, starting with examining the origins of the term can serve as a good way to begin asking students what the grounds for deciding what does and does not constitute *poshlost'* might be, if indeed the decision is not to be based on an us-them notion organized around national culture or class.

What is certain, in any event, is that in "Philistines and Philistinism" Nabokov clearly opposes *poshlost'* to what we might best describe as aesthetic education. Indeed, Nabokov even suggests that it is the latter that generates the former category: "It is possible that the term itself has been so nicely devised by Russians because of the cult of simplicity and good taste in old Russia," he writes.[15] Boym, interestingly, counts this statement as "one of the least ironic sentences in Nabokov, bordering on the banal,"[16] and in her defense Nabokov's subsequent claim, that "in the old days a Gogol, a Tolstoy, a Chekhov in quest of the simplicity of truth easily distinguished the vulgar side of things" strangely suspends, in a way that I like to think is very un-Nabokovian, any concerns we might have about irony when reading all three of the writers he lists in search of "truth."[17] After all, if one concurs with Nabokov's general argument in *Nikolai Gogol*, then Gogol's whole talent and tragedy consists precisely in the fact he could *only* convey the vulgar side of things—when he tried to go further, toward a Russian version of "sweetness and light" with the continuation of *Dead Souls*, he lost his genius as a writer.

Historically speaking, Gogol's failure is part and parcel of a utopian branch of the discourse on *poshlost'* in Russian culture, one that imagines *poshlost'* as a malaise that must be transcended not just in individual works of art but collectively, by society as a whole. Boym's study is particularly attentive to this aspect of the problem, drawing connections between the way nineteenth-century Russian literature dwells on *poshlost'* and how it later becomes a major fixation in the Soviet avant-garde (for example, Mayakovsky, Constructivism), a link Nabokov is not really willing or intellectually equipped to consider. In this regard, though, "Philistines and Philistinism" is also useful in that it gives us a slightly clearer hint than *Nikolai Gogol* does about one of the factors that draws Nabokov away from this utopian tendency, namely, his debt to the French novelist Gustave Flaubert,[18] for it is Flaubert that supplies Nabokov here with one more one-word translation for *poshlost'*, one that Nabokov treats as effectively interchangeable with "smug philistine"—"bourgeois."[19] In both *Nikolai Gogol* and "Philistines and Philistinism" Nabokov warns his reader against confusing the Flaubertian sense of the term with the Marxist one: for Flaubert, "bourgeois" is not a class designation but a synonym for *bêtise* ("I call a bourgeois anyone who thinks basely"), or as Nabokov puts it, it is a "state of mind, not a state of pocket."[20] But what distinguishes Flaubert's war on cliché from the Russian war on *poshlost'* is precisely Flaubert's unrelenting irony. Unlike Gogol's struggle with *Dead Souls*, in *Madame Bovary* Flaubert harbors no aspirations toward rescuing characters like Emma Bovary or Homais from banality, or ultimately even escaping from it himself ("Madame Bovary, c'est moi!"), and the goal of his unfinished *Dictionary of Received Ideas* was even more radical: "If properly done," Flaubert writes, "anyone who ever read it would never dare open his mouth again, for fear of spontaneously uttering one of its pronouncements."[21] We will come back to Flaubert.

3

For my part, as useful as "Philistines and Philistinism" is, when I teach on *poshlost'* I prefer to use Nabokov's definition in *Nikolai Gogol*, first, because it allows for a more sophisticated approach to the topic, and second, because the text demands closer reading—to abuse the old writing and rhetoric classroom cliché, it shows more than it tells.

As said, when Nabokov starts out translating the "idea" of *poshlost'* in *Nikolai Gogol*, or *poshlust*, as he unconventionally proposes transliterating it there, he declares that it has no single-word equivalent in English or the other European languages he knows, even though we know he will come up with ones in English and French later. But, for the moment, when it comes to finding other words to use as brass tacks, so to speak, he doesn't really seem to be attempting to cover all three of the senses found in the dictionary equally:

> English words expressing several, although by no means all aspects of *poshlust* are for instance: "cheap, sham, common, smutty, pink-and-blue, high falutin', in bad taste." My little assistant, *Roget's Thesaurus*, (which incidentally lists "rats, mice" under "Insects"—see page 21 of Revised Edition) supplies me moreover with "inferior, sorry, trashy, scurvy, tawdry, gimcrack" and others under "cheapness."[22]

All the dozen words that Nabokov proposes may overlap with the dictionary entry in one way or another, but of the first six a majority are more explicitly about value, specifically, they measure a devaluation of value, a frayed relation with it—we might see them as qualified versions of dictionary senses one and three. That Nabokov fills out the rest of his dozen with the aid of a thesaurus entry for "cheapness" would seem to confirm that this is the common denominator—and not, say, "smutty," which is the only nod in his list toward dictionary sense two—although the demonstrable unreliability of this "little assistant" also suggests that positing similarities at the expense of differences might be part of the problem as well. *Poshlust* here is sweetener ("pink-and-blue") instead of sugar in your coffee, an inadequate substitute for the real thing, and as Nabokov will explain later, it "is especially vigorous and vicious when the sham is *not* obvious and when the values it mimics are considered, rightly or wrongly, to belong to the very highest level of art, thought or emotion."[23] In short, while values can be said to operate in all three dictionary senses of *poshlost'*, Nabokov's list of provisional English equivalents in *Nikolai Gogol* focuses more narrowly on their mimicry ("To imitate or copy minutely, uncritically, or servilely, usually so as to emulate or aspire to parity with, and frequently with ridiculous effect"—OED).

Nabokov is not alone in situating *poshlost'* as a problem of value. Consider the following, from the Soviet critic Lydia Ginzburg's notebooks from the 1940s:

> *Poshlost'* in essence is a perversion of value, an incorrect handling of value. *Poshlost'* either affirms as a value that which for genuinely cultured consciousness is not a value, or degrades what is valued, or it takes values developed in a cultural milieu inaccessible to it and applies them in the wrong place and in the wrong way; it tears them from an organic connection. *Poshlost'* cannot exist where there is an organic connection among values, i.e., culture. Therefore popular [*narodnoe*] consciousness in its intellectual manifestations cannot be *poshloe*.[24]

Ginzburg's description of the concept has much to recommend it, and in some ways it is more serviceable than Nabokov's—while Nabokov might find it difficult to explain to people why a novel that seems "chock-full of noble emotion and compassion" can be *poshloe*,[25] armed with Ginzburg's criteria we see quite readily how, for instance, Amor Towles's *A Gentleman in Moscow* (a recent Russia-related "bestseller" innocent students keep asking me about) qualifies as such: Towles, a former "investment professional" who might have spent his entire life condemned by the whims of global capital to gaze out at the world from luxury hotels, retires to write novels instead, and, without any convincing knowledge of Russian culture, tries to relay the Soviet experience through the eyes of an imaginary Russian aristocrat sentenced by the Cheka to lifelong imprisonment—in a luxury hotel, of all places. Write about what you know, as they say, but when one's values are utterly twenty-first-century American and bourgeois—that is, when one's command of high culture finds expression above all in an impeccable sense for wine-food pairings—one will have difficulty mimicking the manners of anyone else, much less a Russian count. Mimicking literary values for Towles proves no less of a challenge. As an exercise, one might have students look at an excerpt and imagine what Nabokov would have thought of it:

> ...standing in the empty corridor across from a half-eaten bowl of borscht, the Count felt less like a philosopher than a ghost.
> Yes, a ghost, thought the Count, as he moved silently down the hall. Like Hamlet's father roaming the ramparts of Elsinore after the midnight watch...Or like Akaky Akakievich, that forsaken spirit of Gogol's who in the wee hours haunted the Kalinkin Bridge in search of his stolen coat...
> Why is it that so many ghosts prefer to travel the halls of night?[26]

Without going into specifics, I am reasonably sure Nabokov would fulminate against Towles's writing as "bogus profundity," to use a pejorative from *Strong Opinions*, but with Ginzburg we can diagnose the matter in a less obstreperous and more clinical way. Simply put, *A Gentleman in Moscow* will be perceived as trivial by a reader who enjoys a degree of sensitivity to its ostensible cultural milieu exceeding that of its author. Kendall Jenner defusing a protest against police violence in the United States with a can of Pepsi—the subject of a commercial a number of my students spontaneously identified as *poshlost'* during discussion in a Nabokov course in 2017—seems ridiculous for the same reason, but it is at the same time worse because it depoliticizes values associated with Black Lives Matter more than it simply mishandles them; among critics of the ad, many pointed to the utter banality of the messages on signs held up by the protesters depicted in it (not "End Systemic Racism in the U.S.!" but "Join the Conversation!").[27] Another related example connected to state violence instructive for the classroom: in 2021, during the protests that followed the arrest of Russian opposition leader Aleksei Navalny, the poet Lev Rubinstein called out media personality Ksenia Sobchak for what he saw as a particularly *poshlaia* reaction to events that she posted on Instagram. Sobchak uploaded two videos, one of riot police brutally kicking an elderly woman in the stomach and sending her to the ground, the other of protestors playfully kicking around a riot policeman's helmet as if it were soccer ball. "Personally," Sobchak commented, "I find it unpleasant to watch any cruelty or violence. From either side."

A sentiment we can all endorse, Rubenstein concedes, but if you ask in turn if there was actually a head in that helmet you'll get a furious answer: "What's the difference!"[28] On a much broader scale, the same erasure is at work in the cult of memory that Putinism has constructed around the Soviet victory over fascism in 1945, which over the course of the past decade has absurdly turned fascist itself—it is designed to suppress difference. To the uninitiated, it looks like mere kitsch, but by its own logic it is not perverting values, but preserving them, or rather excluding them from the field of politics. Indeed, its de facto slogan, *Mozhem povtorit'* ("We can do it again," or literally, "we are able to repeat") banks on a conviction that the values of the past can be repeated *without* loss or alteration of meaning, which is to say without *poshlost'*. The practical effect of course is to foreclose any debate in Russian society over the past and condition the country for war.

In this case, then, what is detected as *poshlost'* might seem to depend on context, but we can't "both-sides" the situation either. One tends to perceive differences; the other only enforces similarities. To run through one more example, a student armed with Nabokov's definition of *poshlost'* will probably be unable to account for how Josef Stalin could pencil the word *poshliak* (male personification of the concept) in the margins of the Soviet writer Andrei Platonov's story "For Future Use" when he read it in a Soviet journal in 1931, a scholium that, given the influence of its author, put an almost complete end to Platonov's public career as a writer.[29] But with Ginzburg's framework it is more comprehensible: under Stalinism popular values were held to be identical with Soviet ones, after all, and Platonov was showing them being handled by the proletariat in the wrong way. Of course, I do not think that under the term "popular consciousness" Ginzburg understands quite the same thing as Stalin, but then this is precisely what is at issue. The baseline or context that Ginzburg uses to determine what would and would not be *poshlost'* is itself a concept that is inherently political, that is, open to dispute. Furthermore, as a foundation for culture I suspect Nabokov would reject it entirely—this, after all, is the very stuff of which propaganda photographs of "lovely Kolkhos maidens and windswept clouds" are made.[30] And if we're reading Ginzburg critically ourselves, we'll also register the work the metaphor of organicity performs for her in her definition—it naturalizes a culture, casting it as a living thing with a determinate relation to its origin rather than one that is constantly negotiated and renegotiated as value, a category that is fundamentally abstract, fluctuating, and arbitrary.

Having marked this sleight of hand though, we can also see that Nabokov pulls off something akin to it in his own argument in *Nikolai Gogol*, for just as he links the problem of *poshlost'* to value, he suddenly veers away from it, or, in a rather obscure way, seeks to dehistoricize it. Having cycled through his inventory of English words covering different aspects of the Russian term, Nabokov runs the rule over them again, as it were, and writes:

> All these however suggest merely certain false values for the detection of which no particular shrewdness is required. In fact they tend, these words, to supply an obvious classification of values at a given period of human history; but what Russians call *poshlust* is beautifully timeless and so cleverly painted all over with protective tints that its presence (in a book, in a soul, in an institution, in a thousand other places) often escapes detection.[31]

Where the English terms only denote value judgments contingent upon the historical moment in which they are made, *poshlost'* is "beautifully timeless," it effectively acquires the character of a Platonic form, and, in a kind of Bizarro World inversion of the stated rules of Nabokov's own art ("Find What The Sailor Has Hidden"), its detection becomes a process of camouflage and discovery, an "idea" revealing itself rather than the product of time grinding away at markers of value; *not*, what was once original is cheapened through repetition, but a matter of appearance and essence, outer and inner, falsehood and truth, the delineation of which moreover requires a certain "shrewdness"—talent, genius. The net result is that a historical judgment becomes an aesthetic one.[32]

However, Nabokov's position (which is also in a way ours: it does take talent to identify *poshlost'*) starts to look less secure if we take into account two complications: first, the temporality implied in the etymology of *poshlost'*, which Vasmer traces back to the past tense form of the verb "to go", *poshlo*, making *poshlost'* literally that which "has gone" or "what went"; and second, the fact that the signification of *poshlyi* itself clearly changes in Russian over time.[33] Initially the word indicates nothing more than that which is traditional, habitual, or commonly used, without the negative connotations it accrues later; the relevant entry in Vladimir Dahl's landmark nineteenth-century Russian lexicon, for instance, which was of course Nabokov's constant companion in exile from his Cambridge years on, first lists "old, long-existing, that which has long been customary [*chto izstari vedetsia*]" as an obsolete sense before moving on to others.³⁴ Custom is repetition that would maintain value; we repeat it precisely to this end, *because* others have done so in the past. Just how, historically speaking, this sense of *poshlyi* flips over to its opposite, how it becomes repetition that erases value, is not necessarily clear: Boym contends that the negative sense of *poshlost'*, what she calls "repetition gone sour," develops into a stock idea among the Russian intelligentsia of the nineteenth century in response to anxieties of identity produced by post-Petrine modernization and the premium Romantic-era aesthetics puts on originality. As a concept, *poshlost'* would thus police the boundary between authenticity and imitation, but the underlying fear is that all culture—both traditional Russian and newly imported European—is mere fashioning, ungrounded. As Boym puts it, "How is it possible to distinguish between good and bad repetition? How do we draw the line between the conventions that constitute our cultural situation, and the trivialization that creates culture's malignant doubles?"³⁵

In light of the foregoing we may have ample reason to accuse Nabokov, as Boym does, of critical negligence for leaving most of these historical circumstances out of his account of *poshlost'*, but on the other hand, we might also have to accept that in the main he tends to avoid handling questions through philosophical or historical generalizations when he thinks they can be better addressed through art. After all, that Nabokov recognizes in "Philistines and Philistinism" that *poshlost'* presupposes an "advanced state of civilization" in which "certain traditions have accumulated in a heap and begun to stink" indicates that he is indeed aware of the problem as a historical one, even if the organic metaphor is still at work (instead of a green thumb, the critic of *poshlost'* needs a nose for decomposition).³⁶ Furthermore, we might also want to ask whether Nabokov's fiction does not actually take up in a very complex and singular way some of the same general questions that Boym sees the concept of *poshlost'* posing for Russian culture at large. Is it possible to distinguish between good and bad repetition? In the case of *Speak, Memory*, yes, triumphantly so, but in, say, "Return of Chorb," *The Luzhin Defense*, or *Lolita*, the answers are decidedly less affirmative. Likewise, to return to a contrast I pointed out above, Nabokov exhibits an almost unshakable confidence that he can establish and accurately reproduce in English the contexts and conventions that constitute the Russian cultural situation of *Eugene Onegin*—but what is *Pale Fire* but a malignant double of the same project? Nabokov might well take a measure of refuge in Platonism in his definition of *poshlost'*, but in some of his writings he is more like a Kierkegaard, wondering whether the difference between good and bad repetition is intelligible and, at the same time, whether repetition, properly speaking, is even possible at all once irony has a foot in the door.³⁷

If students have already read a reasonable number of Nabokov's works they should be able to grasp this relationship between *poshlost'* and repetition relatively easily, but if they are just getting started I like to conduct the following exercise, which also doubles as further practice for pronouncing *poshlost'* properly in Russian, beyond the witty instructions Nabokov gives in *Nikolai Gogol*. I play the students a brief clip from 2014 of the Russian film director Nikita Mikhalkov denouncing *poshlost'* (again, the target is Ksenia Sobchak, although this is more of a case of the pot calling the kettle black: Mikhalkov, a loyal mimic of state-sponsored values, even when the state exchanges those values for others, is a notorious arch-*poshliak* himself). In the clip, taken from the cultural commentary program Mikhalkov regularly hosts on Russian state television, he looks solemnly into the camera and, citing a famous line from Chekhov, pronounces three words over Sobchak's questioning the consequences of the Russian war in Ukraine, as if he were a priest closing out a sermon: "*Poshlost'…zveniashchaia poshlost'!*" The clip quickly spread as a meme in Russia, and a number of Internet users uploaded it to Coub, a site that generates gifs with sound so that the video can be run endlessly on a loop. Watch it five or ten times, and each time, as Mikhalkov's intonation rises on the second syllable of *zveniashchaia* ("resounding") and the producers cue up a dramatic melody to complement his pathos, you get a greater sense of what damage sheer repetition can do to the meaning of an utterance.³⁸

4

Thus far we have largely kept to discussion of the first and third dictionary senses of *poshlost'*, but one thing students should also notice while comparing Nabokov's definition in *Nikolai Gogol* with the dictionary is that the second sense given in the latter, "containing something indecent or obscene," receives little direct attention. Those more acquainted with Nabokov's work ought to find this especially odd. After all, a whole series of patently *poshlye* female characters from his novels (for example, Martha in *King, Queen, Knave*, Margot in *Laughter in the Dark*, Marthe in *Invitation to a Beheading*, Mariette in *Bend Sinister*, Armande in *Transparent Things*) are characterized by a casually soulless promiscuity, and Nabokov's male paragons of *poshlost'* are as a rule no less crude when it comes to sex either—the difference perhaps is that their crudeness often attempts to mimic artistic sense. A good local instance of this is M'sieur Pierre's salacious conversation with Cincinnatus during their chess game in *Invitation to a Beheading*, but on a larger, more horrifying scale Humbert Humbert's gestures toward aesthetic bliss as he describes statutory rape exemplify the pattern.[39] Furthermore, that Nabokov skirts around obscenity in *Nikolai Gogol* seems all the more curious if we know something about Gogol, for it is not as if relevant examples of sexual indecency combining with other aspects of *poshlost'* are difficult to find in his work as well (think Pirogov and the prostitute whom his doomed artist friend Piskarev chases after in "Nevsky Prospect," Akaky Akakyevich mysteriously "playing the sybarite" in his bed in "Overcoat," or simply the lewder allegorical angles of "Nose"). One critic suggests that Nabokov is limited in what he can say about the sexual side of *poshlost'* by the more conservative social mores of his American audience in the 1940s, which would be ironic,[40] but it would also explain why, apart from the presence of "smutty" among Nabokov's partial English equivalents, the few references we do get to indecency in Nabokov's definition are oblique: the punning transliteration of *poshlost'* as *poshlust*, by which the Russian word becomes a kind of English portmanteau that fortuitously combines luxury with sensuous, despiritualized desire, or the fact that one of the French words Nabokov proposes as near models for pronouncing the "moist softness" of the final "t" of the Russian is *émoustillant*, "titillating."[41]

Finally, there is one of the more grotesque exhibits of *poshlost'* Nabokov introduces, a photograph in a popular magazine of the "silk hosed dummy legs modeled on those of Hollywood lovelies and stuffed with candies and safety razor blades" that "kind people send our lonely soldiers."[42] It is worthwhile to have students analyze this specimen "cold," and ask them what makes this especially *poshloe* in Nabokov's eyes. Is it really the inordinate amount of "leg" that is being shown, as it were, which might well have scandalized the average upholder of public morals in 1944, or is it the gross incoherence of the image, a pinup turned piñata, that, among other things, points toward a popular ideal of female pulchritude via a "dummy" that unwittingly suggests its dismemberment? The assumption that it is the latter implies that sexual obscenity in and of itself is not the main factor in deciding if something is *poshloe* for Nabokov. It is not that it doesn't matter at all though—it clearly does in the examples from his fiction we have mentioned above, and it is particularly urgent in a work like *Lolita*. But it is nevertheless telling that when Nabokov has to address the question of obscenity more directly in his afterword to the same novel, he rejects the label of "pornography" not on the grounds that its subject matter is indecent but rather that as a rule, as a genre, it is unoriginal, in terms of style it is "limited to the copulation of clichés."[43] If we want to count this as contradiction or an evasion, we can, and we probably should if we don't think that the only thing that matters in *Lolita* is style. But we should perhaps also be aware that the conceptual tension might well be at least in part one that Nabokov inherits from the culture. As Boym writes, "Many Russian native speakers perceive *poshlost'* in relationship to *pokhot'* (lust), although there is no etymological relationship between the two. Others, on the contrary, would deny the sexual connotations of the word (explicitly stated in the dictionary)."[44] In everyday Russian speech, a *poshliak* is more often than not a boor who says crass things about women—think Trump in the *Access Hollywood* tape—but for a good illustration of Boym's second point one can refer to the Russian poet Timur Kibirov, who, in a radio interview from 2004, vehemently insists *poshlost'* and indecency ought to be separated as concepts "once and for all."[45] As support for his argument, Kibirov cites Henry Miller's infamous 1934 novel *Tropic of Cancer*, which in his opinion certainly qualifies as indecent, but should not be considered *poshlyi* for one reason—because in terms of style Miller was doing something new (the choice of Miller as evidence is ironic, though, insofar as Nabokov would most likely have classed it with the modern novels "truffled with obscenities" and "the enlarged pores of dirty words" that he dismisses in *Strong Opinions*).[46] Kibirov's interviewer, the novelist Viktor Erofeev, counters that *poshlost'* and indecency cannot be untangled so easily, that in the concept "one thing is superimposed on another." This is certainly also the case in Nabokov. If morality proceeds from art in Nabokov rather than the other way around, then his reticence toward discussing indecency in any other terms than aesthetic ones makes sense—but if aesthetic values in Nabokov are themselves less stable than we think, where does that leave us?[47]

5

In my course, the classroom discussion on *poshlost'* leads to a short writing assignment (500 words) in which students are asked to isolate and describe one example of *poshlost'* from contemporary culture and then defend their selection according to their understanding of Nabokov's criteria. The three extended cases that Nabokov describes in *Nikolai Gogol*—Gogol's German Lothario, Pop the Proud Donor (U.S. advertising), and the literary "bestseller"—are the primary models, and as these are not straightforward, we read through them together closely before they start the assignment.

As a warm-up, it is a good idea to first browse through a few entries from Flaubert's *Dictionary of Received Ideas*—which Nabokov, in contrast with his own examples, of course refers to as "a more ambitious work." The goal behind each of Flaubert's entries is, in effect, to evoke whatever truth the average bourgeois of his age has been conditioned to utter on a given topic without thinking.

> BIBLE: The oldest book in the world.
> DARWIN: The fellow who says we're descended from monkeys.
> GIFT: It's the thought that counts.
> GRAPESHOT: The only way to make the Parisians shut up.
> MATERIALISM: Utter the word with horror, stressing each syllable.[48]

Then we "brainstorm" (a word fit for an entry itself) to come up with contemporary versions, like these:

> ANTIFA: Stress on the second syllable, or you may have to explain what "fa" stands for.
> CONSERVATIVISM: Quote Winston Churchill.
> INSTITUTIONS: Our real strength.
> INVISIBLE HAND: Only the market has one.
> REFLECT: A nice verb.
> SHOPPING FOR COURSES: Use interchangeably with "deciding between," it's the same thing.[49]

In coming up with their own entries, the focus on words as such will usually lead a few students to connect *poshlost'* with the familiar campus debates around political correctness and free speech. Among other things, what this presents you with is a particularly good moment to discuss whether a concept like *poshlost'*—such as Nabokov understands it, such as Russian culture understands it, such as *we* might understand it—is intrinsically conservative. Historically, as a discourse, in many ways it is: one was reminded of this watching Putin's *Hunger Games*-style war rally for his Special Military Operation in Ukraine, ludicrously titled "For a World without Nazism," at Moscow's Luzhniki stadium in March 2022, when one of its celebrity performers, the film actor Vladimir Mashkov, recited for the crowd one of the nineteenth-century poet Fyodor Tiutchev's more vehement Slavophile poems, which, as it happens, echoes in part Arnold's rhetoric in *Culture and Anarchy*:

> Чем либеральней, тем они пошлее,
> Цивилизация – для них фетиш,
> Но недоступна им ее идея.

> The more liberal they are, the more *poshlye*,
> Civilization for them is fetish,
> But its idea for them is out of reach.

"They" is Europe. Tiutchev's poem ends swearing that in Europeans' eyes Russians will never be seen as "servants of Enlightenment...only as their slaves," and Mashkov wasted no time in connecting the poem to the present: "the slaves today are those who attempt to be politically correct before Europe and America."[50] One has to resist the notion that Tiutchev, or Mashkov for that matter, speaks for all of Russian culture though—Lev Rubinstein provides us with a counter-example above, and as dark as things look in Russia today there are many others.

Even in Flaubert, one of the targets in the early plans for the *Dictionary* is the alleged mediocrity of "the modern democratic idea of equality," and elsewhere in his correspondence he writes: "The entire dream of democracy is to raise the proletariat to the level of bourgeois stupidity."[51] On the other hand, the actual entries in Flaubert's dictionary do not really spare anything ("POLICEMAN: Bulwark of society"). Nabokov himself has more positive views of democracy, of course, though he also has his own vexed issues with equality (see *Bend Sinister*), and some of the items he includes in the inventories of *poshlost'* he shares in *Strong Opinions* ("an overconcern with class or race") sound at best like privilege speaking today, even if Nabokov was a vocal opponent of segregation in the United States; likewise, Nabokov's dismissal of books about "the sorrows of homosexuals" appears incomprehensibly callous, especially given the fate of his brother Sergei in Nazi Germany.[52] The question, for me at least, is whether the way we read Nabokov necessarily has to mimic our idea of who he was, or whether even trying to—emulating Nabokov, in 2022, without recognizing the differences—does not itself end up being a form of *poshlost'*. "I write for myself in multiplicate," Nabokov says at one other juncture in *Strong Opinions*, "a not unfamiliar phenomenon on the horizons of shimmering deserts."⁵³ The first clause seems like a closed circuit, a context that determines values, but the doubles Nabokov creates for himself are by his own admission mirages. They disappear as we get closer. What happens next is reading.

Notes

1. Vladimir Nabokov, *Strong Opinions* (New York: Vintage, 1990), 113.
2. Ibid., 10.
3. Vladimir Nabokov, *Nikolai Gogol* (New York: New Directions, 1961), 70.
4. See, for example, Sergei Davydov, "Poshlost'," in *The Garland Companion to Vladimir Nabokov*, ed. Vladimir E. Alexandrov (New York: Routledge, 1995), 628. Davydov's short essay provides an excellent road map for tracking the concept through Nabokov's oeuvre.
5. "In Russian it means vulgarity or triteness, but...Nabokov so expands the definition that it makes one wonder how the English language ever got along without it." "And Now, Poshlost," *Time* (December 1, 1967), 118; https://content.time.com/time/subscriber/article/0,33009,712044,00.html
6. "The aspect under which [Gogol] sees reality is expressed by the untranslatable Russian word *poshlost'*, which is perhaps best rendered as 'self-satisfied inferiority,' moral and spiritual." D. S. Mirsky, *A History of Russian Literature from the Earliest Times to the Death of Dostoyevsky (1881)* (London: A.A. Knopf, 1927), 193–194. It is worth noting that both Mirsky and Nabokov, in emphasizing the role of *poshlost'* in Gogol's art, are taking a cue from Dmitry Merezhkovsky's Symbolist-era study *Gogol and the Devil* (1906).
7. *Bol'shoi tolkovyi slovar' russkogo iazyka*, ed. S. A. Kuznetsov (St. Petersburg: Norint, 1998), 950. All translations from Russian are mine unless indicated.
8. Svetlana Boym, *Common Places: Mythologies of Everyday Life in Russia* (Cambridge, MA: Harvard UP, 1994), 3.
9. Nabokov, *Nikolai Gogol*, 63.
10. Vladimir Nabokov, "Philistines and Philistinism," in *Lectures on Russian Literature*, ed. Fredson Bowers (San Diego: Harcourt Brace, 1981), 313.
11. Ibid., 309–310.
12. Vladimir Nabokov, *The Annotated Lolita* (New York: Vintage, 1991), 315.
13. "Now, the use of culture is that it helps us, by means of its spiritual standard of perfection, to regard wealth as but machinery, and not only to say as a matter of words that we regard wealth as but machinery, but really to perceive and feel that it is so. If it were not for this purging effect wrought upon our minds by culture, the whole world, the future as well as the present, would inevitably belong to the Philistines. The people who believe most that our greatness and welfare are proved by our being very rich, and who most give their lives and thoughts to becoming rich, are just the very people whom we call Philistines. Culture says: 'Consider these people, then,

their way of life, their habits, their manners, the very tones of their voice; look at them attentively; observe the literature they read, the things which give them pleasure, the words which come forth out of their mouths, the thoughts which make the furniture of their minds; would any amount of wealth be worth having with the condition that one was to become just like these people by having it?'" Matthew Arnold, *Culture and Anarchy*, edited by J. Dover Wilson (Cambridge: Cambridge UP, 1966). On the origins of the word, see *OED*.

14 Nabokov, "Philistines and Philistinism," 310.
15 Ibid., 313.
16 Boym, *Common Places*, 41.
17 Nabokov, "Philistines and Philistinism," 313–314.
18 "I am re-reading *Bovary* for the hundredth time. So good, So good!" Vladimir Nabokov, *Letters to Véra* (New York: Vintage, 2017), 173.
19 "A bourgeois is a smug philistine." Nabokov, "Philistines and Philistinism," 310.
20 Gustave Flaubert, *Lettres de Gustave Flaubert à George Sand*, précédées d'une étude par Guy de Maupassant (Paris: G. Charpentier, 1884), lxxiv; Nabokov, "Philistines and Philistinism," 310. On distinguishing between the Marxist and Flaubertian senses of "bourgeois," see also *Lectures on Literature*, edited by Fredson Bowers (San Diego: Harcourt Brace, 1980), 126–127.
21 Gustave Flaubert, *The Letters of Gustave Flaubert 1830–1857*, selected, edited, and translated by Francis Steegmuller (London: Faber & Faber, 1979), 176.
22 Nabokov, *Nikolai Gogol*, 64.
23 Ibid., 68.
24 Lidiia Ginzburg, *Zapisnye knizhki, vospominaniia, esse* (St. Petersburg: Iskusstvo-SPb, 2002), 165.
25 Nabokov, *Nikolai Gogol*, 69–70.
26 Amor Towles, *A Gentleman in Moscow* (New York: Viking, 2016), 123.
27 Pepsi ultimately withdrew the commercial, but the full version is still available on YouTube: www.youtube.com/watch?v=uwvAgDCOdU4.
28 Rubinstein also cites Ginzburg's definition of *poshlost'* in his essay. See Lev Rubenshtein, "'Sami-to ponimaiut?' Lev Rubinstein o poshlosti i shevelenii khvostami," *MBKh Media*, February 27, 2021; https://mbk-news.appspot.com/sences/sami-to-ponimayut/. Sobchak's Instagram post: www.instagram.com/p/CKZd0cslreV/?utm_source=ig_web_copy_link.
29 Platonov's story first appeared in *Krasnaia nov'* 3 (March) 1931; the copy of the journal with Stalin's marginal notes can be viewed here: https://kkos.ru/blog/all/platonov-1931/.
30 Nabokov, *Nikolai Gogol*, 67. "Frankly," Nabokov confesses in one interview, "a national, folklore, class, masonic, religious, or any other communal aura involuntarily prejudices me against a novel…."; Nabokov, *Strong Opinions*, 113.
31 Nabokov, *Nikolai Gogol*, 64.
32 It is certainly not a coincidence that, in the course of defining *poshlost'*, the only other thing to which Nabokov grants immortality is "authentic literature." Ibid., 68.

33 Max Vasmer, *Russisches etymologisches Wörterbuch* (Heidelberg: C. Winters, 1953–1958), II:422; see also Boym, *Common Places*, 42.
34 Vladimir Dal', *Tolkovyi slovar' zhivogo velikorusskogo iazyka*, 4 vols. (Moscow: Russkii iayzk, 1990), III:374.
35 Boym, *Common Places*, 46.
36 Nabokov, "Philistines and Philistinism," 309–310.
37 See Søren Kierkegaard, *Repetition* and *Philosophical Crumbs*, trans. M. G. Piety (London: Oxford, 2009).
38 One of the posts on Coub: https://coub.com/view/259flm. The original broadcast of Mikhalkov's program, BesogonTV, on YouTube: (www.youtube.com/watch?v=LRG0 FPqSepE; see 26:45).
39 "When people ask me for advice" about sex, says Pierre to Cincinnatus, who has not asked for advice, "I always tell them, 'Gentlemen, be inventive. There is nothing more pleasant, for example, than to surround oneself with mirrors and watch the good work going on there—wonderful!'" Vladimir Nabokov, *Invitation to a Beheading* (New York: Vintage, 1989), 145.
40 John Burt Foster Jr., "Poshlust, Culture Criticism, Adorno, and Malraux," in *Nabokov and His Fiction: New Perspectives*, edited by Julian W. Connolly (London: Cambridge UP, 1999), 225.
41 Nabokov, *Nikolai Gogol*, 63, 64. The other French word Nabokov suggests is *restiez* (one assumes these are not chosen altogether at random).
42 Ibid., 67.
43 Nabokov, *The Annotated Lolita*, 314, 313.
44 Boym, *Common Places*, 303n49.
45 "Chto takoe poshlost'?" *Radio Svoboda*, October 30, 2004, www.svoboda.org/a/24197 194.html.
46 Nabokov, *Strong Opinions*, 4, 151.
47 On this, see Leland de la Durantaye, *Style Is Matter: The Moral Art of Vladimir Nabokov* (Ithaca, NY: Cornell UP, 2010).
48 Gustave Flaubert, *The Dictionary of Accepted Ideas*, translated by Jacques Barzun (New York: New Directions, 1968).
49 For a good attempt at other updates of Flaubert's dictionary, see Teju Cole, "In Place of Thought," *The New Yorker*, August 27, 2013. www.newyorker.com/books/page-turner/in-place-of-thought.
50 "Kak pered nei ni gnites', gospoda, Vam ne sniskat' priznan'ia ot Evropy," *Rossiiskaia gazeta*, March 19, 2022, https://rg.ru/2022/03/18/kak-pered-nej-ni-gnites-gospoda-vam-ne-sniskat-priznania-ot-evropy.html.
51 Flaubert, *The Letters*, 176, 183.
52 Nabokov, *Strong Opinions*, 101, 116. Sergei Nabokov was first arrested by the Nazis for his homosexuality in 1941 and died in Neuengamme concentration camp in 1945.
53 Ibid., 113.

Teaching Nabokov in a Virtual Time of Trouble

Tim Harte

As someone who has taught a "Nabokov in Translation" course at Bryn Mawr College for over fifteen years, I have long felt sheepish about my eager involvement in faculty governance at our all-women's college. Deep down, I know that my attendance at all those requisite weekly meetings for this or that committee would have been something dismissively shunned by the Russian-American writer. Vladimir Nabokov's flagrant disregard for faculty assemblies and the like while at Cornell University has been well documented.[1] In the summer of 2020 my Nabokov-inspired angst over active participation in everyday faculty affairs would come to a head, as I took on the central administrative role of provost (chief academic officer) at Bryn Mawr. It was a scholarly and professional contradiction I could certainly live with, but it did feel like an affront to my Nabokovian sensibilities. Amidst an ongoing pandemic that necessitated daily Zoom meetings from morning to night, I suddenly had little time for the creative, playful spirit of Nabokov's fiction and the invigorating *joie de vivre* (*zhizneradostnost'* in Russian) that I have always found unique to his writing and that I have enjoyed imparting to my students over the years. The pride I experienced when taking on such a prominent leadership role at the College was, alas, tempered by my inner Nabokov voice.

It would be several months into my tenure as Bryn Mawr's provost, moreover, when, seemingly out of the blue, I had on my hands what emerged as a student-led strike—or widespread boycott of classes—that was supported as well by a not-so-insignificant portion of the Bryn Mawr faculty. Centered around issues of race at the college and the Black Lives Matter movement (and, in particular, the police shooting of a Black man, Walter Wallace Jr., in nearby Philadelphia), this strike originated at neighboring Haverford College before spreading quickly to Bryn Mawr College, whereby we experienced over two weeks of controversy and class cancellations amidst a wide range of demands for racial justice and equity on campus from the striking students. That the strike started in late October before continuing into the first half of November was a Russian Revolution–related coincidence not lost on me. Against the backdrop of not only the pandemic and the Black Lives Matter movement but also a national presidential election that had everyone on edge on our semi-virtual campus (over half of all courses that semester were conducted via Zoom, even though approximately three-quarters of the student body was living on campus at the time), the strike provided a test of my academic ideals and administrative steel. As provost I had leadership duties that I needed to carry out, but I also had my own pedagogical perspective as someone teaching Nabokov at the college. Although the middle-of-the-road embrace of complexity championed by Anton Chekhov (whose short stories and plays I also teach) had its appeal as I navigated the situation, it was impossible not to view the situation through the lens of Nabokov and to envision, it stands to reason, how I might teach Nabokov at a post-strike college. Eventually the strike came to an end, as a somewhat beleaguered Bryn Mawr administration—myself included—agreed to a good portion of the striking students' demands. Yet the repercussions of the strike can still be felt today. As I prepare to teach my Nabokov course in spring 2022 (even as provost, I am still able to teach a course or two each year), I cannot help but gauge the political climate on campus and wonder how Nabokov's fiction might possibly suit the moment—or not.

It almost goes without saying that Nabokov would have looked askance at Bryn Mawr's student strike. Even though he often adopted a combative, defiant stance against injustice, Nabokov was hardly one to join in any broad social movement or go along with the so-called crowd. "Nabokov is a freedom fighter," Brian Boyd writes in his definitive biography of the Russian-American writer, "but his fight is philosophical and metaphysical, not social."[2] That so many students rushed to join the strike and boycott their Bryn Mawr courses en masse would have undoubtedly perturbed this stridently anti-Soviet writer who dismissed collective action like few others. "My aversion to groups," Nabokov stated in a 1967 interview, "is rather a matter of temperament than the fruit of information and thought. I was born that way and have despised ideological coercion instinctively all my life."³ Yet any hypothetical stance Nabokov may have taken against Bryn Mawr's strike might be seen as somewhat of a red herring here and ultimately not that important, for it is in Nabokov's fiction and aesthetic worldview that we can find more resonance and grounds for analyzing what it means to teach the Russian-American writer on a college campus today, especially one so recently roiled by the cultural and social politics of the day.

A natural question that immediately comes to mind is whether students would even want to take a Nabokov course following all the turmoil of the past year and amidst the ongoing reevaluation of the academic canon throughout higher education. Surely the decolonizing of the curriculum happening on campuses nationwide could be seen as knocking an outspoken aesthete—and elitist—such as Nabokov from his lofty perch and relegating his playful prose to the sidelines. That Nabokov was born into one of Russia's wealthiest families before the Revolution, enjoying a most privileged childhood while benefiting from a second-to-none education, would hardly align him with today's egalitarian academic sensibilities, even if the Nabokovs lost all their riches after the 1917 Russian Revolution and then endured the tragic death of Vladimir Nabokov Sr., the writer's father and an active politician-in-exile who fell victim to an assassin's bullet in 1920s Berlin. By the time the middle-aged Nabokov reached the shores of America in the early 1940s, he was far from the epitome of the pampered White Russian thumbing his nose at a democratic United States. Nevertheless, it stands to reason that a course devoted to the work of one writer with little direct relevance to the racial reckoning transpiring on Bryn Mawr's campus would have only limited appeal to students. To my pleasant surprise, however, a healthy batch of twenty undergraduates preregistered for this spring 2022 course, which suggests that an interest in the Russian-American writer—and author of *Lolita*, it should not be forgotten—to this day persists (although it does not hurt that my course counts for credit in both the Russian and English majors). Indeed, I would like to think that Nabokov's imaginative writing, playful take on the modern novel, and maximalist approach to life will always have a place on college campuses.

Yet the question remains: how does one go about teaching Nabokov in the post–George Floyd, post-strike environment existing at Bryn Mawr? And should the course be amended to suit the times? The task at hand has long been to delve into Nabokov's writings with my students, and that will always remain the central aim of the course, yet surely some discussion of race, prejudice, and a questioning of the status quo can be worked into the course. Following analysis of several early Nabokov stories ("A Letter that Never Reached Russia," "Beneficence," "Christmas," and "A Guide to Berlin"), my "Nabokov in Translation" course commences in full with the autobiographical *Speak, Memory*, a work that provides an excellent overview of Nabokov's pre-America life as well as his aesthetic, philosophical, and even social concerns. That the celebrated *Speak, Memory* was initially published in *The New Yorker* under the careful eye of Nabokov's editor at the magazine, Bryn Mawr graduate Katharine White, makes this wide-ranging memoir all the more special and unique for my students. More importantly, at the start of his memoir Nabokov takes an insubordinate stance against "common sense" and restraint that might, in certain respects, resonate with our current environment on campus:

> Imagination, the supreme delight of the immortal and the immature, should be limited. In order to enjoy life, we should not enjoy it too much.
> I rebel against this state of affairs. I feel the urge to take my rebellion outside and picket nature.[4]

Not exactly the rebellion Bryn Mawr students had in mind last year, but such words prove a clever, useful reminder that an artistic agenda can be as defiant as any social platform. Whether or not Nabokov's imaginative stance against common sense would satisfy those students who virtually picketed classes last year, the rebellious chord the writer strikes in *Speak, Memory* and elsewhere in his oeuvre could indeed provide fertile ground for reflection on the strike and its polemical spirit.

Also of note in *Speak, Memory* are Nabokov's remarks on his own progressive schooling in pre-Revolutionary Petrograd (St. Petersburg). Here the writer underscores the education prescribed for him by his socially conscious, politically astute father: "Belonging, as he did by choice, to the great classless intelligentsia of Russia, my father thought it right to have me attend a school that was distinguished by its democratic principles, its policy of nondiscrimination in matters of rank, race and creed, and its up-to-date educational methods."[5] Yet modern-day students ought to be wary of such pronouncements from Nabokov, for in the same breath, he remarks, "I would not have found the whole business too dismal if only my teachers had been less intent in trying to save my soul."[6] What emerges here and elsewhere in *Speak, Memory* is a certain skepticism toward established practices and norms, as Nabokov prompts readers to question the educational ideals of his pre-Revolutionary era (and, it follows, of our own era). He was, it should also be noted, never one to disavow or downplay his aristocratic privilege. On the other hand, those "democratic" ideals taught to Nabokov at the Teneshev School in St. Petersburg would in fact pervade his fiction.

Nabokov may have been averse to sanctimonious doctrine and just about any brand of moral teaching, yet he did stake his ground on certain ethical principles, albeit in an indirect, mischievous manner. One early Nabokov novel I teach in the course, *Despair* (*Otchaianie*), has long provided a good pivot point to an ethical sensibility in Nabokov's work that would inform much of his subsequent fiction, particularly *Lolita*, and it does so in a way that clearly reverberates with today's social *Zeitgeist*. Whereas the doomed protagonist of *Despair*, Herman Karlovich, generalizes in a way that diminishes physical differences, the novel's wayward artist, Ardalion, arguing with Herman, highlights the protagonist's crass impulse to see similarities in people, a tendency that will lead to Herman's precipitous downfall: "'You'll say next that all Chinamen are alike. You forget, my good man, that what the artist perceives is, primarily, the *difference* between things. It is the vulgar who note their resemblance.'"[7] Students might argue about how significantly such *differences* pertain to last year's racial reckoning on campus, but Nabokov's fiction nevertheless serves as a reminder that no one benefits from those (over)generalizations lumping a certain race or class of people together. Good art, in Nabokov's not-so-humble estimation, offers an antidote to the human impulse to discriminate.

Amidst discussion of Nabokov's fiction and his mid-career move to the United States just as World War II was commencing, it might behoove me to add to the course a thing or two that speaks directly to our contemporary era and matters of race. The writer was a keen observer of the everyday and sporadically offered insight into a country long grappling with racial strife. Case in point would be several letters Nabokov wrote to his wife, Véra, as he traveled through the American South; in these letters Nabokov alludes to some of the racism that he could not help but witness in 1940s America. Here we encounter an émigré writer keenly aware of the inequity and racism underlying American society. Describing his 1942 tour of several southern colleges, including Coker College (now University) in Hartsville, South Carolina, the historically Black, all-women's Spelman College (as Nabokov put it, "a Black

Wellesley"), and Georgia State Women's College, Nabokov would write the following to Véra in October of 1942:

> To the west, cotton plantations, and the prosperity of the numerous Cokers, who seem to own half of Hartsville, is founded on this very cotton industry. It is picking time now, and the "darkies" (an expression that jars me, reminding me distantly of the patriarchal "Zhidok" [Yid] of western Russian landowners) pick in the fields, getting a dollar for a hundred "bushels"—I am reporting these interesting facts because they stuck mechanically in my ears.[8]

Although hardly a searing condemnation of southern racism, this letter underscores the Russian-trained ear that Nabokov brought to his initial observations of American life. In this same letter to Véra, he goes on to note, "In the evenings, those who have children rarely go out because (despite their wealth) they have no one to leave the kids with; Negro servants never sleep over in the whites' homes—it is not allowed—and they cannot have white servants because they cannot work with blacks."[9] It is hard to see anything but disapprobation in these remarks, even if they are of an understated nature, and it is a similar form of observations on American life that Nabokov would eventually conjure in his notorious *Lolita*. Although in no way should these letters or other similar writings overshadow or supplant the artistic prose, surely the students could benefit from some assurance that Nabokov was not blind to the social and racial inequities of his adopted country.

During his 1942 stay at Spelman College, meanwhile, Nabokov lectured on Alexander Pushkin, emphasizing the African roots of the great Russian poet (Pushkin's maternal great-grandfather was brought as a slave to Russia from Africa and given to Peter the Great as a gift).[10] In his keynote Spelman lecture on Pushkin, Nabokov would dwell at length upon the benefits of a mixed-race lineage. Pushkin, Nabokov declared before a large, enthusiastic crowd, "provides a most striking example of mankind at its very best when human races are able to freely mix."[11] Although slightly dismissive of the "almost comical enthusiasm" with which the Spelman College audience greeted his lecture, Nabokov would reiterate his anti-segregationist, pro-miscegenation beliefs in later years.[12] Most notably, in his 1956 essay "On a Book Entitled *Lolita*," he wrote that in addition to the taboo of pedophilia in the United States, there was also the off-limits subject matter of "the Negro-White marriage which is a complete and glorious success resulting in lots of children and grandchildren" (as well as "the total atheist" who leads a happy, useful life to a ripe old age).[13] One of the aims of Nabokov's controversial *Lolita* would certainly be the writer's desire to ruffle some feathers in the United States and call into question some of American society's censorious social mores.

When teaching *Lolita*, it is initially hard to get past the pedophilia that is at the heart of the novel; nevertheless, discrimination slowly emerges as an important motif amidst Humbert Humbert's confessional screed. Although the concerns of the novel are ostensibly disconnected from Bryn Mawr's racial reckoning of 2020, various allusions to anti-Semitism in *Lolita* point to a Nabokovian brand of social justice that expands out to issues of race and gender. At an early point in the novel, Charlotte Haze, Lolita's mother, questions Humbert Humbert's racial lineage, suspecting he is Jewish ("Looking down at her fingernails, she also asked me had I not in my family a certain strange strain"), and amidst some banter among Humbert, Charlotte, and her friends, Jean Farlow interrupts an anti-Semitic remark her husband, John, is about to blurt out: "We talked of the school. It had its drawbacks, and it had its virtues. 'Of course, too many of the tradespeople here are Italians,' said John, 'but on the other hand we are still spared—' 'I wish,' interrupted Jean with a laugh, 'Dolly and Rosaline were spending the summer together.'"[14] The implication here being that John is about to say "Jews," yet one might easily substitute the word "Blacks." And later in the novel, when Humbert absconds with his "nymphet" and travels across the United States, subsequent anti-Semitism is encountered at the fateful Enchanted Hunters hotel, where the hotel staff mistakes Humbert's surname for Humberg and initially denies him a room in the hotel. *Lolita*, at its core, may be a novel about delusion and the harm that comes when someone cannot see beyond his obsessions, but it also grapples with imperfections underlying—and undermining—American society.

After *Lolita*, the course concludes with two of Nabokov's later American novels, *Pnin* and *Pale Fire*, both of which transpire on fictional college campuses. Given the contemporary time period Nabokov sets these novels in (the late 1950s/early 1960s), Nabokov's colleges are not exactly rife with dissension and racial strife, yet both works and their respective settings can be seen as amplifying some of the same narrowness of college life that Bryn Mawr's students rebelled against in the fall of 2020. Bryn Mawr's striking students might have been fed up with Zoom and the pandemic, but like Nabokov, they could see ample room for improvement throughout their rarefied college environment, a milieu that has persisted throughout the second half of the twentieth century up to this day. For Nabokov, the university system of the United States offered great opportunity, but he never shied away from showing the ugly warts of both his adopted country and its universities, be it the racism, anti-Semitism, cruelty (*Pnin*), or pettiness and homophobia (*Pale Fire*).

As I prepare to teach "Nabokov in Translation" in the coming semester, I cannot help but think that Nabokov would have resisted any obligation to focus on the systemic racism at play in American society and American universities, yet he could hardly complain that students might now be bringing such a discerning eye to their own academic environment.[15] What remains to be seen is how "Nabokov in Translation" will resonate with students this time around and to what extent the students will choose to link Nabokov's writing to campus events and contemporary society in class discussion or in their written work for the course. It is my hope that the fact of my being provost and thus at the heart of last year's events at Bryn Mawr will elicit—rather than stymie—such discussion of race and rebellion within Nabokov's fiction, nonfiction, and letters. Irrespective of where the discussion leads and what works and themes the students opt to focus on for their midterm and final papers, I would like to think that the imaginative, probing essence of the Russian-American's fiction will ultimately provide the students—and the Provost—a way to hone our creative perspective on the tumultuous events of the last two years and what it means to read Nabokov today.

Notes

1. According to biographer Brian Boyd, Nabokov never attended a faculty meeting during his eleven years at Cornell University. Boyd, *Vladimir Nabokov: The American Years* (Princeton, NJ: Princeton UP, 1991), 134.
2. Brian Boyd, *Vladimir Nabokov: The Russian Years* (Princeton, NJ: Princeton UP, 1990), 309.
3. Vladimir Nabokov, *Strong Opinions* (New York: McGraw Hill, 1973), 64.
4. Nabokov, *Speak, Memory: An Autobiography Revisited* (New York: Vintage International, 1989), 20.
5. Ibid., 185.
6. Ibid., 185.
7. Nabokov, *Despair* (New York: G.P. Putnam's Sons, 1969), 51.
8. Nabokov, *Letters to Véra*, edited and translated by Olga Veronina and Brian Boyd (New York: Alfred A. Knopf, 2015), 465.

9 Ibid., 467.
10 For more on Pushkin's maternal great-grandfather, Abram Petrovich Gannibal, see T. J. Binyon, *Pushkin: A Biography* (London: Harper Collins, 2002), 2–6.
11 Cited in Boyd, *Vladimir Nabokov: The American Years*, 50. For more on this Pushkin lecture and Nabokov's time at Spelman College, see Jennifer Wilson, "Was 'Lolita' About Race? Vladimir Nabokov on Race in the United States," *Los Angeles Review of Books*, October 31, 2016.
12 Nabokov, *Letters to Véra*, 470. In a 1967 interview with *The Paris Review*, Nabokov declared, "In home politics I am strongly anti-segregationist." See Nabokov, *Strong Opinions*, 98.
13 Vladimir Nabokov, "On a Book Entitled *Lolita*," in *The Annotated Lolita*, ed. Alfred Appel Jr. (New York: Vintage Books, 1991), 314.
14 Nabokov, *Annotated Lolita*, 75, 79.
15 As Nabokov remarked in a 1968 interview, "The dreary principles once voiced in the reign of Alexander the Second and their subsequent sinister transmutation into the decrees of gloomy police states…come to my mind whenever I hear today's retro-progressive book reviewers in America and England plead for a little more social comment, a little less artistic whimsy." See Nabokov, *Strong Opinions*, 112.

Nabokov's Haunted Screen: The Exilic Uncanny in Weimar Film

Luke Parker

One of the joys of reading and teaching the "early" Nabokov is his precocious intelligence and worldly prescience. Who today can resist references to readers and historians in the '20s of the twenty-first century? A brilliant undergraduate himself only several years earlier, Nabokov as an émigré writer in 1920s Berlin seemingly sees everything and cannot resist cataloguing it. At once detached and engaged, Nabokov's stance in the 1920s affords access to both the Berlin he found and the Berlin he created.

I teach a course on Nabokov's Russian fiction and Weimar cinema as parallel reactions to and recreations of 1920s Berlin. In European exile, first as a student at Cambridge and then, from 1922 on, as a twentysomething in Berlin, Nabokov regularly attended local cinemas, watching mostly German and American movies. His knowledge of film, as both spectator and participant (occasional extra and screenwriter), informs his Berlin fiction, which employs the cinema as setting, topic, and style.[1] What is more, even his earliest works revel in allowing the reader to observe the process of fictionalizing exile. In media terms, a Nabokov story contains the feature, the "making of" featurette, and the voiceover commentary.

The beauty of watching Weimar film alongside Nabokov's fiction in their shared historical context is that the filmmakers' cheerful yet market-savvy bricolage is a match for Nabokov's playful humor.[2] These films, like Nabokov's early fiction, are products of Weimar's media environment, designed to be enjoyed in one night, perhaps (but not necessarily) revisited, and intended to prime their audience for the next installment. An understanding of Berlin's cinematic culture—that is, not only the films but also the stories, spaces, and images of the cinema as a lynchpin of Weimar culture—is key to teaching Nabokov's career as a young writer in exile. As students quickly grasp, Nabokov's ambitions grew as the decade progressed, writing not only for Russian émigré readers but also for European audiences in translation and, aspirationally, international viewers in screen adaptations.

Nabokov's youth and sensitivity to his media environment make his Russian fiction and Weimar film an appealing combination for today's undergraduates. Most intriguingly, his fiction addresses a question foremost in our own cultural context—in an age of digital media, is literature (and the study of fiction) relevant to the present? Does it speak to our contemporary moment, or do its answers all belong to the past? Nabokov's response in his Russian work is that to attempt to label our "moment" (the 2020s no less than the 1920s) is begging the question—our historical significance is available only to the hindsight of the future historian. And yet literature, in so powerfully shaping how we process our ever-changing present, contributes to that future definition—experience is an ineluctably aesthetic phenomenon.

The Cinema as Exile's Double

In the first unit of my course on the Russian Nabokov, I focus on the uncanniness of exile, teaching Nabokov's early fiction alongside German films of the era. Typically, scholars have focused on Nabokov's "cinematic style" and allusions and homages to films.[3] In my course I offer students a different angle: the ghostliness of the émigré encounter with Weimar film is about the spectrality of exile itself, where Europeanized Russians found themselves at once "at home" and "not at home." In this unit, our discussions focus on the theme of the uncanny in its historical (World War I, Russian exile), aesthetic (horror films, "shell shock cinema"), and psychological aspects (trauma, grief, memory). In this way, we balance an understanding of the larger forces acting on the individual with the diversity of their potential affective and creative responses.

Sigmund Freud's essay "The Uncanny" (1919) and its companion piece *Beyond the Pleasure Principle* (1920) have been read as an answer to questions raised by war trauma. Even if one attempts to ward off Freud the clinician by bracketing the importance of grief and mourning for Nabokov's characters,

Freud the cultural critic inevitably remains as a marker of how the citizens of the defeated Central Powers also suffered revolution and socioeconomic collapse. These concerns, then, were shared by Russian émigrés and Weimar Berliners. The fact of this shared experience—the very proximity and cohabitation of Russians and Germans in mid-1920s Berlin—supplies the enduring interest of the émigré perspective, both insider and outsider.

As Anton Kaes has argued, film's multiplicatory technique and gift for doubling gives it a unique capacity to represent and produce the uncanny: "How is one to distinguish between reality and hallucination, since 'reality' itself is, after all, part of the fictional universe created by the very act of filming?... Film qua film—that is, its technological capacity for lifelike representation—is the ultimate double, an uncanny experience in itself to which we submit ourselves."[4] For Kaes, Weimar cinema is a response to historical crisis, a "shell shock cinema" that works through the trauma of the First World War. In approaching Nabokov's early fiction through the uncanny, I suggest a similarly contextual reading, replacing war with exile. As Barbara Streuman writes, "In analogy to the experience of the uncanny and its resurfacing of an alien knowledge about the most intimately familiar, exilic displacement rearticulates a secret contradiction by which one's site of belonging has been inhabited all along."[5] In making the absent present or returning what was lost, forgotten or discarded, the uncanny plays a key role in the émigré experience.

The first unit of the course lasts three weeks, moving from historical context (war, revolution, exile) to the uncanny and on to Berlin itself. In week one the students read Nabokov's short story "A Letter that Never Reached Russia" (1925) and his talk "On Generalities" (1926) alongside Alexander Dolinin's article "Clio Laughs Last: Nabokov's Answer to Historicism." We also watch the final episode of the BBC series *The First World War,* entitled "War Without End." In week two, students read Nabokov's story "The Return of Chorb" (1925) and selections from his first novel *Mary* (1926) that pertain to the cinema. They also attend screenings of the Weimar films *The Cabinet of Dr. Caligari* (1920) and *Nosferatu* (1922). We tie film and fiction together with Freud's contemporary theoretical piece "The Uncanny," Maxim Gorky's seminal Russian reaction to the uncanniness of silent cinema (1896), and Zinaida Gippius's polemical essay "Cinema" written in emigration in Paris ("Sinema" (1926), in my own unpublished English translation). Finally, in week three students read "A Guide to Berlin" (1925), "A Nursery Tale" (1926), and selections from *King, Queen, Knave* (1928) while watching F. W. Murnau's *The Last Laugh* (1924) and Walter Ruttmann's *Berlin: Symphony of a Great City* (1927). In addition to screening the films, it is worth using the "playlist" function on Kanopy or equivalent campus streaming service to create a series of film clips for close viewing, centering discussion on individual scenes and even frames. I also highly recommend the BFI Film Classics series.[6]

Developed in the context of a course on Nabokov's Russian fiction, this unit on the exilic uncanny could also be excerpted in a course on Russian Berlin or the Russian emigration. The screenings could be supplemented with further films such as Paul Wegener's *The Golem*, Murnau's *The Haunted Castle*, or Robert Wiene's *The Hands of Orlac* (see the filmography at the end of this essay). The unit could be amplified in these contexts with supplementary material on Russian émigrés and psychoanalysis or on the Nabokovian Weimar theme of doubles and automata. On psychoanalysis, students could read Nabokov's 1931 parody of commercial Freudianism "What Everyone Should Know," watch the 1926 UFA "culture film" *Secrets of a Soul*, and read Freud's case histories of the "Wolf Man" and the Russian aristocrat-turned-émigré Sergei Pankejeff or perhaps Pankejeff's own later memoirs. On automata and doubles, alongside Nabokov's 1928 novel *King, Queen, Knave* (ideally in the original Russian version, so different from the rewritten English version of forty years later), students could watch either the 1913 or 1926 versions of *The Student of Prague*, Ernst Lubitsch's *The Doll* (1919), and Paul Leni's *Waxworks* (1924).

Discussing the Uncanny

In his literary responses to Berlin's cinematic culture, Nabokov drew on a Russian tradition of artistic responses to the cinema. As early as 1896, Maxim Gorky's response to a screening of the Lumière Brothers films in the provincial town of Nizhny Novgorod set in motion a series of Russian writers' responses to film as uncanny. Famously, Gorky highlighted the spectrality of cinema as a shadow world, a theme continued in the poet Zinaida Gippius's ironic attack on the cinema as a "danse macabre" of lifeless figures. This assertion of the phantasmic and spectral quality of film experience, typical of the Symbolists of the 1910s, became the theme of Gippius's provocative 1926 essay "Cinema."

In *Mary*, Nabokov borrowed this stance, which was by now passé for members of the younger generation, and ingeniously applied it to the status of exile itself. For the protagonist Ganin, his encounter with his own image on screen provokes "a shudder of horror" as he realizes that he is "watching something vaguely yet horribly familiar"—a textbook case of Freud's uncanny.⁷ *Das Unheimliche* is a dynamic term describing the forceful return of an image or idea or the unexpected reappearance of an outdated ("surmounted") belief or overcome relic of earlier historical, artistic, or cultural development. In both cases, what we have put out of mind is not yet done with us.

In the passages of *Mary* the students and I focus on in class (9, 21–22, 110, 113–114), the cinema becomes a metaphor of the émigrés' role as extras in their own drama, whose images are condemned to wander, like their own doubles, throughout the movie theaters of the world. Nabokov's focus on the medium's power to not alleviate but perpetuate their suffering suggests that the cinema is itself an uncanny force. In this, Nabokov uncharacteristically sides with Freud, who had pointed out that fiction films and narratives offer even greater scope for the uncanny than real life: "the story-teller has a *peculiarly* directive power over us; by means of the moods he can put us into, he is able to guide the current of our emotions, to dam it up in one direction and make it flow in another, and he often obtains a great variety of effects from the same material."⁸ It is this peculiar power of the director and author that Nabokov explores in "Return of Chorb" and would later develop in his first and second novels, *Mary* and *King, Queen, Knave*.

In films like *Caligari* and *Nosferatu*, students directly encounter the "haunted screen" of Weimar film. While Lotte Eisner's "*écran démoniaque*" has become an historical cliché, it nonetheless describes a commonplace of Russian émigré writing of the period.⁹ The uncanny spectrality of Weimar film reflected back to its Russian viewers the ghostliness of exile. As a fiction writer, Nabokov started his career in the context of considerable personal and communal loss. After being dispossessed of his estate, inheritance, and homeland in 1919, Nabokov lost his father to a violent and public, even heroic, death in 1922. His marriage to Véra Slonim in 1925 was preceded by a broken-off engagement to Svetlana Siewert that had thrown him into a depression overcome only by manual labor in the south of France. In his poetry, Nabokov directly treated a lost Russia and a possible return, allowing his lyric persona to express an exile's longing. Yet in his fiction of these years, Nabokov preferred to avoid directly autobiographical trauma, portraying not a father's death but that of a wife ("The Return of Chorb") or son ("Christmas," 1925) or even featuring the main character's own demise ("Details of a Sunset," 1924). Émigrés like Nabokov, working through personal and communal trauma, encountered in Weimar cinematic culture an artistic medium that aestheticized and commercialized death, loss, disorientation, and alienation. The confluence of historical experience and artistic trends lent to German film of the early 1920s a discernible style, traces of which have rightly been discovered in Nabokov's fiction of these years.

Yet more recently scholars have shown that Expressionism was less a serendipitous "artistic outlet" for timeless German national characteristics than a calculated choice of an "art" style that would distinguish their products on the international market.[10] In a similar way, Nabokov's use of "Expressionist" features can be read less as a formative influence on his aesthetics than a conscious marker of his engagement with the cultural commonplaces of his German exile. Since films like *Caligari*, produced by the transnational figure Erich Pommer, were not naively influenced by a German national heritage but consciously adopted elements of it, we might want to refine our model of how Nabokov was "influenced" by these films. Just as German filmmakers made strange their own productions in order to differentiate them from Hollywood on the international market, Nabokov would in turn adopt such features as markers of his own early work in exile. Stories like "A Nursery Tale" announce themselves as the work of a Berlin writer, whose references to (E.T.A.) Hoffmannstrasse could play multiple roles: inside jokes for Russian Berliners, local color for Russian Parisians, and seeds for translation into German. On this reading, Weimar film is a subset of Nabokov's larger encounter with the cultural and urban landscape of Weimar Berlin.

It is such an encounter that a course on Nabokov's Russian fiction should ideally facilitate. Happily, for today's students the strangeness of silent film approximates the strangeness of Weimar film confronted by Russian émigrés like Nabokov. If the uncanny is a case of repetition, then we can say that for Russian émigrés, as for American undergraduates, the encounter with Weimar film centered less around unfamiliarity than around a strange familiarity.

Silent Film as Historical Uncanny

For today's student, silent film is the cinematic undead. Familiar in the form of GIFs, clips, samples, and remakes, the images of silent film continue to circulate, filtering into the peripheral awareness of consumers. Rarely screened as part of regular movie theater programming, silents have long been largely confined to museums, cinematheques, and specialist festivals. Streaming media are optimized to the small screen—so minimized, the aesthetic and affective hold of silent films is severely diminished. Nothing could be further from the youthful Nabokov's encounters with film.

Just as today Nabokov's early fiction can be read in carefully collated and annotated Russian (and to some extent English) editions, so can many significant silent films of the Weimar era be viewed in restored versions accompanied by critical commentary. As Paolo Cherchi Usai, former senior curator at the George Eastman Museum, has argued, these films' apparent lack of color, sound, and visual clarity is now understood to be less a product of their own defects than of our own uneven archival and screening practices.[11] The effect of such a recovery can, however, be not only an artistic restoration but also a return of the technologically and even aesthetically "surmounted," as formerly buried and lifeless images reemerge in all their complexity and potency.

As students can experience firsthand, these were rarely "black and white" productions but were instead colored in various ways, including hand-coloring, stenciling, tinting, and toning.[12] The film historian Rashit Yangirov has discovered a direct reference to such colored silent film in Nabokov's poetry, showing that the 1925 poem "Kuby" refers to an "emerald" scene of a close-up of Cesar's face in *The Cabinet of Dr. Caligari*.[13] Yangirov convincingly argues that Nabokov's famously sensitive use of color can be correlated with the chromatic experiences of a moviegoer of the 1920s, in which, for example, yellow tinting connoted daytime, blue nighttime, red a fire or battle.[14] Color, then, is both a "normal" and aesthetically significant feature of silent film, which had for many years been lost or forgotten due to early museum and archival practices of copying films onto black and white stock.[15]

Students experience the uncanniness of Weimar film in both historical and personal terms. Historically, they experience the return of the apparently antiquated and outmoded: the technology and style of silent film. And this return is amplified by the experience of silent film projected on a large screen, where it becomes the equivalent, as event and valid artwork, to contemporary sound and color productions. Furthermore, students' experience of restored color, where the historical becomes present, facilitates the personal uncanny experience of silent film's undiminished power to affect its viewer. *Caligari* and *Nosferatu* continue to grip and disturb the spectator: supposedly defanged by the passage of time, these films lose nothing by comparison with cinema's subsequent technological and artistic progress. Lying in wait for today's younger viewers, they coax a belief in their power which, to our surprise, has not in fact been surmounted and cannot easily be overcome.

Of course, the archive is not the crypt, and as film historians have pointed out, digital "restoration" is as much translation and adaptation. Yet the payoff in teaching is not intended to be historical authenticity but experiential equivalence. A large-format digital encounter with silent film levels the playing field, rendering its charms comparable and assimilable to the media experience of a generation for whom the image is almost never analogue. Rolls and reels of film, tangible records: these treasured markers of recovered authenticity belong to another realm of aesthetic experience entirely. Digital media are precisely an unmarked presence, under the cloak of which silent film can truly begin to work on a new generation.

Conclusion

Nabokov's Russian fiction of the mid-1920s—what has been termed "early" Nabokov—has often been approached like "early" cinema: a series of sketches for the later canon. Simpler and rougher, these early works, the story goes, allow a glimpse of future artistic mastery in more elemental form. Yet teaching Nabokov's Russian work in translation offers students a set of responses to the present that are as artistically valid and integral as silent film is now (and was originally) recognized to be. In this sense, the Russian Nabokov represents a product of the 1920s, which, like silent film, can seem far timelier today than the long-familiar American Nabokov and his later contemporary, the classical Hollywood of the sound era.

Nabokov, born at the very turn of the century, was in his twenties in the 1920s, and saw nothing unnatural in the media saturation of Weimar urban culture. Nabokov's responsiveness to Berlin's cinematic culture was part of his generation's youthful encounter with western European modernity as the setting of their exile. Among the younger émigrés, their Russian childhood was the artistic subject of imaginative returns—both public, through a fantasized border crossing, and private, through reconjured memories. At the same time, for this younger generation, born in the late 1890s and early 1900s, as for their German counterparts in Berlin, the cultural break of war and revolution created a time marked less by nostalgia than by novelty. Nabokov shared this willingness to engage the present and to anticipate a future that would treasure, through his art, the unnoticed and undervalued details of exile. It was the cinema, a symbol of modernity and contemporaneity (a single word, *sovremennost'*, in Russian), which ultimately stood for the exilic present—film as encounter.

For students of today, then, Nabokov both embodies a kind of generational attitude to an already mediated present—cinematic culture as *our* moment—and shows how, in his promotion of the irreducible uniqueness of the individual, to resist the idea of generational belonging altogether. In teaching, I find this ambivalence particularly valuable: Nabokov provides a test case for how a young, educated artist and intellectual recognizes and resists their own historicization.

Notes

1 See Alfred Appel Jr., *Nabokov's Dark Cinema* (New York: Oxford UP, 1974); Gavriel Moses, *The Nickel Was for the Movies: Film in the Novel from Pirandello to Puig* (Berkeley: U of California P, 1995); Barbara Wyllie, *Nabokov at the Movies: Film Perspectives in Fiction* (Jefferson, NC: McFarland, 2003); Luke Parker, *Nabokov Noir: Cinematic Culture and the Art of Exile* (Ithaca, NY: Cornell UP, 2022).

2 See Thomas Elsaesser on the distinctive playfulness and self-awareness of Weimar filmmaking, a feature of the broader ironic irreverence Peter Sloterdijk has seen in Weimar culture at large. Thomas Elsaesser, *Weimar Cinema and After: Germany's Historical Imaginary* (New York: Routledge, 2000); Peter Sloterdijk, *Critique of Cynical Reason*, trans. Michael Eldred (Minneapolis: U of Minnesota P, 1987).

3 It has been noted the extent to which Nabokov's fiction appears indebted to Weimar Expressionist film. See especially "The Impact of German and Soviet Film on Nabokov's Russian Fiction" in Wyllie, *Nabokov at the Movies*, 11–44.

4 Anton Kaes, *Shell Shock Cinema: Weimar Culture and the Wounds of War* (Princeton, NJ: Princeton UP, 2009), 126.

5 Barbara Streuman, *Figurations of Exile in Hitchcock and Nabokov* (Edinburgh: Edinburgh UP, 2008), 18.

6 On these two films in particular, see Kevin Jackson, *Nosferatu: Eine Symphonie des Grauens* (London: British Film Institute, 2013); David Robinson, *Das Cabinet des Dr. Caligari*, 2nd edition (London: British Film Institute, 2013).

7 Vladimir Nabokov, *Mary*, trans. Michael Glenny (New York: Vintage, 1970), 21–22.

8 Emphasis in original translation. Sigmund Freud, "The Uncanny," in *The Standard Edition of the Complete Psychological Works of Sigmund Freud. Volume XVII (1917–1919): An Infantile Neurosis and Other Works*, ed. James Strachey (London: Hogarth Press, 1955), 251.

9 See Lotte Eisner, *The Haunted Screen: Expressionism in the German Cinema and the Influence of Max Reinhardt*, translated by Roger Greaves (Berkeley: California UP, 1969).

10 Robinson, *Caligari*, 45.

11 See especially his chapter "Pixels" in Paolo Cherchi Usai, *Silent Cinema: A Guide to Study, Research, and Curatorship*, 3rd edition (London: British Film Institute, 2009), 6–20.

12 See Cherchi Usai's chapter on this entitled "Chroma" in Usai, *Silent Cinema*, 43–61.

13 Rashit Iangirov, "'Chuvstvo fil'ma.' Zametki o kinematograficheskom kontekste v literature russkogo zarubezh'ia 1920-1930-kh godov," in *Imperiia N. Nabokov i naslednki. Sbornik statei*, ed. Iurii Leving and Evgenii Soshkin (Moscow: Novoe literaturnoe obozrenie, 2006), 421.

14 Ibid., 422, 422n15.

15 Usai, *Silent Cinema*, 43–44. For the richness of this color world, see the work of Yoshua Yumibe, in particular his *Moving Color: Early Film, Mass Culture, Modernism* (New Brunswick, NJ: Rutgers UP, 2012) and Sarah Street and Joshua Yumibe, *Chromatic Modernity: Color, Cinema, and Media of the 1920s* (New York: Columbia UP, 2019).

Filmography

Berlin, Symphonie einer Großstadt (1927, dir. Ruttman)—Flicker Alley Blu-ray

Das Cabinet des Dr. Caligari (1920, dir. Wiene)—Kino Blu-ray

Geheimnisse einer Seele (*Secrets of a Soul*, 1926, dir. Pabst)—Kino DVD

Der Golem, wie er in die Welt kam (1920, dir. and starring Wegener)—Kino Blu-ray

Der leztze Mann (*The Last Laugh*, 1924, dir. Murnau)—Kino Blu-ray

Orlacs Hände (1924, dir. Wiene, starring Veidt)—Kino Blu-ray

Die Puppe (*The Doll*, 1919, dir. Lubitsch)—Kanopy

Schloß Vogelöd: Die Enthüllung eines Geheimnisses (*The Haunted Castle*, 1921, dir. Murnau)—Kino Blu-ray

Der Student von Prag (1913, starring Wegener; 1926, starring Veidt)—YouTube

Nosferatu, eine Symphonie des Grauens (1922, dir. Murnau)—Kino Blu-ray

Das Wachsfigurenkabinett (*Waxworks*, 1924, dir. Leni, starring Veidt, Jannings, Krauss)—Flicker Alley Blu-ray

PART III

DISABILITY STUDIES AND QUEERINGS

Reading Disability in "A Guide to Berlin"

Roman Utkin*

"Despite its simple appearance, this *Guide* is one of my trickiest pieces," Nabokov warned in a note to readers of the English translation of his short masterpiece "A Guide to Berlin."[1] At first glance, this seemingly benign, plotless story of a man's journey across Berlin appears to be at a safe remove from Nabokov's complex and controversial novels. By the end of the short story, the narrator's friend verbalizes what some readers may already feel: "That's a very poor guide....Who cares about how you took a streetcar and went to the Berlin Aquarium?"[2] As is frequently the case with Nabokov, the author provokes and challenges the reader to let go of assumptions, to look for clues, to re-read. Indeed, tracing the tricks of "A Guide to Berlin" can serve as an effective introduction to Nabokov and to literary analysis: the short story displays a mastery of literary craft that underpins the fraught Nabokovian interplay of aesthetics and morality.

At issue here is the fact that the narrator of the "Guide" is a disabled man. This disability appears subtly, and fully grasping it requires noticing and pondering details, the sort of readerly attention Nabokov prized.[3] At first, we learn that the narrator walks with a "thick rubberheeled stick"; then he secures a seat on a tram by the window thanks to a "compassionate woman" who avoids looking too closely at him; and, in the story's final vignette, the description of the narrator's reflection in a mirror reveals that he is missing an arm ("an empty right sleeve") and has a scarred face. No explanation for this bodily disfiguration is provided, though some scholars have suggested that perhaps the narrator is a war veteran.[4] In my experience, students often make this same comment—after all, the short story takes place in Weimar-era

Berlin, the most enduring pictorial representations of which inevitably feature disabled World War I veterans.

However, the discussion of why the narrator is disabled takes a sharp turn when students learn that there is no mention of the narrator's disability in the original Russian and that Nabokov intentionally cripples his narrator in the English version. The societal and scholarly understandings of disability have changed so substantially since Nabokov wrote the short story in 1925 and translated it in 1976 that a conversation about the implications of the narrator's disability must go beyond suggestions of historical effect. What role does the character's physical condition play in the narrative? How does the character's disability shape his spatial awareness of Berlin? Why does Nabokov mark his narrator with corporeal difference without changing much else in the translation?

I regularly teach "A Guide to Berlin" in a seminar for first-year students with a focus on academic writing and in a seminar on Nabokov. In both cases, the discussion of disability is essential. Most students associate Nabokov with *Lolita,* often without having read the novel but knowing that it is somehow scandalous and disturbing (before college, many of them were unable to search for the very word "lolita" on child-locked search engines at home). In reading the "Guide," my students expect some form of perversity and never fail to seize on the sexualized depiction of trams, their "uncoupling" and "coupling on" in the second vignette, where one tram is described as a "male" and the other a "submissive female."[5] (The offensiveness of the latter description is rarely redeemed by the ensuing discussion of this scene and the realization that the trams trade positions each time they reach the end of the line.) Whereas the students have strong opinions about Nabokov's use of "submissive female," they hesitate to discuss the narrator's disability with the same vigor. They sense that the presence of disability in the narrative is very important, but they tend to be much more cautious in commenting on disability than on sexuality. Meanwhile, the discussion of disability is key to understanding this text and its structure.

In this essay, I will share some strategies for framing contemporary readings of the "Guide" in the classroom. Nabokov's handling of his character's disability shares certain features of disability's conventional literary use as a shorthand for trauma. But Nabokov's approach also showcases him as a writer attuned to disability as a potent source of knowledge. Before turning to the discursive tools of disability studies for suggesting possible approaches to reading the short story with students, I will review some of its existing interpretations.

"The Costs of Character"

Of all Nabokov's Russian short stories, the "Guide" received the most attention from literary scholars, who have argued that its Russian and English versions reflect the evolution of the author's aesthetics concerning beauty, pain, and exile as well as his views on contemporary literature. Eric Naiman has addressed the appearance of the narrator's physical injuries in the translation head on, asking, "Why does an author cripple a character?"[6] For Naiman, answering this question is crucial, because by adding "the author-character violence" in the translation, Nabokov announces his authorial presence and therefore raises the stakes of interpreting his actions.

In his perceptive analysis of the "Guide," organized around the idea of the "costs of character," Naiman argues that the mature Nabokov's introduction of disability indicates the author's sharpened "concern with the relationship between pain and beauty, between the inflicted deformity and crafted order."[7] The "Guide's" guide appears mutilated to account for the later Nabokov's penchant for punishing his narrators, disciplining them "for the attempted hubris to tell a tale," as in *Lolita*, *Pnin*, "The Vane Sisters," and the translation of *Despair*.[8] The trouble is, as Naiman concedes, that unlike the narrators who morally deserve punishment, the "Guide's" narrator has done nothing unethical.

Naiman resolves this paradox somewhat paradoxically by invoking Humbert Humbert's quotation from a fictional "old poet" in *Lolita*: "The moral sense in mortals is the duty / we have to pay on mortal sense of beauty." Naiman finds that in the "Guide's" English version composed fifty years after the Russian original, Nabokov maims his narrator as payment for "the mortal sense of beauty." But reading the "Guide" via *Lolita* raises more questions than it answers, since the "mortal sense of beauty" is used in the novel euphemistically: it stands for illicit desire and amoral pleasure that should be constrained by the "tax" of morality. As the only ostensible transgression of the "Guide's" narrator is an attempt to depict Berlin, it remains unclear what makes him deserve severe punishment. Although Naiman classifies his take on the "Guide" as "reading preposterously," such a reading presents Nabokov as an unduly cruel author—unless the duty of "the moral sense" is a test of readerly empathy, similar to the story's "compassionate woman" who offers her window seat to the narrator without staring at him.

Naiman's reading builds upon preceding analyses of the story that focus on Nabokov's translation of the "Guide" as an instance of authorial return to the past for commenting on the present. Jacob Emery has suggested that Nabokov mutilates his narrator to show the extent of his exilic trauma as someone who lost both his native country and language. Whereas in the Russian version of the "Guide," the "Bolshevik-instigated exile from Edenic *Russia* produces grief," in the English translation, "the exile from Edenic *Russian* actually disables the narrator."[9] To support his claim, Emery points to Nabokov's choice to translate as "cripple" the Russian verb "*trevozhit*'" (to trouble, to provoke anxiety) in the sentence encapsulating the author's contempt for communism conveyed in the fourth vignette. In commenting on the image of the red five-pointed star at the ocean's bottom, the narrator says that it represents "topical utopias and other inanities that cripple us today." Emery uses evidence from Nabokov's interviews as well to support his interpretation of disability as the consequence of the author's double exile, but it is still hard to square Nabokov's life at Montreux—where he lived at the time of translating the short story—with the notion of being "crippl[ed] today."

Omry Ronen also identifies a contemporary concern in the story, associating it not with the communist regime as such but with the Soviet writer and formalist critic Viktor Shklovsky. Ronen argues that there is an intertextual-cum-biographical relationship between Nabokov's "Guide" and Shklovsky's 1923 Berlin novel *Zoo, or Letters Not about Love*. Ronen's argument is twofold. First, he observes that in the Russian original Nabokov turns to the same Berlin landmarks as Shklovsky and writes about them in a formalist way, employing the signature formalist techniques of defamiliarization and "the laying bare of the device."[10] Second, Ronen contends that Nabokov cripples his narrator in the English translation as a way of condemning Shklovsky's collaboration with the Soviet regime. Not only did Shklovsky beg to be allowed to return to Russia in the last chapter of *Zoo*, he also censored the subsequent editions of his popular novel; one could say his censorship mutilated those editions. In Ronen's view, the 1964 version of *Zoo* was especially problematic as it lacked the novel's final lines following the author's application to repatriate to Russia. Those lines depicted surrendering soldiers killed by blows to the right arm and the head. This was Shklovsky's allegorical reference to his surrender and a request to be spared. Shklovsky removes this reference from *Zoo*; Nabokov installs a mutilated soldier with a scarred face and the missing right arm in his translation of the "Guide." Ronen concludes that Nabokov thus visualizes the moral scars of Shklovsky's accommodation with Soviet power in the image of his badly disfigured narrator.

Ronen's interpretation finds an admiring but unconvinced reader in Naiman. Although Naiman calls Ronen's reasoning ingenious, he doubts that Nabokov would have known about, much less read the 1964 Soviet edition of Shklovsky's *Zoo*. Instead of considering the details of the narrator's physical disability, Naiman probes the first part of Ronen's argument concerning Nabokov's use of defamiliarization. He follows Maxim Shrayer's observation that Nabokov does not simply follow Shklovsky's formulation of defamiliarization in art but polemicizes with it. Shklovsky famously put forth the idea that the purpose of art is to represent objects in an unfamiliar way, to defamiliarize them such that they can be seen rather than merely recognized.[11] As Shrayer points out, Nabokov adds a temporal dimension to the process of making things strange.[12] In the "Guide," Nabokov articulates an almost theoretical statement about "the sense of literary creation," which is "to portray ordinary objects as they will be reflected in the kindly mirrors of future times."[13] In Nabokov's conception, time itself acts as the agent of defamiliarization. The author's role is to capture accurately the sense of time. One example of this temporal defamiliarization can be found in Nabokov's portrayal of the tram, which is on the cusp of acquiring a charming "air of antiquity."[14]

Naiman synthesizes the preceding analyses to suggest that perhaps in the "Guide's" English translation Nabokov extends the principle of temporal defamiliarization to defamiliarization itself. He writes, "Memory has itself become a distorting mirror and, when compared with the original version, the translation may serve as a parable about the unreliable, distorting vision—the creative trauma—of the kindliest of mirrors."[15] Looked at this way, the literary device backfires, because revisiting the past, especially in twentieth-century Berlin, can be difficult to bear. Some quaint-looking trains, for example, also transported people to death camps. As a result, the able-bodied narrator of the 1920s cannot retain his corporeal integrity when the author travels back in time from the postwar present.

All the interpretations summarized above have taken the presence of disability for a static signifier of trauma, lack, and otherness. They have also treated the addition of disability in the English translation as a riddle in need of a solution. But what if disability also deserves a closer inspection as a narrative device? In the field of disability studies, scholars have scrutinized the conventional use of disability in narrative as "a stock feature of characterization" and "an opportunistic metaphorical device."[16] David Mitchell and Sharon Snyder have highlighted the main problem of exploiting disability for its metaphorical potential: "while stories rely upon the potency of disability as a symbolic figure, they rarely take up disability as an experience of social or political dimensions."[17] As any Nabokovian knows, the author reserved nothing but scorn for anyone attempting to extract social or political dimensions from his writings. However, a consideration of his "Guide" through the prism of disability studies generates another possible explanation of the change in the narrator's bodily appearance—one that is centered not on determining *why* he is disabled but on *how* his disability influences the experience of reading.

A Guide to "Narrative Prosthesis"

To explain the problematic use of disability in literary texts, Mitchell and Snyder provide a range of examples. One of them is drawn from Sophocles' tragedy *Oedipus Rex*, which they view as paradigmatic for literary approaches to disability. In the famous episode known as the Riddle of the Sphinx, Oedipus faces the chimeric beast who challenges him to solve a riddle: "What is the creature that walks on four legs in the morning, two legs at noon, and three in the evening?" Oedipus's correct answer is "man" as humans crawl on all fours in infancy and then walk on two legs in adulthood until needing a cane in old age. This episode highlights the greatness of Oedipus's intelligence. But Mitchell and Snyder remind us that Oedipus himself has a disability—he has a limp and even his name means "swollen foot." Therefore, Mitchell and Snyder assert, Oedipus solves the riddle thanks to his own disability, which served as an experiential source for his interpretative mastery. While Oedipus's disability represents a mode of experience-based knowledge in the Riddle of the Sphinx, Sophocles leaves unexplored the "relationship of the body's mediating function with respect to Oedipus's kingly subjectivity."[18] Although the protagonist's disability clearly shapes and advances the narrative, it remains, for the most part, a one-dimensional metaphorical signifier of otherness.

Mitchell and Snyder call such use of disability "narrative prosthesis," or "a crutch upon which literary narratives lean for their representational power, disruptive potentiality, and analytical insight."[19] In modern narratives, the disabled body usually appears when there is a need to intensify a character's individual and/or moral collapse, which the character either overcomes or to which it succumbs—compare Tiny Tim in *A Christmas Carol* and Captain Hook in *Peter Pan*. There is a myriad other, more and less complex examples of disability in literary texts, but what unites them all is that disability reflects and reinforces cultural expectations: victims are normally redeemed, and villains are almost always punished. The trouble is that in both positive and negative portrayals a disabled character is inevitably otherized and thus excluded from a shared social identity. In failing to understand disability on its own terms—and to explore how disability would influence a particular character's experience of the fictional world—literary narratives ultimately reinforce harmful stereotypes about individuals with disabilities. That is precisely why it is important to approach Nabokov's "Guide" in the classroom with an awareness of disability studies criticism, which also helps to arrive at a richer interpretation of the short story.

There is a structural relationship between disability's rendering in fictional and societal narratives. The socio-political concerns of disability studies scholars have demonstrated that disability is a product of social conventions as much as of bodily conditions. That is, environmental and societal factors shape what counts as a disability (wearing glasses vs. walking with a cane) and how disability is approached (an isolated individual condition vs. universal malleability of human bodies). Accordingly, treating disability as a marker of isolation leads to stigma, while an understanding of disability as a positive identity category becomes a mode of situating one's understanding of self.[20] This principle can be extended to reading literary texts, even if they ostensibly use disability as a "narrative prosthesis." Let us see this principle at work in Nabokov's short story.

Disability in "A Guide to Berlin"

As mentioned earlier, the narrator in the "Guide" conveys his bodily disfigurement gradually. Although he does not call direct attention to it until later in the text, the narrator's disability immediately adds depth to the story. For a reader familiar with the Russian version, that the narrator now walks with a "thick rubberheeled stick" represents a riddle, not unlike an inverted version of the Riddle of the Sphynx.[21] But for a less informed reader, the presence of the cane signals that the narrator is someone requiring assistance with walking, perhaps an elderly gentleman. The detailed description of the cane makes it apparent that it is not a fashionable accessory but a utilitarian device. The presence of the cane announces a temporal lag—the narrator walks slowly and cautiously. If taken beyond its status as a feature of characterization, the thick and sturdy cane prompts the reader to slow down and to pay close attention to the "treacherous glaze of the sidewalk"—*and* of the textual surface. In a manner resembling defamiliarization, the slowing down prolongs the length of perception and therefore enhances it. The first sign of the narrator's disability thus marks not his puzzling marginality but his physically embodied perspective onto the urban space.

The narrator mentions his bodily difference for the second time when he is riding the tram in the third vignette. Here he situates his disability in a social setting. The tram is crammed, and the narrator gets a seat by the window, which allows him to observe what happens on the street and move the story along. Although the description of the view from the window is ostensibly more important, the brief scene inside the tram reveals the narrator's acute awareness of his corporeality. Notably, the narrator rehearses a social script already familiar to him: he knows that a "compassionate woman" will always offer him her seat and that she will try not to look too closely at him.[22] But in trying not to look *too* closely, the compassionate woman still must look closely. The narrator preempts any manifestation of pity or disgust by asserting his agency: the awkward gazing is the price he pays for the seat he wants. In underscoring the compassionate passenger's gender, the narrator also implicitly comments on the lack of empathy or any other response in the male passengers on the tram. This absence of understanding will materialize in the fifth and final vignette, in the failure of the narrator's friend to comprehend why this guide to Berlin is worth reading.

The narrator's disability is finally made visible in the mirror in the pub where the "Guide" ends. Again, Nabokov presents the disabled body very matter-of-factly, though the details of his disfigurement are disturbing. Not only does the narrator walk with a cane, he is also missing an arm and has a badly damaged face. Given how incrementally the narrator's disability appears in the text, one wonders if his bodily damage is limited to the frugal details the reader glimpses in the three external observations: the walking stick, what the compassionate woman sees, and the reflection in the mirror. The existing scholarly interpretations of this story have not considered the possibility that, perhaps, the narrator's disability extends beyond its external manifestation. In this connection, the story's final lines provide rich interpretative material.

The narrator's friend cannot understand why the narrator finds so special the way the child observes the pub's interior in the mirror. The narrator exclaims, "How can I demonstrate to him that I have glimpsed somebody's future recollection?"[23] This enigmatic ending has been understood as part of the narrator's preoccupation with art, memory, and the passage of time encapsulated in the earlier formulation about "the kindly mirrors of future times."[24]

However, if we bear in mind the narrator's aside about the treacherous glaze of the surfaces in this text, the narrator's final exclamation can be read literally as his inability to communicate verbally. To be sure, the story begins with the narrator "telling [his] friend about utility pipes, streetcars, and other important matters."[25] It is nevertheless noteworthy that the narrator and his friend never engage in a dialogue. All of the narrator's observations take the shape of an interior monologue, including the final statement, which he addresses to the reader, who accesses it via the printed text. The friend makes judgments and asks questions, but the narrator answers them only indirectly.

There is an explicit reference to speech, moreover, that is incoherent to observers in the fourth vignette, "Eden." While at the zoo, the narrator encourages the reader to watch the feeding of the giant tortoises. From the contemporary point of view, the description of one of the tortoises and "his [sic] monstrous speech" is insensitive.[26] But the analogy functions to exemplify the extreme difficulty of verbal expression. Additionally, the narrator makes sure to note that the tortoises have been brought to the city's zoo from the Galápagos Islands. In other words, they are foreigners in Berlin—like the narrator and his friend. As a result, the whole of the "Guide"—a utilitarian device in its own right—becomes a story about searching for an appropriate language. On the conceptual plane, the "Guide" maps a search for representational means capable of demonstrating that which defies conventional representation.

By establishing the connection between the narrator's disability and his subjectivity, we can see that the added details in the "Guide's" English translation sharpen the narratorial perspective. The narrator's disability becomes a way of seeing and experiencing Berlin. His bodily difference still carries a great deal of metaphorical potential, but that does not necessarily come at the expense of reaffirming negative stereotypes. Tracing the implications of the narrator's changed appearance in the story's English version defamiliarizes the very process of reading the text—a process that, in turn, becomes a journey of self-discovery.

Notes

* I would like to thank Erin Davenport, Susanne Fusso, Charles Gershman, and Priscilla Meyer for their valuable feedback while I was drafting this essay.
1 Vladimir Nabokov, *Details of a Sunset and Other Stories* (New York: McGraw-Hill, 1976), 90. Nabokov's brief foreword to the English translation to "A Guide to Berlin" is omitted from the story itself and published as a commentary in the Vintage International edition of his short fiction.
2 Vladimir Nabokov, "A Guide to Berlin," in *The Stories of Vladimir Nabokov* (New York: Vintage International, 1997), 159.
3 Vladimir Nabokov, "Good Readers and Good Writers," in *Lectures on Literature* (New York: Harcourt Brace Jovanovich, 1980), 1–6.
4 See Eric Naiman, *Nabokov, Perversely* (Ithaca, NY: Cornell UP, 2010), 224.
5 Nabokov, "A Guide to Berlin," 156–157.
6 Ibid., 221.
7 Ibid., 232.
8 Ibid., 231.
9 Jacob Emery, "Guides to Berlin," *Comparative Literature* 54, no. 4 (2002): 304.
10 Omry Ronen, "Viktor Shklovsky's Tracks in 'A Guide to Berlin,'" trans. Susanne Fusso, in *The Joy of Recognition: Selected Essays of Omry Ronen*, ed. Barry P. Sherr and Michael Wachtel (Ann Arbor: Michigan Slavic Publications, 2015), 202–231. Maxim Shrayer has also analyzed "A Guide to Berlin" as Nabokov's response to Shklovsky. See his *The World of Nabokov's Stories* (Austin: U of Texas P, 1999), 78–81. Alexander Dolinin likewise noted the Shklovskian connection in the short story in his commentary to Nabokov's collected works in Russian. See Vladimir Vladimirovich Nabokov, *Sobranie sochinenii russkogo perioda v piati tomakh*, vol. 1 (St. Petersburg: Simpozium, 2004), 764.
11 Viktor Shklovsky, "Art as Device," in *Viktor Shklovsky: A Reader*, ed. and trans. Alexandra Berlina (New York: Bloomsbury Academic, 2016), 73–96.
12 Shrayer, *World of Nabokov's Stories*, 79. See also Brian Boyd, *Vladimir Nabokov: The Russian Years* (Princeton, NJ: Princeton UP, 1990), 250–251.
13 Nabokov, "A Guide to Berlin," 157.
14 Ibid., 156.
15 Naiman, *Nabokov, Perversely*, 230. Regarding the imagery of mirrors and mirroring in the text, D. Barton Johnson's examination of palindrome as the short story's central linguistic device offers an excellent guide for analyzing Nabokov verbal tricks with students. See D. Barton Johnson, "A Guide to Nabokov's 'A Guide to Berlin,'" *Slavic and East European Journal* 23, no. 3 (1979): 353–361.
16 David Mitchell and Sharon Snyder, "Narrative Prosthesis and the Materiality of Metaphor," in *The Disability Studies Reader*, ed. Lennard J. Davis (New York: Routledge, 2006), 205.
17 Ibid., 205.

18 Ibid., 214.
19 Ibid., 206.
20 See the entry on "Disability" in Rachel Adams, Benjamin Reiss, and David Serlin, *Keywords for Disability Studies* (New York: New York UP, 2015), 30–44.
21 Nabokov, "A Guide to Berlin," 155.
22 Ibid., 157.
23 Ibid., 160.
24 See Naiman, *Nabokov, Perversely*, 230; Shrayer, *World of Nabokov's Stories*, 80.
25 Nabokov, "A Guide to Berlin," 155.
26 Ibid., 159.

Nabokov, Creative Discussion, and Reparative Knowledge

Sara Karpukhin

> It is sometimes the most paranoid-tending people who are able to, and need to, develop and disseminate the richest reparative practices.
>
> Eve Kosofsky Sedgwick

My course on Vladimir Nabokov's Russian and English novels in the fall of 2016 at Notre Dame was one of the first courses I designed on my own after getting my doctorate the previous year. Eleven years earlier, I had come to the United States from the city of Irkutsk in eastern Siberia, where I was born, socialized, and educated, and when I started teaching, it turned out that both my background and my experience as a graduate student in the United States had instilled a certain kind of reading in me, which in turn had prepared me for a certain kind of teaching.

My reading centered on the trueness and fullness of knowledge, and since for a writer like Nabokov both attributes seemed to be predicated on the reader's access to the author and his intentions, I opted for a lecture-style delivery. Having spent almost my entire reading life with Nabokov and written a dissertation about him, I believed that I was in a privileged interpretive position compared to the rest of the class. But probably due to the novelty of the experience and the fact that I had only eleven students in that first class, in practice the method shifted more and more toward discussion during the semester. I couldn't yet say how exactly, but I immediately felt that, to my surprise, it was affecting my way of reading. I tried to preserve that element of discussion even when I started teaching a fifty-student class on Nabokov at the University of Wisconsin-Madison in 2017.

When I reflected on my first impressions, they came down, I thought, to what Seneca the Younger described as *docendo discimus* and what modern pedagogy calls the "protégé effect." Teaching Nabokov to American undergraduates in 2016 and 2017 was a learning experience for me. My students enjoyed what Brian Boyd calls the game of cognitive challenges and rewards in Nabokov's prose but tended to remain unresponsive to—even mildly annoyed at—the interpretive prescriptions in the author's forewords, lectures, and interviews. After witnessing their reaction, I, too, walked away with a surprising new belief that Nabokov and I as his representative in the classroom were not the ultimate authorities on how to read his works. This questioning attitude to authority in my students seemed like a quality of their generation as well as a reaction to the political and cultural events of those years, specifically the election of Donald Trump in November 2016 and the beginning of the global #MeToo movement in October 2017.

Equally surprising to me was the fact that there were several words in Nabokov's American works that demanded translation, intergenerational rather than interlingual, for my students: those words were *vulgarity, texture, pity,* and *colored*. In this essay, I will first address these keywords and then see whether a pedagogical generalization can be made based on my experience.

Vulgarity

When we read in *Pnin* (1957) about the religious veneer and cultural pretentions of the semi-fictional St. Bartholomew Preparatory School where "there was the Reverend Hopper's mellow voice, nicely blending vulgarity with refinement," I point out in class that the Reverend does not allow himself any obscene language, as the word seems to be used most often in American parlance today.[1] What he means is "smugly unrefined." The same applies to the other four times Nabokov uses the words "vulgar" and "vulgarity" in the novel.

Nabokov's "vulgarity" is directly related to the Russian *poshlost'*, or what he translates as *poshlust* (the lust for things posh) and defines, in his book on Nikolai Gogol, as "the falsely important, the falsely beautiful, the falsely clever, the falsely attractive."[2] The origins of the Russian literary obsession with *poshlost'* can be traced to Alexander Pushkin's aristocratic disdain for what was best described for him by the English word "vulgar," namely, the misguided presumption of low-born professional critics who passed judgment on the work of aristocratic authors. This presumptuousness or, to use the definition of Prince Dmitry Mirsky, "self-satisfied inferiority," was particularly galling in daily behavior.[3] When the critic Nikolai Nadezhdin picked up a handkerchief dropped by Pushkin, this gesture was enough for the poet to call Nadezhdin "vulgar" (in English) in a letter. Curiously, when in the next generation of Russian aristocracy Count Lev Tolstoy denounced this kind of superficial preoccupation with manners, he found the opposite of English *vulgar* in the French *comme il faut* but still based his moral judgment on fundamental aristocratic entitlement.

Nabokov commented on the class origin of this quality when he wrote in "On a Book Entitled *Lolita*" in 1956 that "in regard to philistine vulgarity there is no intrinsic difference between Palearctic manners and Nearctic manners. Any proletarian from Chicago can be as bourgeois (in the Flaubertian sense) as a duke."[4] The English word encapsulated for him a cultural tradition founded on the idea of social class as an indication of inborn merit—but perpetuated beyond the limits of the original social conditions. The writer exerted considerable effort in trying to convince his readership in egalitarian America that his cultural reflexes (Russian aristocratic contempt, British class consciousness, French artistic hauteur) were a universal moral quality of *any* artist.

It is worth asking during class discussion whether Nabokov was aware of the ethical problem inherent in the fact that for him, his privileged upbringing was never unearned, a presumption of innate intellectual and moral superiority. Even when students do not rush to judge the author, they can reflect on his (and their) positionality.[5]

Texture

Then, in reverse alphabetical order, comes the word "texture" in *Pale Fire* (1962). Even though the word is relatively uniform in meaning, it seemed to confuse the students in my first classes, because it was not the familiar contemporary meaning, "the feel, appearance, or consistency of a surface or substance." Nabokov spoke not of surfaces but of patterns and organization. In that, he followed his favorite Second Edition of the Webster's International Dictionary, where the definition ranged from "a woven web" to "the disposition of filaments" to "the disposition of the several parts of any body in connection with each other, or the manner in which the constituent parts are united; structure."

In the novel, the word is foregrounded when Nabokov's main character, the poet John Shade, describes an epiphany he had regarding the afterlife: "not text, but texture; not the dream / but topsy-turvical coincidence, / Not flimsy nonsense, but a web of sense. / Yes! It sufficed that I in life could find / Some kind of link-and-bobolink, some kind / Of correlated pattern in the game, / Plexed artistry, and something of the same / Pleasure in it as they who played it found."[6]

Apart from "texture," the words "web," "link," "correlated," "pattern," and "plexed" all emphasize structural connections and pattern design. The poet formulates a theory of the afterlife and literary art as the realms, not of texts, but textures, or textual patterns, where the actual meaning of an element is of less consequence than the meaning generated in the patterning of this element with another. In the process, connections between textual details inevitably postulate the existence of a space outside them, and it is in this fugitive "outside" that meaning is born. The outside is so much more important than the inside that it does not matter that Shade's being "reasonably sure" about his survival turns out to be an error in the text, where he is killed in a tragic case of mistaken identity: mistakes and lethal accidents become cognitively powerful in the magical texture of things, intimated by the poet.

The narrative paradox of fictional self-representation and in general the conditional reality of representational art distributed across levels from "less true" to "more true" constitute one of the main themes of *Pale Fire* and one of its inner springs. It thus problematizes the relations between real life and fiction, already suspicious for this generation of readers. In class, to show the significance of textures in the book, I compare the endlessly receding enfilade of "outsides" implied in the leap from text to texture to the philosopher and AI theoretician Douglas R. Hofstadter's "strange loop."[7] "Not text, but texture" is an expression of the shift from one level of reflection to another, "more general" level. The self-referential looped chain of "outsides" in "not text, but texture" can be taken as Shade's (and arguably Nabokov's) metaphor for consciousness, a universal model that can with equal justice apply to the poet's thinking on creativity and mortality. When Shade presents human consciousness as the ability to create a succession of meta-levels and jump from one of them to the next, the poet in effect suggests that a *meta*physical realm is an inevitable consequence of the existence of conscious life. "Texture" serves as the password both to the novel and to the theory of consciousness expressed in it.

Pity

How strange, then, that John Shade offers a different password, when challenged by his interlocutor and novel's narrator Charles Kinbote. On the explicit textual level, Shade's "password" is "pity."[8]

In class we speculate whether it can be a case of self-translation, of the writer recycling for his mature English-language work the imagery, devices, and concepts from his young Russian novels. Can "pity" from *Pale Fire*, a novel published in 1962 in English, have migrated from the first novel we read, *The Defense* (*Zashchita Luzhina*), written in 1929 in Russian, where it was the defining psychological trait of the wife of the mad grandmaster Luzhin? And if so, is the pity in *Pale Fire* as problematic as the characterization in *The Defense*? Critics are divided on whether to read it as a positive or negative trait.[9] Indeed, looking for an authorial endorsement to take Mrs. Luzhin's sentimental, self-abnegating pity at face value, students encounter instead a noncommittal ambiguity, for the heroine's well-meaning sentimentality is associated with the hackneyed compassion of old novels with their mediocre plots and inevitable happy endings—the kind of novels that Luzhin's father wrote, Luzhin's wife read, and Luzhin's author derided.

It feels doubly ambiguous when we talk about the odd tone of the second canto of Shade's poem in *Pale Fire*. The canto tells the story of the poet's unattractive and morose daughter Hazel and her suicide. The scene where Shade is crying in the men's room only because his homely teenage daughter was cast as Mother Time in a school play is disturbing. Where my students expect unconditional love and tireless parental support, there are instead, memorably, "the demons of our pity" that speak still,[10] and the parents' oddly urgent helplessness in the face of the "new defeats, / New miseries"[11] occasioned by their child's lacking conventional good looks.

Neither my tolerant, inclusive, body-positive audience nor I knew at first how to reconcile the pitying, guilt-ridden Shades' attitude to their suicidal daughter and Shade's unequivocal ethical password, "pity." Why is "pity" the password if it is personified by "demons"? Does Shade understand that his pity comes across as condescension, judgment, and parental disappointment and as such is probably not the best way to assuage the girl's "defeats" and "miseries"? One of the students in my class at Notre Dame suggested that Shade's account might be a kind of atonement, because he feels guilty for having pitied his daughter in life and, at least partially, responsible for her suicide. I thought this was an astute proposition but what to do with *pity* as password?

Once we broach the subject of pity, we cannot escape the subject of cruelty. As optional secondary reading for my Nabokov class in 2017, I assigned the philosopher Richard Rorty's "The Barber of Kasbeam: Nabokov on Cruelty." Rorty points out that Nabokov is not indifferent to moral issues, but artistically he is more interested in the absence of pity in selves, the cruelty of artists, whose point of view readers are invited to share in order to examine the consequences.[12] In her response to Rorty's reading, Leona Toker added that Nabokov often portrays, not cruelty, or a deliberate rejection of pity, but callousness, or, in the words of Humbert Humbert with respect to the barber of Kasbeam, inattention, a more fitting attitude perhaps for superior consciousness.[13]

Webster's Second, too, comparing compassion, sympathy, and pity, indicates that "pity regards its object not only as suffering, but weak, and hence as inferior." If Nabokov was aware of this definition, his word choice was a deliberate invocation of the idea of superiority.

In the course of discussion that year, we concluded that pity in *Pale Fire* was the proud man's empathy, a way to feel for, and relate to, others without fully sharing in their experience, without compromising one's sense of self. Shade's pity is empathy and detachment merged in one moral experience. It is, in Rorty's terms, a way of reminding ourselves of the pain we cause by our pursuit of autonomy *without* relinquishing this pursuit. In *Pale Fire*, the writer dramatizes the oscillation between these two mutually exclusive aspects of pity when he distinguishes between the "password pity" of the commentary, which embodies the empathic side and is applied to Kinbote, and the "demon pity" of the poem, which can be a form of inattention and callousness and is applied to Hazel. Insisting on the vital role of pity, then, is tantamount to declaring it the moral obligation of natural privilege, the connate duty of superior consciousness. Can one go further and say that Shade's "password pity" for Kinbote is an atonement for his earlier "demon pity" for his daughter?

Nabokov has more to say about pity in his lectures on literature, which I mention briefly in class. In the Dickens lecture, pity, or "specialized compassion," distinguishes the British novelist from Homer. Nabokov goes so far as to claim that the "divine throb of pity" was totally unknown to Homer.[14] Assuming that this is the same moral category as the pity of *The Defense* and *Pale Fire*, this "specialized pity," this self-aware compassion of the moderns, different from the "generalized compassion" or the supposed knee-jerk morality of the Greeks, is, to the best of my knowledge, the clearest expression of the importance of this emotion in Nabokov.

Yet, the clarity is blurred once again in the lecture on Franz Kafka. Nabokov famously states there: "*Beauty plus pity*—this is the closest we can get to a definition of art." But in the full context of the lecture's opening paragraph, pity, to the reader's increasing surprise, unlike beauty, remains indefinable:

> "To take upon us the mystery of things"...this is also my suggestion for everyone who takes art seriously. A poor man is robbed of his overcoat...; another poor fellow is turned into a beetle...—so what? There is no rational answer to "so what." We can take the story apart, we can find out how the bits fit, how one part of the pattern responds to the other; but you have to have in you some cell, some gene, some germ that will vibrate in answer to sensations that you can neither define, nor dismiss.[15]

If beauty can be pulled asunder as texture, pity is as irreducible as it is imperious. It comes from "the mystery of things." Despite the generic difference between a college lecture and a novel, Nabokov essentially expresses the same double meaning of pity here. People need to exercise compassion for other people, but because this need cannot be explained in the coordinates of the artist's overarching imperative to hold on to his or her sense of autonomy, compassion can turn out to be no more than a productive mistake, and other people are often undeserving.

When the "white fountain" from John Shade's vision of the afterlife finds a confirmation in the newspaper report of a similar vision that a "Mrs. Z." had under similar circumstances, Shade sets out to find the woman, excited to ask her about it. However, when they meet, he cannot bring himself to articulate the all-important question, because "if (I thought) I mentioned that detail / She'd pounce upon it as upon a fond / Affinity, a sacramental bond, / Uniting mystically her and me, / And in a jiffy our two souls would be / Brother and sister trembling on the brink / Of tender incest."[16]

In class discussion we talk about the palpable distaste, even disgust that Shade shows at the thought of sharing his treasured experience with a stranger. We also use this framework to contextualize the insight Shade experiences when he learns from the journalist who wrote the report that there was a misprint in it and the woman's "white fountain" was actually a "white mountain."

What Shade sees proves less important than the fact that he believes in a coincidence for a while; an element receives its purpose from a meaningful outside, "not text, but texture." But the reader notices, yet again, the incommunicability of the discovered meaning, unsharable and indefinable in human terms, and the poet feels relief at not having to relate to another person directly, at going back to his solitary experience, at being able, after all, to extract mystical meaning from his autonomy. Texture here is not formed by a connection between individuals but by two thoughts within a single mind, and the revealed meaning must remain occult to the rest of the world for the mind to remain secure in its autonomy. At the end of the poem, the reader realizes that, given other instances where Shade explicitly pits private against public, this may be the secret engine of the work, the crux where compassion, autonomy, and consciousness come together and make apparent the intimate connections between vulgarity, texture, and pity.

Pity, or the tension between the autonomy of superior consciousness and that consciousness's moral obligation to be able to relate to others, finds a correlative in texture or a shimmering possibility of a connection between the mind and something outside it. But texture is still localized in the poet's mind, and there is hardly more than a shimmer of another mind outside it, even when it comes to the minds of his wife and his daughter. Both pity and texture express the pregnant paradox of the unspoken need of the morally (but not epistemologically?) "useful" Other in a writer who categorized himself as an "indivisible monist"[17] and whose character claimed that "the only real number is one and the rest are mere repetition."[18]

Colored

Nabokov's monism was particularly jarring in the classroom conversation we had in the fall of 2020 about the gloss on the word "Negro" in *Pale Fire*. The narrator of the novel puts the word in the context of the conversation he had with John Shade about prejudice and American anti-Semitism. Shade is said to loathe racial prejudice generally, but "as a man of letters" prefers "is a Jew" and "is a Negro" to "is Jewish," and "is colored."[19] Lumping these two identities together, furthermore, according to Shade, is careless, demagogic (and is "much exploited by Left-Wingers"), because it obscures the difference between "two historical hells."[20]

Most revealingly in that passage, Shade objects to the use of word "colored" even though "many competent Negroes...considered it to be the only dignified word, emotionally neutral and ethically inoffensive; their endorsement obliged decent non-Negroes to follow their lead, and poets do not like to be led."[21] Shade, "as a dealer in old and new words," objects to the epithet because it is "artistically misleading" and because its meaning "depended too much upon application and applier."[22] The "artistic objection," Shade further explains, has to do with the fill-in plates in books on flora and fauna and the actual colors that he sees in his mind's eye when he hears it.[23] The kind of freedom Nabokov construes here out of the unique richness of an artist's individual experience proves once again unsharable.

This stance came across as politically supercharged in 2020, after the racial reckoning and the protests of that summer, and the author's choice to make his high standards of creative insight dependent on the exclusion of other people had painfully obvious political consequences. Shade's refusal to "be led" here sounded to me and my students too much like contemporary conservative media that bemoaned having to give up some of its historically hegemonic power to name people as it pleased. It was particularly disappointing that Shade, a character Nabokov otherwise seems to treat with sympathy, uses his literary vocation to justify divesting himself of ethical answerability in naming others. In this passage alone, the suspect status of affective relations between individuals, the prioritization of a (white) poet's autonomy over ethical answerability to a marginalized Other, and the critique of "lumping" identities together by "Left-Wingers" all clashed with one of the most important values of this generation of readers: affect-based solidarity.

Pale Fire, *Lolita*, and *Pnin* all connected, usually implicitly as in the usage "competent Negroes" in the quote from *Pale Fire* above, race with class and power.[24] The unreflecting acceptance of the connection on Nabokov's part was pointed out in our class discussions in 2020 either by my students or myself, as a generational difference between Nabokov and today's reader. My purpose in facilitating the discussion was then to ask what use could the reader find for this pointing out? Judgment as a boost to our own sense of self-worth? Creation of an ethical space in which to explore and define positionality? Something else entirely?

Teaching

As I am writing this in the spring of 2022, reflecting on the real-life events that my students and I have witnessed since I started teaching in 2016, from Trumpism to #MeToo to George Floyd to Black Lives Matter to the trauma of the pandemic and social isolation to the Russian invasion of Ukraine, the questions that still present themselves are: Is my method of attending to surprise pedagogically productive? Can I generalize a pedagogy out of several very local keywords and close readings? And more broadly, what is my pedagogical responsibility in the face of trauma? How does one teach a writer such as Nabokov now in the first place?

One answer would be to look at how that writer taught others. When Nabokov's *Lectures on Literature* (1980), *Lectures on Russian Literature* (1981), and *Lectures on Don Quixote* (1983) were published, they were seamlessly integrated into the canon. From students' memoirs, we know that they liked Nabokov, and at least one of them, Alfred Appel Jr., cherished the memory, remained attached to Nabokov the man, and was inspired to become a scholar himself.[25]

However, Nabokov's very method of teaching—almost always reading from one of the thousand pages which he had prepared in the beginning of his career in America—confirmed the impression of teaching as a temporary inconvenience in the daily routine of a creative artist. In an interview given after he had retired from teaching, Nabokov stated that "for some reason" his most vivid memories from his time as a college professor concerned examinations. He then gave a masterfully Nabokovian description of the intellectual helplessness and body odor of the crowd in front of the examiner.[26]

Although in that published interview Nabokov said that he loved teaching, in 1952, after twelve years as a college instructor in America, he memorably confessed in a private letter to Edmund Wilson that he was "sick of teaching, sick of teaching, sick of teaching."[27] In the next decade, one of the pioneers in the Anglo-American genre of the academic novel, he published three books where teaching was portrayed as a distraction or a ruse barely tolerated by creative characters, while non-creatives abused it and turned their academic posts into hotbeds of mediocrity. In *Pnin*, to take one example, one of the most poignant aspects of the main character's life is the disconnect between what he knows and what he is compelled to teach, between his live memory and matchless knowledgeability on the one hand and the dull robotic nonsense of Russian grammar on the other. Teaching in *Pnin* is funnily absurd, and not just because of the language barrier. The teacher can be replaced by a machine because the riches of his inner world remain intrinsically incommunicable. Tellingly, while the narrator makes fun of the word "group," the otherwise noncombative Pnin balks at the temerity of contemporary psychology that impinges on individual privacy to alleviate individual sorrows. To both the narrator and Pnin, the sharing of knowledge and emotion is a sham. The best teacher in *Pnin*, if not in all of Nabokov's fiction, is a painter named Lake, and as if to compensate for his pedagogical talent, Nabokov writes that "while endowed with the morose temper of genius, he lacked originality and was aware of that lack."[28]

Paradoxically, if Nabokov's poetics depends on instruction, the premise of sharing knowledge in actual instruction clashes with his epistemology, which privileges detachment (specificity, individual perception, mystical epiphany) over involvement (generalization, connection, sharable knowledge).[29] If one concludes that, in teaching Nabokov today, the instructor has little use for the strategies that Nabokov himself once adopted, what method should one choose?

In the last five years, the years of #MeToo, feminist readings of Nabokov have revitalized Nabokov studies and Nabokov pedagogy. Feminism seems congenial for the classroom where students never need help in "calling out" Nabokov as an occasionally sexist, homophobic, and racist writer. Indeed, reading Nabokov today almost always means reading him "symptomatically."[30] Such readings often collapse the distinction between real life and fiction by foregrounding fiction's real-life implications and treat a failure to do so as a politically and morally fraught choice. This stance culminates in posing, if not answering, one of today's most pressing pedagogical questions: Why include Nabokov in the college curriculum at all?[31]

When, as in my case as academic staff, the instructor has little control over whether to teach Nabokov or not, a somewhat different set of questions (or the same questions differently asked) presents itself: Is there *no* responsible way to teach someone like Nabokov except with the purpose of rejecting him on all fronts? How does the reader account for the surprise they may feel when reading/teaching Nabokov distracts them from nursing their own autonomy? And why even in their pedagogical anxiety and their impostor syndrome does the instructor sometimes sense an opportunity, rather than a neurosis?

Personally, my assumed privileged position among Nabokov's intended readership has always been a safety object of sorts. And it never felt more so than when I came across the work of Eve Kosofsky Sedgwick. In the essay "Paranoid Reading and Reparative Reading, or, You're So Paranoid, You Probably Think This Essay Is About You," written in the 1990s during the AIDS epidemic and concerned with finding means for communal repair, she famously proposes to distinguish between paranoid reading, embedded in what Paul Ricoeur called the "hermeneutics of suspicion" and preoccupied with establishing whether knowledge is true, from reparative reading, which focuses on the uses, that is, the performativity of knowledge.[32] According to Sedgwick, paranoid reading has become a virtually ubiquitous approach to knowledge and uncertainty. It is (1) anticipatory (deliberately eliminates surprise and tautologically already knows what it will find when it sets out searching for meaning); (2) reflexive and mimetic (knows its object by imitating it); (3) "strong" as a theory (creates a large domain of disparate elements); (4) negative in terms of the affects it prioritizes (becomes stronger by finding more and more instances of humiliating mistakes); and (5) exposure-oriented (believes in demystification and revealment as always leading to improvement to the point where it does not notice when revealment itself becomes a form of violence).[33]

To imagine an alternative, one begins by agreeing that "to have an unmystified, angry view of large and genuinely systemic oppression does not intrinsically or necessarily enjoin that person to any specific train of epistemological and narrative consequences."[34] A focus on the use of knowledge then allows Sedgwick to theorize reparative reading as one that leaves room for surprise, is less contagious, is a "weak" or local theory, admits a seeking of pleasure as one possible interpretive motive, and does not blindly place faith in demystification. In sum, the goal of reparative epistemology is not so much to uncover and confirm the painful truth as to respond to it with care.

Aside from the reassuring implications that reparative position might have for keyword-oriented, discussion-based pedagogy, I want to conclude this essay with a plan for reading Nabokov reparatively.

First, the reader acknowledges that reparative readings are hermeneutic experiments, creative, open-ended, and non-totalizable. The reader chooses not to imitate Nabokov in prescribing overarching interpretive control and "hermophobic" rejection with respect to certain interpretations. The reader recognizes their own interpretive fears—fear of humiliation and fear of disappointing the author or any other interpretive authority—but at the same time asserts joy and other positive affects as derivable from and motivating their own reading. The reader "weakly," locally agrees with Nabokov's epistemology resistant to generalizations and looks at close reading as an occasional productive strategy. The reader locally acknowledges Nabokov's well-documented critique of the deterministic and demystifying impulses in Freud and Marx but looks for opportunities to break out of the monopolizing (and therefore exclusionary) optics of *other* projects of exposure, even some feminist and antihomophobic projects, while remaining mindful of the role such projects play in the self-determination of disempowered communities.[35]

Lolita, or rather the interpretive space around it, would seem to be an unavoidable testing ground for these positions. In the 1966 interview by Alberto Ongaro, published in English in 2019, Nabokov claimed that he did "not believe the patriarchal structure of society has prevented women from developing in their own way" and that "the reality is that women are biologically weaker than men." When Ongaro objected that Nabokov had made Lolita stronger than Humbert Humbert, the writer replied: "She's stronger only because Humbert Humbert loves her. That's all."[36] The failure to de-essentialize strength in humans and the unreflecting attempt to justify patriarchy as rooted in "biological" (physical?) difference are exposure-worthy, especially when the reader invokes the real-life interview of the singer Fiona Apple who was raped at age twelve: "How much strength does it take to hurt a little girl? How much strength does it take for the girl to get over it? Which one of them do you think is stronger?" An opportunity for reparative reading emerges from the fact that Fiona Apple's words appear in Kate Elizabeth Russell's 2020 novel *My Dark Vanessa*, directly inspired by *Lolita* and intended as a kind of contemporary response to it.[37] (The reader almost wishes that Russell consciously included Apple's poignant quote in her novel as a retort to Nabokov's embarrassing statement.) The reparative questions for discussion then would be: What can be said about the role of fiction as a medium for this response? Does one *have* to agree that, because rape irrevocably contaminates or displaces by violence the joy of sex for the victim in real life, the creation and interpretation of theories and fictions about abuse and rape *have* to be centered around negative affect and *cannot* admit a self-soothing and a seeking of the joy of relief as legitimate motivations for imagining violence? Is there a space for this ethical possibility in contemporary readings of *Lolita*? And more generally, what can be said about Nabokov's notion of love? How is it different from that of today's audience and why?

The classroom would be a perfect space for such reparative inquiries precisely because classroom discussions admit surprise, and surprise and hope are Sedgwick's primary reparative affects:

> Hope, often a fracturing, even a traumatic thing to experience, is among the energies by which the reparatively positioned reader tries to organize the fragments and part-objects she encounters or creates. Because the reader has room to realize that the future may be different from the present, it is also possible for her to entertain such profoundly painful, profoundly relieving, ethically crucial possibilities as that the past, in turn, could have happened differently from the way it actually did.[38]

While both paranoid and reparative epistemologies are "rooted in deep pessimism," what they seek—and their motive for seeking it—"differ widely."[39] Sedgwick suggests that thanks to this reorientation toward repair, the excluded wounded reader can sometimes find means to heal and help themselves in the very same culturally prestigious texts that wound and exclude them:

> No less acute than a paranoid position, no less realistic, no less attached to a project of survival, and neither less nor more delusional or fantasmatic, the reparative reading position undertakes a different range of affects, ambitions, and risks. What we can best learn from such practices are, perhaps, the many ways selves and communities succeed in extracting sustenance from the objects of a culture—even of a culture whose avowed desire has often been not to sustain them.[40]

Of course, stories like *Lolita* can re-traumatize students who have experienced abuse, and addressing real-life trauma while teaching the novel includes a content warning on the syllabus and alternate assignments for those who need them (in my class I use *The Real Life of Sebastian Knight* in that capacity). Otherwise, under this approach, spontaneous discussion, preferably in small groups, starts to play a central role, as do creative writing assignments, which I include in my course as an optional alternative to academic papers. In them, students are encouraged to rewrite Nabokov's narratives, write prequels and sequels, as well as fan fiction. The evaluative criteria for such assignments, then, if applicable at all, would be grounded in queering reparative reading. In the case of *Lolita*, it would be reparative reading to loosen, in the words of

Joseph Litvak, "the traumatic, inevitable-seeming connection between mistakes and humiliation" and treat mistakes queerly as "sexy, creative, even cognitively powerful";[41] to find in Nabokov's novel what Sedgwick describes with regard to camp as "the startling, juicy displays of excess erudition...the passionate, often hilarious antiquarianism, the prodigal production of alternative historiographies; the 'over'-attachment to fragmentary, marginal, waste or leftover products; the rich, highly interruptive affective variety; the irrepressible fascination with ventriloquistic experimentation; the disorienting juxtapositions of present with past, and popular with high culture" and with regard to D. A. Miller as "surplus beauty" and "surplus stylistic investment";[42] to ask if such surpluses in *Lolita* could be potentially nourishing to the reader traumatized by depictions of violence and abuse in it; to imagine how the book's limitations can be transcended in other possible fictions; and to challenge the book's exclusions with a hope for solidarity among its audience.

Notes

1. Vladimir Nabokov, *Pnin* (New York: Vintage International, 1990), 94–95.
2. Vladimir Nabokov, *Nikolai Gogol* (New York: New Directions, 1944), 70.
3. D. S. Mirsky, *A History of Russian Literature, From Its Beginnings to 1900*, ed. Francis James Whitfield (Evanston, IL: Northwestern UP, 1999), 158.
4. Vladimir Nabokov, *The Annotated Lolita,* edited, with preface, introduction and notes, by Alfred Appel Jr. (London: Penguin Books, 1991), 315.
5. For more on *poshlost'* in Nabokov, see Matthew Walker's essay in this volume.
6. Vladimir Nabokov, *Pale Fire* (New York: Vintage International, 1989), 63.
7. Douglas Hofstadter, *Gödel, Escher, Bach: An Eternal Golden Braid* (New York: Basic Books, 1999).
8. Nabokov, *Pale Fire*, 225.
9. Eric Naiman, *Nabokov, Perversely* (Ithaca, NY: Cornell UP, 2010), 188.
10. Nabokov, *Pale Fire*, 44.
11. Ibid., 45.
12. Richard Rorty, *Contingency, Irony, and Solidarity* (Cambridge: Cambridge UP, 1989), 159.
13. Leona Toker, "Liberal Ironists and the 'Gaudily Painted Savage': On Richard Rorty's Reading of Vladimir Nabokov," *Nabokov Studies* 1 (1994): 195–206.
14. Vladimir Nabokov, *Lectures on Literature*, ed. Fredson Bowers (San Diego: Harcourt Brace Jovanovich, 1980), 86.
15. Ibid., 251.
16. Nabokov, *Pale Fire*, 62.
17. Vladimir Nabokov, *Strong Opinions* (New York: Vintage International, 1973), 85.

18 Vladimir Nabokov, *Novels and Memoirs* (New York: Library of America, 1996), 81. For important critical analyses of the philosophical and political implications of Nabokov's position, see Leona Toker, "'The Dead Are Good Mixers': Nabokov's Versions of Individualism," in *Nabokov and His Fiction: New Perspectives*, ed. Julian Connolly (Cambridge: Cambridge UP, 1999), 92–108; Dana Dragunoiu, *Vladimir Nabokov and the Poetics of Liberalism* (Evanston, IL: Northwestern UP, 2011), esp. chapter 4.

19 Nabokov, *Pale Fire*, 217.

20 Ibid.

21 Ibid.

22 Ibid.

23 Ibid., 218.

24 For an insightful and sensitive analysis of these connections, see Galya Diment, "Masters and Servants: *Up*stairs and *Down*stairs in Nabokov," in *Nabokov Upside Down*, ed. Brian Boyd and Marijeta Bozovic (Evanston, IL: Northwestern UP, 2017), 131-142.

25 Recent summaries of Nabokov's attitude to academia can be found in Elizabeth Susan Sweeney, "Academia," in *Nabokov in Context*, ed. David Bethea and Siggy Frank (Cambridge: Cambridge UP, 2018), 51–58; Ben Dhooge and Jürgen Pieters, eds., *Vladimir Nabokov's Lectures on Literature. Portraits of the Artist as a Reader and Teacher* (Leiden, Netherlands: Brill Rodopi, 2018).

26 Nabokov, *Strong Opinions*, 22.

27 Vladimir Nabokov and Edmund Wilson, *Dear Bunny, Dear Volodya: The Nabokov – Wilson Letters, 1940–1971*, ed. Simon Karlinsky (Berkeley: U of California P, 2001), 300.

28 Nabokov, *Pnin*, 96.

29 See Kate Kokinova, "Lolita Reading *Lolita*: Rhetoric of Reader Participation," *Nabokov Studies* 14 (2016): 59.

30 For the origin and meaning of the terms "surface reading" and "symptomatic reading," see Stephen Best and Sharon Marcus, "Surface Reading: An Introduction" in *Representations* 108, no. 1 (2009), 1–21. For examples of how the concepts can be applied to Nabokov see Eric Naiman, "Nabokov and #MeToo: Consent, Close Reading, and the Sexualized Workplace," in *Teaching Nabokov's* Lolita *in the #MeToo Era*, ed. Elena Rakhimova-Sommers (Lanham, MD: Lexington Books, 2021), 136–137, and Meghan Vicks's essay in this volume.

31 Two recent feminist cases for including *Lolita* in the curriculum are given in Marilyn Edelstein, "(How) Should a Feminist Teach *Lolita* in the Wake of #MeToo?" in *Teaching Nabokov's* Lolita *in the #MeToo Era*, ed. Elena Rakhimova-Sommers (Lanham, MD: Lexington Books, 2021), 11–29; Anne Dwyer, "Why I Teach *Lolita*," in *Teaching Nabokov's* Lolita *in the #MeToo Era*, 31–41.

32 In her essay published in this volume, Meghan Vicks identifies Sedgwick's reparative and paranoid reading as a productive interpretive strategy as well. Dr. Vicks and

I worked completely independently from each other and had remained unaware of the similarity of our approaches until our first drafts had already been written. I draw attention to this meaningful coincidence by way of emphasizing the timely relevance of Sedgwick's work for Nabokov studies and encouraging the readers to familiarize themselves with it. The value of reparative thinking in culture at large can be gauged from two recent books: Olivia Laing, *Funny Weather: Art in an Emergency* (New York: W. W. Norton, 2020), which quotes Sedgwick directly, and Sarah Schulman, *Conflict Is Not Abuse: Overstating Harm, Community Responsibility, and the Duty of Repair* (Vancouver: Arsenal Pulp Press, 2017), esp. the introduction, "A Reparative Manifesto."

33 Linking paranoid reading to paranoid politics, Sedgwick suggests that paranoia is "so indelibly inscribed in the brains of baby boomers that it offers us the continuing illusion of possessing a special insight into the epistemologies of enmity" (Eve Kosofsky Sedgwick, "Paranoid Reading and Reparative Reading, Or, You're So Paranoid, You Probably Think This Essay Is About You," in *Touching Feeling: Affect, Pedagogy, Performativity* [Durham, NC: Duke UP, 2003], 127); given the proliferation of conspiracy theories in the age of social media and, for example, the cultural critic Natalie Wynn's analysis of incel culture as rooted in what she terms "masochistic epistemology" (if it hurts, it must be true) ("Incels | ContraPoints," Natalie Wynn, accessed August 9, 2021, www.youtube.com/watch?v=fD2briZ6fB0), one suspects that paranoia-like positions define the thinking of at least some groups among millennials and Gen Z, too.

34 Sedgwick, "Paranoid Reading and Reparative Reading," 124.

35 Sedgwick names Judith Butler's *Gender Trouble* (1990) and D. A. Miller's *The Novel and The Police* (1988) among such monopolizing projects. The goal of reparative reading would be to mitigate the *exclusion* of certain perspectives and identities from interpretive effort rather than gloss over underlying *differences* between them, such as "sexual difference," difference of gender presentation, race, economic and educational background, citizenship, etc. Differences are still there, but reparative reading is possible across differences, and understanding does not depend on their reification.

36 Vladimir Nabokov, *Think, Write, Speak: Uncollected Essays, Reviews, Interviews, and Letters to the Editor*, ed. Brian Boyd and Anastasia Tolstoy (New York: Alfred A. Knopf, 2019), 219.

37 Kate Elizabeth Russell, *My Dark Vanessa* (New York: William Morrow, 2020), 193–194.

38 Sedgwick, "Paranoid Reading and Reparative Reading," 146.

39 Ibid., 138.

40 Ibid., 150–151.

41 Quoted in ibid., 147.

42 Ibid., 150.

Paranoid Reading, Reparative Reading, and Queering *The Real Life of Sebastian Knight*

Meghan Vicks*

In the last quarter century, literary criticism has become increasingly interested in textual "surfaces." This surface turn has been accompanied by critiques of symptomatic reading, which has enjoyed enormous authority in the field. Simply put, symptomatic reading asserts that "proper interpretation" must ferret out "a latent meaning behind a manifest one,"[1] locating a text's truest meaning in its depths, while imagining the critic as "wrestling meaning from a resisting text or inserting it into a lifeless one."[2] In contrast, the turn to the surface supposes and witnesses many things, among them: that the most meaningful meanings are not necessarily the deepest ones; that the forces of repression or domination often operate openly, requiring no unveiling; or that in addition to understanding a work through its content or form, the *experience* of reading a text—one's *affective* response to it—matters.

Of the symptomatic approaches, what Eve Kosofsky Sedgwick terms "paranoid reading" merits singling out. Sedgwick identifies paranoid practices as those that uncover hidden truth by employing a "hermeneutics of suspicion," be it unconscious drives undergirding literary forms or oppressive historical forces camouflaged by liberal aesthetics—basically, what Marxist, psychoanalytic, and deconstructive analysis have in common. Pointing to the hegemony of paranoid reading in criticism, Sedgwick wonders what other ways of knowing are consequently muffled by it. She advocates for a reading practice that pivots from the paranoid position to one she calls "reparative," from where it is possible to build psychic wholeness and positive affects out of reality—even out of one revealed to be hostile or depressing.

The benefits and drawbacks of symptomatic and paranoid reading, as well as the interpretive horizons opened by a surface turn and the reparative mode, are rewarding topics in classes that study works by Vladimir Nabokov.[3] For one, plenty of Nabokov's characters are themselves readers, and interpretation is thematized in his works. But the argument may also be made that symptomatic reading has reigned among scholarly approaches to Nabokov. As Eric Naiman writes, it is not only that "Nabokov's world is charged with hermeneutic paranoia";[4] the world of Nabokov studies is also characterized by a kind of hermeneutic performance anxiety, or "hermophobia."[5] Thus, bringing discussion of these reading practices into a study of Nabokov sheds light on his characters and how they read *and* also on how we—Nabokov's readers—understand and experience Nabokov. It allows us to think carefully about what is gained or lost by our paranoid and symptomatic approaches to Nabokov and to access ways of reading him that encourage the reparative moment: an experience of joy and wholeness in relation to the text, unencumbered by fear of "missing something" or "getting it wrong."

The Real Life of Sebastian Knight (henceforth *RLSK*) is particularly well suited for an analysis of these issues. It features a quest for a hidden truth or concealed reality (to learn the *real* life of Sebastian Knight) and a quester in the form of a reader, interpreter, and writer (Sebastian's half-brother, V.). V. operates, often, as a paranoid reader, even like a "hermophobic" Nabokovian scholar, but toward the novel's end embraces a reparative reading practice, one that allows for psychic reconciliation without solving epistemic or empirical crisis.[6] As a corollary to this, the novel is fertile ground for queer readings and reading queerly, which have emerged lockstep with both paranoid and reparative reading practices.

Frameworks

To set the stage for *RLSK*, students consider the question *What is real?* together with two theoretical frameworks we'll work with: the first from Nabokov and the second from Sedgwick.

Nabokov's "Reality"

I provide a handout featuring some of Nabokov's statements on reality (Appendix A). Students consider these remarks with three tasks in mind.

First, we attempt to understand Nabokov's comments on their own. What does it mean when he writes "reality" is "one of the few words which mean nothing without quotes"? Or if, as he claims, "The word 'reality' is the most dangerous word there is," what makes it so? Often, the more we discuss his comments the queerer they become, offering multiple potential interpretations while eschewing commonsensical, normative understandings of reality.

Second, we put these comments into conversation with a general class discussion about *What is real?*, involving contemporary concepts such as post-truth, disinformation, alternative facts, fake news, and so on. Compared with notions such as these, Nabokov's "reality" is perhaps more positively drawn, even though he emphasizes that to perceive "true reality" is impossible. For many, Nabokov's comments open our original question up to more philosophical and aesthetic considerations.

Third, we explore how these comments impact a reading of the novel's title. I ask what students assumed *RLSK* might be about knowing only its title. Did this assumption shift once they were clued into Nabokov's statements on reality? How do these statements inevitably transform the title into a cipher that requires deciphering? (Who here is starting to feel suspicious?)

In adding depth to the novel's title, we establish questions that will accompany our reading of *RLSK*: How does the narrator V. define what's real? What counts, for him, as "the real life" of Sebastian—and what doesn't count? What methods does he use to discover Sebastian's "real life"? What sources does he trust, and which ones does he dismiss? With these I encourage students to develop a complex and suspicious understanding of the novel's ideas about reality *and* to see V. as a kindred reader on a similar quest to theirs. After all, V. interprets anecdotes, memories, rumors, and even *his own imaginings* about Sebastian; analyzes Sebastian's literary texts; and critiques an earlier biography on Sebastian, a newspaper obituary, and reviews of Sebastian's work—all as part of his mission to uncover Sebastian's "real life."

Paranoid Reading and Reparative Reading

The notion of V. as a reader leads to the second theoretical framework taken from Sedgwick's "Paranoid Reading and Reparative Reading, or, You're So

Paranoid, You Probably Think This Essay Is About You."[7] Ideally, students read and discuss this piece in preparation for our conversations about *RLSK*; otherwise, I provide a summary.

To provide a genealogy of paranoid reading, Sedgwick points to what Paul Ricoeur designated the "hermeneutics of suspicion" as a way of categorizing the position of Marx, Nietzsche, and Freud. "Beginning with them," Ricoeur explains, "understanding is hermeneutics: henceforward, to seek meaning is no longer to spell out the consciousness of meaning, but to *decipher its expressions*"; their "distinguishing characteristic" is "the general hypothesis concerning both the process of false consciousness and the method of deciphering."[8] Like other symptomatic reading practices, the "hermeneutics of suspicion" locates the most meaningful aspect of a text in what it represses. However, what distinguishes it from religious models of revealed meaning (such as in Gnosticism) is its emphasis on demystification or the "reduction of illusion."[9]

Sedgwick observes in the "hermeneutics of suspicion" a "concomitant privileging of the concept of paranoia."[10] Even Freud, Sedgwick reminds us, noted a remarkable correspondence between a patient's "systematic persecutory delusion" and Freud's own theoretical system.[11] Paranoid practices are thus methods that lean toward deciphering, diagnosis, and unveiling, operating under the suspicion that the truest (most real) meaning must be plumbed from the depths beneath a false and deceptive surface (be it a text, culture, consciousness, historical record, etc.).

While acknowledging that her own writings have leaned upon paranoid practices (as other scholars have noted[12]), in this essay Sedgwick thinks carefully about their potential disadvantages. One is that the only positive affect the paranoid position seeks is the avoidance of humiliation; otherwise, it is enjoined entirely with negative affect, especially anxiety. Another is that its faith in exposure seems, in retrospect, stunningly naïve: On the one hand, "What is the basis for assuming that it will surprise or disturb, never mind motivate, anyone to learn that a given social manifestation is artificial, self-contradictory, imitative, phantasmatic, or even violent?";[13] on the other hand, why fetishize unveiling when clear signs of violence and oppression are easily, ubiquitously evident? ("Why bother exposing the ruses of power in a country where, at any given moment, 40 percent of young black men are enmeshed in the penal system?").[14] Still another is that paranoid reading is hyper-privileged in cultural and historical studies, likely at the expense of other possible modes of knowing—in particular, a kind she calls *reparative*.

To describe reparative reading, Sedgwick finds useful Melanie Klein's concept of paranoid and depressive positions. For Klein, the psyche in the paranoid position is one of "terrible alertness to the dangers posed by the hateful and envious part-objects that one defensively projects into, carves out of, and ingests from the world around one."[15] Meanwhile, the depressive position is "the position from which it is possible in turn to use one's own resources to assemble or 'repair' the murderous part-objects into something like a whole—though,...*not necessarily like any preexisting whole*....Among Klein's names for the reparative process is love."[16] As Ellis Hanson puts it: "Faced with the depressing realization that people are fragile and the world hostile, a reparative reading focuses not on the exposure of political outrages...but rather on the process of reconstructing a sustainable life in their wake."[17] Hence, in contrast to paranoid reading and its demystification, suspicion, decoding, and unveiling of hidden meaning, reparative practices work toward *pleasure* and *amelioration*—the act of trying and trying again to take joy and make whole even in the midst of hostile meaning.

As we study *RLSK*, one major goal is to come to a better understanding of reparative reading and what it enables us to do, while also honoring what paranoid reading does well and acknowledging where it falls short. To this end, students keep notes regarding V.'s "knowledge-seeking modes": when does V. employ paranoid practices to seek knowledge about Sebastian, and when does he demonstrate reparative ones? The latter, at least for me, produces the most beautiful moments in the novel, even though these moments are suffused with empirical and epistemological uncertainty (moments when "reality" is deeply in question). Finally, our task will also be to read in both paranoid and reparative modes, exploring how these produce different knowledges about and experiences of the novel.

RLSK and Paranoid Reading

Reality's False Bottoms

Nabokov's statements on reality compel students to re-read the title of *RLSK* suspiciously. What could the real (without quotation marks) life mean, if reality means nothing without quotation marks? As Gennady Barabtarlo first discovered, anagramming "Sebastian Knight" offers up *A Knight Is Absent*, feeding our hermeneutic frenzy.[18] Both the title and the title character's name contain false bottoms, riddles, or traps nestled within them. Through this, what I most want students to grasp is the beginning of a pattern where seemingly stable bits of reality (supposedly solid surfaces), when read in the paranoid mode, become unstable (beneath these surfaces are conflicting, self-sabotaging depths).

To develop this pattern, students keep a list of facts about Sebastian introduced in the first chapter. By "facts," I mean information about him seemingly not up for debate (in the spirit of the saying, "Everyone is entitled to their own opinion, but not their own facts"). Here are just three of the most common ones that produce interesting discussion:

1. "Sebastian Knight was born on the thirty-first of December, 1899, in the former capital of my country."[19]
2. The names of Sebastian's mother (Virginia Knight), her father (Edward Knight), her cousin (H. F. Stainton), her lover (Palchin), a friend of the family (Captain Belov), and an old Russian lady (Olga Olegovna Orlova). Meanwhile, the names of some characters are not given, including Sebastian's father, stepmother, and half-brother.
3. How, where, and when Sebastian's mother died: "She died of heart-failure (Lehmann's disease) at the little town of Roquebrune, in the summer of 1909."[20]

All of these, with very little paranoid reading, transition from facts into questions.

Regarding Sebastian's birthday, seasoned readers of Nabokov are conditioned to wonder which calendar (Gregorian or Julian) is intended whenever a pre-Revolution date is given in connection with Russia. Until 1918, Russia used the Julian calendar and therefore "lagged twelve days behind the rest of the civilized world in the nineteenth century, and thirteen in the beginning of the twentieth."[21] Like Sebastian, Nabokov was born in Saint Petersburg in 1899, a year that further complicates the transposition of the Julian day into the Gregorian system—if one is born in 1899 (when from Julian to Gregorian it is a twelve-day difference), they inevitably celebrate all their birthdays in the twentieth century (when the difference from Julian to Gregorian is thirteen days). Nabokov notes these imperfectly shifting dates between calendars in *Speak, Memory* to explain why his birthday is sometimes April 10, other times April 22, and still other times April 23, but he also plays with such slippery dates in his literary works.[22] Which calendar, therefore, does V. have in mind when he tells us Sebastian's birthdate, and what different meanings do the various possibilities enable?

There is then the curious fact that so many peripheral characters are named in the first chapter, and yet we never learn the name of the father, the stepmother, or the narrator—three who would share the same last name, in all likelihood a Russian one. Observing this, we remember that this Russian family name would also, by tradition, be Sebastian's. Hence the name's absence becomes curiouser still. It moreover sharpens focus on "Knight," the maiden name of Sebastian's mother. Is "Sebastian Knight," then, the title character's birth name? Or is it his pen name? And is "the real life of *pen name*" the same thing as "the real life of *birth name*"—or are these different enterprises?

We are now on high alert and tackle the third fact: Sebastian's mother died of heart failure, specifically Lehmann's disease. We are fastidious, good readers; we will caress the truth out of every detail, so we look this up. We discover that Lehmann's disease does not exist (at least not according to any medical dictionary in our world). We massage it even more. "Lehmann's" sort of sounds like "layman's." Could this be a layman's heart disease, or lovesickness? Another student finds "Hansel" anagrammatically tucked away in "Lehmann's": could we be following breadcrumbs?[23] One of these will eventually lead to Sebastian, who also suffers from Lehmann's disease, mentioned by V. when describing the earliest signs of trouble in Sebastian and Clare's relationship.[24] Did Sebastian die from lovesickness?

As we go through these details, we become less convinced that we can establish even the basic facts about Sebastian. The novel seems on a mission to undermine any *real* certainty about its subject (or maybe, one student remarks, V. is just bad at his job). We consider why this might be its mission. What is to be gained by making suspicious what V. writes in a text about a "real life," and what possible interpretations are enabled here? It says something, of course, about "reality" and how well we can ever know it. But this paranoid method also opens the novel up to several queer possibilities, one of which I turn to now.

Queering the Narrative

Paranoia and paranoid reading have enjoyed an intimate relationship with queer studies. Like feminist resistant readings, which undertook against-the-grain interpretations of canonical texts to expose misogyny, early queer readings engaged in the symptomatic/paranoid tradition to unveil queer "leakages"—"cracks and fissures in supposedly heteronormative surfaces, which revealed subversive queer connotations."[25] Even before becoming a method of queer analysis, during the mid-1980s paranoia was an *object* of "antihomophobic theory," a way of understanding "not how homosexuality works, but how homophobia and heterosexism work—in short, if one understands these oppressions to be systemic, how the world works."[26] In *RLSK*, a queer narrative can be accessed both through the paranoid practice, which reveals queer leakages in the novel, as well as by considering V.'s paranoia as an *object* (and not just as one of his interpretive methods)—an object that announces his homophobia.

After demonstrating how the paranoid practice throws into suspense what seem to be the novel's basic facts, the paranoid impulse dictates we question what V. believes to be key—"the missing link"—to learning the "real life" of Sebastian. This is that Sebastian fell in love with a mysterious woman and left Clare Bishop for her. As V. tells Roy Carswell, underscoring the importance of this to his project: "I must find that woman. She is the missing link in his evolution, and I must obtain her—it's a scientific necessity."[27]

In this quest to find the "missing link," V. adopts radically paranoid methods, from decoding a fictitious letter in *Lost Property* to searching across the continent for Nina Rechnoy. The energy and urgency he puts into this quest can pull readers in as well, so much so that we risk overlooking some basic questions. Namely, why does V. feel so strongly that this affair is key to understanding Sebastian? Or, put another way: why does V. put so much weight into answering *this* question? We consider what V. takes for granted about the affair: that it was with a woman. Could he be wrong?

Once we entertain the possibility that the mysterious woman might be a mysterious man, abundant textual evidence can be called to substantiate it.[28] Queer leakages emerge in multiple moments, among them:

1. Sebastian's journey with the futurist poet Alexis Pan and his wife Larissa.

V. dismisses the possibility that Sebastian had an affair with Larissa, which might explain why he went on the trip: "Why he had joined in that ludicrous show and what in fact had led him to pal with that grotesque couple remained a complete mystery (my mother thought that perhaps he had been ensnared by Larissa but the woman was perfectly plain, elderly and violently in love with her freak of a husband)."[29] Here, a "complete mystery" is tantalizingly put before the reader, but V. allows it to remain unsolved after rejecting just one potential solution. Why not entertain other possibilities, or at least the next one: perhaps it was with Alexis that Sebastian had an affair. V.'s epithet for Alexis—"freak"—may expose subconscious homophobia. In any case, a rigidly assumed heteronormativity is revealed to be operating in V.'s narrative.

2. V. pinpoints the beginning of trouble in Sebastian and Clare's relationship to a mysterious trip Sebastian took with a Russian man.
Clare arrives at a resort and learns that Sebastian has unexpectedly left for "an unknown destination."[30] When Sebastian returns, he "was certainly glad to see her but there was something not quite natural in his demeanor. He seemed nervous and troubled, and averted his face whenever she tried to meet his look. He said he had come across a man he had known ages ago, in Russia, and they had gone in the man's car to—he named a place on the coast some miles away."[31] We ponder what is "not quite natural" about Sebastian here. And as with the mystery of the futurist trip, we marvel that V. allows this episode to remain cloaked in ambiguity—from the unnamed location, to the identity of the Russian man, to Clare's worry that Sebastian's not telling the truth. In other words: what makes some mysteries worthy of solving, and others worthy of forgetting? We see a pattern where V. opts not to search when a queer, homosexual reality is a possibility.

3. V. meets a Russian man who drives—the so-called Uncle Black, cousin of Pahl Pahlich Rechnoy.
While this character appears on the periphery of the chapter with Pahl Pahlich, he is strikingly brought into the narrative's focus multiple times. He is introduced through the black knight chess piece (which reminds us of another Knight—Sebastian!) that Pahl Pahlich tosses to him.[32] For his nephew he draws "with incredible rapidity and very beautifully a racing car,"[33] whereupon Pahl Pahlich comments: "Oh, he's an all round genius. He can play the violin standing upon his head, and he can multiply one telephone number by another in three seconds, and he can write his name upside down in his ordinary hand." The nephew adds, "And he can drive a taxi."[34] As V. is leaving, Uncle Black and the nephew are returning from a walk. V. notes: "'Once upon a time,' Uncle Black was saying, 'there was a racing motorist who had

a little squirrel; and one day …'"[35] These details—the knight, the triple mention of driving or racing cars, the uncle's charming talents—along with the paranoid imperative, encourage a connection between Uncle Black and the mysterious Russian man who drove a car, whom Sebastian knew "ages ago," and with whom he traveled when he should have been meeting Clare. Could Uncle Black and this unknown man be the same person?[36] And if so, could he, and not Nina Rechnoy, be the real object of V.'s search (unknown to V.)?

These and other details crack the heteronormative surface of *RLSK*. What's revealed is not only the possibility that Sebastian was queer but also that V.'s paranoia over finding the mysterious woman is more about desperately and homophobically asserting Sebastian is *not* gay than knowing and accepting who Sebastian may really be. What emerges is the tragedy of heteronormativity that devalues, others, ignores, silences, and harms LGBTQ people (as if this isn't bad enough) and that also limits our ways of knowing the world and perceiving what's possible.

RLSK and Reparative Reading

Reparative "Undestanding"

As demonstrated, a paranoid reading of *RLSK* may reveal the depressing and angering possibility that V. does not accept Sebastian's queerness and hence the tragic reality of homophobia. I ask students: Where do we go from here as readers? What do we do with this interpretation? We might be tempted to reject V. with the proverbial finger and to question how complicit Nabokov is in V.'s homophobia. These are, without doubt, legitimate responses, and we spend time exploring them. But I think a more reparative response is also potentialized here. Sedgwick reminds us that the reparative position is "[n]o less acute than a paranoid position, no less realistic, no less attached to a project of survival, and neither less nor more delusional or fantasmatic," but it "undertakes a different range of affects, ambitions, and risks."[37] Thus, the reparative reader is, for example, keenly aware of the depressing reality of homophobia, but they "help [themselves] again and again"[38] to craft something sustaining and positive "from the objects of a culture—even of a culture whose avowed desire has often been not to sustain them."[39]

One valuable inroad toward a reparative reading for students is through some biographical notes, which also further queer the novel. When Nabokov writes about his younger brother Sergey in *Speak, Memory*, he mentions *RLSK*: "For various reasons I find it inordinately hard to speak about [Sergey]. That twisted quest for Sebastian Knight..., with its gloriettes and self-mate combinations, is really nothing in comparison to the task I balked in the first version of this memoir and am faced with now."[40] Of the few anecdotes provided, Nabokov describes how he discovered Sergey was gay and, effectively, outed him to their father: "a page from his diary that I found on his desk and read, and in stupid wonder showed to my tutor, who promptly showed it to my father, abruptly provided a retroactive clarification of certain oddities of behavior on his part."[41] The discovery was not met with sympathy or acceptance by the family. Nabokov's biographer Brian Boyd detects here "belated self-reproach" for invading Sergey's privacy and outing him, which I worry might be too generous of an interpretation.[42] But we ponder whether the novel's potential closeting of Sebastian might be Nabokov's way of *not* repeating the deep harm he caused when he read Sergey's diary and betrayed his privacy—perhaps an attempt to atone for this transgression, though not an unproblematic one?

We also notice that Nabokov's description of his relationship with Sergey during their childhood years echoes the portrayal of Sebastian and V.'s childhood relationship, but with certain traits of theirs inverted.[43] Sebastian, like Nabokov, is the older sibling born in 1899, the future famous author, adventurous and beloved as a child; but like Sergey, Sebastian is queer. When we get to the novel's finale, where V. describes having put on Sebastian's likeness and in so doing has become Sebastian, we return to the idea that Nabokov inversely grafts onto Sebastian and V. his own relationship with Sergey. We couple this with the idea that Nabokov composed *RLSK* in the wake of a period when he and Sergey were "on quite amiable terms in 1938–1940, in Paris."[44] Could *RLSK* therefore be Nabokov's way of working through their relationship and coming to a kind of reconciliation, albeit an imperfect one?[45]

In these discussions it is essential to nevertheless acknowledge Nabokov's discomfiture concerning Sergey's homosexuality:

> Sergey's homosexuality had always made Vladimir awkward, and the brothers' first meeting in Paris had not been a success. Nevertheless Sergey indicated he wanted to speak seriously to Vladimir and confront their differences, and a week later they lunched near the Luxembourg Gardens with Sergey's partner. "The husband, I must admit, is very pleasant, quiet,

not at all the pederast type, attractive face and manner. All the same I felt rather uncomfortable, especially when one of their friends came up, red-lipped and curly." A week after the public reading, Vladimir and Sergey talked together earnestly, calmly, even warmly. That warmth—never present between them until now, even in childhood—would endure when they met in the future.[46]

It is difficult to read Nabokov's characterizations of Sergey's partner and friend, the homophobic backhands "not at all the pederast type" and "red-lipped and curly" couched meanly among compliments. A reparative response fully recognizes this despairing and homophobic reality, and it does not attempt to fix or explain it away. Rather, it leans toward the hopeful possibility that Nabokov demonstrates both love for Sergey and regret for his past actions, while not excusing or remedying his homophobia.

Nabokov concludes his remarks about Sergey with the following:

I know little of his life during the war. At one time he was employed as translator at an office in Berlin. A frank and fearless man, he criticized the regime in front of colleagues, who denounced him. He was arrested, accused of being a "British spy" and sent to a Hamburg concentration camp where he died of inanition, on January 10, 1945. It is one of those lives that hopelessly claim a belated something—compassion, undestanding [sic], no matter what—which the mere recognition of such a want can neither replace nor redeem.[47]

I always wonder if the misprint of "undestanding" is somehow intentional or at least a telling slip. It underscores, after all, an unknowing that remained between Nabokov and Sergey, Nabokov's inability to understand or fully accept him.[48] It is, perhaps, the perfect means to state that Nabokov, in some fundamental ways, misunderstood his brother—or, to circle back to our original topic, that he could not access his real life.[49]

Mistakes and "Reading Queer"

In "Paranoid Reading and Reparative Reading," Sedgwick quotes a personal communication with Joseph Litvak, who proposes that, while mistakes often condition a paranoid fear of being wrong, ignorant, left out, or humiliated, queer thinkers have found mistakes to also be sites where a reparative impulse is ripe:

It seems to me that the importance of "mistakes" in queer reading and writing...has a lot to do with loosening the traumatic, inevitable-seeming connection between mistakes and humiliation. What I mean is that, if a lot of queer energy, say around adolescence, goes into what Barthes calls "le vouloir être intelligent" (as in "If I have to be miserable, at least let me be brainier than everybody else"), accounting in large part for paranoia's enormous prestige as the very signature of smartness (a smartness that smarts), a lot of queer energy, later on, goes into...practices aimed at taking the terror out of error, at making the making of mistakes sexy, creative, even cognitively powerful. Doesn't *reading queer* mean learning, among other things, that mistakes can be good rather than bad surprises?[50]

In parsing these comments, it is helpful to recall Klein's characterization of the depressive position. From the depressive position, one witnesses the fractured, hostile, erroneous world (e.g., heteronormative society, racism, etc.) and yet, rather than expose that world (e.g., through parody, delegitimization), attempts to construct there an experience of joy and wholeness. A good example of this is Sedgwick's discussion of the queer-identified practice of camp, which she argues is seriously misrecognized when understood through paranoid optics as a way of mocking and denaturalizing dominant culture. Instead, Sedgwick sees camp as a practice of the reparative impulse: "Its fear, a realistic one, is that the culture surrounding it is inadequate or inimical to its nurture; it wants to assemble and confer plenitude on an object that will then have resources to offer to an inchoate self."[51] What Litvak's comments propose, together with Sedgwick's discussion of the depressive position and camp as reparative, is that the queer subject, by virtue of being *queer*, may be ontologically positioned to create positive affects out of mistakes, fractured worlds, hostile environments. This is what it means to *read queer*.[52]

These comments offer a valuable way to approach mistakes in *RLSK*. Students keep a list of mistakes, misreadings, distortions, failings, and losses that appear in the narrative. While V. sometimes leans upon the paranoid mode to unravel information they harbor regarding Sebastian's "real life" (as with his response to Mr. Goodman's misreadings of Sebastian's remarks),[53] I ask students to pay special attention to mistakes that inspire a reparative response, either from V. or from us.

Of these many moments, there are three I find essential to discuss: (1) Sebastian's trip to the wrong Roquebrune;[54] (2) the summary of Sebastian's *The Doubtful Asphodel* and V.'s response to it;[55] and (3) the final scene, where

V. learns that the sleeping patient he thought was Sebastian is someone else and that Sebastian died the previous day.[56]

Sebastian's trip to the wrong Roquebrune—where he visited what he erroneously believed to be the house where his mother died and experienced there a queer, spectral vision of his mother—inspires both paranoid and reparative responses. While Mr. Goodman argues that Sebastian viewed this incident cynically, V. insinuates that Sebastian embraced the emotions and ghostly vision he experienced, even after realizing the mistake.[57]

The Doubtful Asphodel describes a dying man who realizes the "answer to all questions of life and death" but fails to pass on this "absolute solution" to the reader. V.'s first response to this is paranoid. He muses, "are we mistaken? I sometimes feel…that the 'absolute solution' is there, somewhere, concealed in some passage…,"[58] anticipating that closer reading could decipher it. But later in the chapter, in response to critical reviews of *The Doubtful Asphodel*, V. exclaims: "Yes, I think of all his books this is my favorite one. I don't know whether it makes one 'think,' and I don't much care if it does not. I like it for its own sake. I like its manners."[59] In the face of the book's potential failure, V. doesn't argue the failure away but instead embraces the book "for its own sake"—turning away from thinking to feeling in doing so. If we return to this scene after reading the novel's finale, there is moreover an undeniable sense that V. is also responding reparatively to Sebastian here: he likes Sebastian for his own sake, for his manners, and without thinking about any "absolute solution."

The final scene enjoys a special place in our discussion regarding mistakes. Students often notice it has two antecedents—Sebastian's trip to the wrong Roquebrune and *The Doubtful Asphodel*. In this scene, V. fully embraces the reparative mode. Even when faced with the empirical fact that the patient before him is not Sebastian, V. nevertheless does not disown but rather accepts the profound emotions he experienced before the revelation of the mix-up: "those few minutes I spent listening to what I thought was his breathing changed my life as completely as it would have been changed, had Sebastian spoken to me before dying."[60]

During discussion of this scene, there are four points I advance if students don't develop them themselves. The first: V.'s realization that the soul is "not a constant state" but a "manner of being"[61] queers the concept of identity, transforming identity from a stable phenomenon to a fluid one, making transition and wonder intrinsic to it.[62] Second: the final sentence where V. admits that "perhaps we both are someone whom neither of us knows"[63] elicits yet another reevaluation of the novel's title and what is meant by the *real* life. Third: V.'s realization (the secret he uncovers) not only happens thanks to the mistake but is accompanied by acceptance of deep epistemic uncertainty. After all, the final sentence suggests that V. doesn't know Sebastian and Sebastian doesn't know V. — and also that they may not know themselves. Epistemic certainty is not a prerequisite to revelation and discovery. And fourth: I introduce Nabokov's comments on reading with "one's spine."

These comments are taken from the lectures "Good Readers and Good Writers" and "L'Envoi." In the first, his opening one, Nabokov characterizes the "good reader" as capable of reading in a way that produces a "sensual and intellectual" pleasure. "A wise reader," Nabokov says,

> reads the book of genius not with his heart, not so much with his brain, but with his spine. It is there that occurs the telltale tingle even though we must keep a little aloof, a little detached when reading. Then with a pleasure which is both sensual and intellectual we shall watch the artist build his castle of cards and watch the castle of cards become a castle of beautiful steel and glass.[64]

In "L'Envoi," the closing lecture, Nabokov returns to the spine and its tingle, advocating a way of knowing that allows one to rise at least a little above existence to catch a moment of wholeness and thrills:

> The main thing is to experience that tingle in any department of thought or emotion. We are liable to miss the best of life if we do not know how to tingle, if we do not learn to hoist ourselves just a little higher than we generally are in order to sample the rarest and ripest fruit of art which human thought has to offer.[65]

I detect in these comments what Sedgwick might characterize as the pleasure and amelioration of reparative reading. As Nabokov encourages his students to seek out a way of knowing the world that allows them to access pleasure and wholeness, V. shows us how this is accomplished in the novel's final scene, which is flushed with the reparative moment.

Of course, students often argue that this moment inevitably kickstarts another cycle of paranoid reading: a conspiracy that V. is just a character invented by Sebastian. He never gives us his name, after all, is curiously missing from Mr. Goodman's biography, and so on. As we indulge this line of thinking, I ask students to consider what's at stake in it: that is, what is to be gained if we can uncover a hidden truth that V. doesn't actually exist? And we wonder: would this truth be more meaningful or real than the reparative one?

Appendix A: Some of Nabokov's Statements on Reality

> Reality is a very subjective affair. I can only define it as a kind of gradual accumulation of information; and as specialization. If we take a lily, for instance, or any other kind of natural object, a lily is more real to a naturalist than it is to an ordinary person. But it is still more real to a botanist. And yet another stage of reality is reached with that botanist who is a specialist in lilies. You can get nearer and nearer, so to speak, to reality; but you never get near enough because reality is an infinite succession of steps, levels of perception, false bottoms, and hence unquenchable, unattainable. You can know more and more about one thing but you can never know everything about one thing: it's hopeless. So that we live surrounded by more or less ghostly objects....[66]

> The word "reality" is the most dangerous word there is....The reality of art? It is an artificial, a created reality that is only reality within the novel. I do not believe in such a thing as objective reality.[67]

> "reality" (one of the few words which mean nothing without quotes)[68]

> I tend more and more to regard the objective existence of *all* events as a form of impure imagination—hence my inverted commas around "reality." Whatever the mind grasps, it does so with the assistance of creative fancy, that drop of water on a glass slide which gives distinctness and relief to the observed organism.[69]

Notes

* I am grateful to Sara Karpukhin and José Vergara for inviting me to write an essay for this collection and for their generous and thoughtful feedback on early drafts.

1. Fredric Jameson, *The Political Unconscious: Narrative as a Socially Symbolic Act* (Ithaca, NY: Cornell UP, 2014), 60.
2. Stephen Best and Sharon Marcus, "Surface Reading: An Introduction," *Representations* 108, no. 1 (2009): 5.
3. Sara Karpukhin, whose essay is included in this volume, also finds Sedgwick's reparative reading to be a productive method for interpreting Nabokov, especially for contemporary students. It is a telling coincidence that in thinking about approaches to Nabokov in today's classroom, we each independently turned to Sedgwick. We are hopeful that our complementary essays together demonstrate the timeliness of Sedgwick for Nabokov studies today, in and outside of the classroom.
4. Eric Naiman, "Hermophobia (On Sexual Orientation and Reading Nabokov)," *Representations* 101, no. 1 (2008): 127.
5. Ibid., 124.
6. Using *RLSK* as a case study, Priscilla Meyer argues that indeterminacy is central to Nabokov's work: "Nabokov's art was a quest for that unattainable knowledge.... [B]ecause such knowledge can never be conclusive, Nabokov's novels are never closed, in plot, theme, or resolution....Nabokov's indeterminacy is constructive rather than destructive of meaning." Priscilla Meyer, *Nabokov and Indeterminacy: The Case of "The Real Life of Sebastian Knight"* (Evanston, IL: Northwestern UP, 2018), 4, 9.
7. An earlier version of this essay was published in 1997 under the title "Paranoid Reading and Reparative Reading; or, You're So Paranoid, You Probably Think This Introduction Is about You," in *Novel Gazing: Queer Readings in Fiction* (Durham, NC: Duke UP, 1997), 1–37. I use Sedgwick's 2003 version of the essay, published in *Touching Feeling* (see note 10 below).
8. Paul Ricoeur, *Freud and Philosophy: An Essay on Interpretation*, trans. Denis Savage (New Haven: Yale UP, 1977), 33–34.
9. Ibid., 56.
10. Eve Kosofsky Sedgwick, "Paranoid Reading and Reparative Reading, or, You're So Paranoid, You Probably Think This Essay Is About You," in *Touching Feeling: Affect, Pedagogy, Performativity* (Durham, NC: Duke UP, 2003), 125.
11. Ibid., 125.
12. *Epistemology of the Closet* (1990), considered a founding text of queer studies, shows Sedgwick as a "full-on symptomologue." Emily Apter and Elaine Freedgood, "Afterword," *Representations* 108, no. 1 (2009): 144. See also Best and Marcus, "Surface Reading," 6.
13. Sedgwick, "Paranoid Reading and Reparative Reading," 141.
14. Ibid., 140.
15. Ibid., 128.
16. Ibid. Emphasis in the original.
17. Ellis Hanson, "The Future's Eve: Reparative Reading after Sedgwick," *South Atlantic Quarterly* 110, no. 1 (2011): 105.

18 Gennady Barabtarlo, "See Under Sebastian," *The Nabokovian* 24 (1990): 24–28. Barabtarlo further develops the meaning of this anagram in "*Taina Naita*: Narrative Stance in Nabokov's *The Real Life of Sebastian Knight*," *Partial Answers: Journal of Literature and the History of Ideas* 6, no. 1 (2008): 57–80.
19 Vladimir Nabokov, *The Real Life of Sebastian Knight* (New York: Vintage International, 1992), 3.
20 Ibid., 9.
21 Vladimir Nabokov, *Speak, Memory: An Autobiography Revisited* (New York: Vintage International, 1992), 13.
22 For an exploration of just a few of the calendar anomalies in Nabokov's works, see Stephen H. Blackwell, "Calendar Anomalies, Pushkin and Aesthetic Love in Nabokov," *The Slavonic and East European Review* 96, no. 3 (2018): 401–431.
23 Many critics have attempted to crack the "Lehmann" code, and there exist multiple "solutions" (too numerous to enumerate here, but see, for example, Meyer, *Nabokov and Indeterminacy*, 26, 76, 96, 157n23, 161n32). Students have enjoyed researching this problem on their own, while comparing their findings with those offered by scholars.
24 Nabokov, *RLSK*, 87.
25 Jenny Björklund, "Queer Readings/Reading the Queer," *Lambda Nordica* 23, nos. 1–2 (2018): 8.
26 Sedgwick, "Paranoid Reading and Reparative Reading," 126.
27 Nabokov, *RLSK*, 118.
28 Gerard de Vries observes that many of the novel's motifs "point to homosexuality" and argues that "the inner story of the novel" could be that Sebastian had an affair with a man, in all likelihood the character dubbed "Uncle Black." See de Vries, *Silent Love: The Annotation and Interpretation of "The Real Life of Sebastian Knight"* (Boston: Academic Studies Press, 2016), 173, 193. See also note 36 below.
29 Nabokov, *RLSK*, 28.
30 Ibid., 85.
31 Ibid., 86.
32 Ibid., 140.
33 Ibid., 142.
34 Ibid.
35 Ibid., 146.
36 As far as I know, de Vries was the first to propose that "the man Sebastian met [in Germany] is most probably 'Uncle Black' as V. calls him, or the 'chess player Schwarz' as he is named by Sebastian." He further makes the case that Uncle Black was modeled on Hermann Thieme, Sergey Nabokov's lover. See *Silent Love*, 174, 192.
37 Sedgwick, "Paranoid Reading and Reparative Reading," 150.
38 Ibid.
39 Ibid., 150–151.
40 Nabokov, *Speak, Memory*, 257.
41 Ibid., 257–258.

42 Brian Boyd, *Vladimir Nabokov: The Russian Years* (Princeton, NJ: Princeton UP, 1990), 106.
43 Students enjoy comparing the description of the brothers' childhood relationship on page 257 of *Speak, Memory* with the first two chapters of *RLSK*.
44 Nabokov, *Speak, Memory*, 258.
45 Numerous scholars have made this case. For example, Susan Elizabeth Sweeney considers *RLSK* to be just one of Nabokov's "*Doppelgänger* fictions" that play out versions of his relationship with Sergey: "complementary and interdependent roles are reversed; names, personalities, narrative voices, and histories are exchanged; each brother suffers or enjoys the other's fate. … Both [*Despair* and *RLSK*] repeat Nabokov's childhood relationship with Sergey, but each corrects it in a different way: *Despair* through fantasies of role reversal and mistaken identity, and *Sebastian Knight* by asserting the underlying affinity of the two brothers despite their apparent differences. Thus Nabokov has indeed transformed his anxious memories of Sergey into 'transcendent fiction.'" See "The Small Furious Devil: Memory in 'Scenes from the Life of a Double Monster,'" in *A Small Alpine Form: Studies in Nabokov's Short Fiction*, ed. Charles Nicol and Gennady Barabtarlo (New York: Garland, 1993), 208.
46 Boyd, *Russian Years*, 398–399.
47 Nabokov, *Speak, Memory*, 258.
48 It is worthwhile to note what Nabokov leaves out of his description of Sergey's arrest and death in *Speak, Memory*. Prior to his arrest for being a "British spy," in 1943 Sergey was arrested in Berlin for homosexuality. A cousin was able to secure his release five months later, whereupon Sergey relocated to Prague. There, he was arrested once again after his co-workers turned him in for openly voicing contempt for Hitler. The fact that Nabokov does not mention that Sergey fell victim to the Nazi persecution of homosexuals reads here as a pregnant absence, as yet another way that Nabokov fails to know and accept Sergey. His papering over Sergey's sexual orientation is especially troubling considering that Sergey was persecuted for it. Thus, "undestanding" manifests through what is not said or acknowledged here. For more on Sergey's arrests and death, see Simon Karlinsky, *Dear Bunny, Dear Volodya: The Nabokov–Wilson Letters, 1940–1971*, revised and expanded edition (Berkeley: U of California P, 2001), 174; and Brian Boyd, *Vladimir Nabokov: The American Years* (Princeton, NJ: Princeton UP, 1991), 88–89. See also note 49 below.
49 For more on Nabokov's homophobia and Sergey, see Lev Grossman, "The Gay Nabokov," *Salon*, 2000, www.salon.com/2000/05/17/nabokov_5/; and Dieter E. Zimmer, "What Happened to Sergey Nabokov," January 2, 2017, www.d-e-zimmer.de/PDF/SergeyN.pdf.
50 Sedgwick, "Paranoid Reading and Reparative Reading," 147. Emphasis added.
51 Ibid., 149.
52 See also Jack Halberstam, *The Queer Art of Failure* (Durham, NC: Duke UP, 2011).
53 Nabokov, *RLSK*, 62–63.
54 Ibid., 16–18.
55 Ibid., 174–180.

56 Ibid., 199–203.
57 Ibid., 18.
58 Ibid., 178.
59 Ibid., 180.
60 Ibid., 202.
61 Ibid.
62 Susan Fromberg argues that V.'s final speech "is a deliberate and conscious echo of the final speech in *Alice in Wonderland*." See Fromberg, "The Unwritten Chapters in *The Real Life of Sebastian Knight*," *Modern Fiction Studies* 13, no. 4 (Winter 1967–1968): 439. Meyer, on the other hand, suggests that it may crib elements of Bernard's final soliloquy in Virginia Woolf's *The Waves*. Meyer, *Nabokov and Indeterminacy*, 66. Comparative analysis of *RLSK*'s final scene with the relevant quotes from *Alice in Wonderland* and *The Waves* is productive in class discussions.
63 Nabokov, *RLSK*, 203.
64 Vladimir Nabokov, "Good Readers and Good Writers," in *Lectures on Literature*, ed. Fredson Bowers (San Diego: Harvest, 1982), 6.
65 Vladimir Nabokov, "L'Envoi," in *Lectures on Literature*, 382.
66 Vladimir Nabokov, *Strong Opinions* (New York: Vintage, 1990), 10–11.
67 Interview with Pierre Dommergues, translated from the French and quoted in Leland De La Durantaye, "Kafka's Reality and Nabokov's Fantasy. On Dwarves, Saints, Beetles, Symbolism, and Genius," *Comparative Literature* 59, no. 4 (2007): 322.
68 Vladimir Nabokov, "On a Book Entitled *Lolita*," in *The Annotated Lolita*, ed. Alfred Appel Jr. (New York: Vintage Books, 1991), 312.
69 Nabokov, *Strong Opinions*, 154.

PART IV

PARATEXTS AND ARCHIVES

Patterns and Paratexts: Teaching Nabokov's Autobiography

Robyn Jensen

Truth be told, I have taught Nabokov primarily to the current generation of college students. I cannot speak to the ways that classroom dynamics have shifted over generations. And while I imagine that the students in my classroom are different from those who sat in Nabokov's own lecture halls (in short: more diverse, online, and in debt), I have come to think that there are also certain curious affinities between Nabokov and this new generation. These affinities come into sharper focus, I think, when the work in question is Nabokov's autobiography *Speak, Memory*.

Consider Nabokov's authorial persona. Students may bristle at his avowedly tyrannical level of control over his works and their reception (he likened himself to a "perfect dictator" and his characters to "galley slaves").[1] But while Nabokov positioned himself as the God-like creator of an entire universe, where everything is set in motion at his behest and meaning resides firmly in his hands, this can be seen as a compensatory move, charged with an awareness of *losing* such authorial power. Pitched out of the insular community of Russian émigré writers and readers in Western Europe, Nabokov was forced to confront the limits of singular control over his works upon entering the literary marketplace in America. The production of the physical book, to be sold as a commodity that must compete for readers' attention alongside new media, is a collaborative process shaped by market forces as well as aesthetic concerns—a process that Nabokov could not fully control but increasingly tried to.[2] During his American period, Nabokov made use of various forms adjacent to the text itself to reassert authorial control: forewords, indexes, book covers, annotations, commentaries, and interviews. In these paratextual elements, he performs the role of the fearsome writer, often to comic effect.

These dynamics of the literary marketplace have only intensified with the rise of social media. The cultivation of a commanding authorial persona with "strong opinions" is, after all, a requisite for the contemporary author in the age of the Internet. If a student today were to say that Nabokov was "trolling" his interviewers, they wouldn't be entirely wrong. Or we can imagine that the public feud between Nabokov and Edmund Wilson might transpire today online at an accelerated pace and with others chiming in. And while Nabokov placed the precarious position of the author at the center of works like *Pale Fire*, the logic of contemporary social media multiplies the ways in which an author can lose control over their work once it has been published. Indeed, this may be an aspect of Nabokov's authorial anxiety that our students understand rather well. The awareness of being read (and thus, potentially, misread) is one that social media sites train their users in. Twitter, in particular, breeds an acute sense of self-awareness about how one's statements will be read, assessed, and commented upon—a process of critical judgment that the author and the wider public can see play out in real time.

This is also a generation for whom the idea of continually reworking one's self-narrative over a thirty-year period, as Nabokov did, is not so outlandish. The accretion of each new selfie creates a composite self-portrait that shifts over time. Today's students are adept at self-fashioning, at crafting a version of the self through text and image for a public audience. As such, they are also highly attuned to the practices of deception at the heart of Nabokov's poetics. Given the ways in which people have come to perform versions of the self online (whether idealized, fictionalized, professionalized, ironized, or something else entirely) and, in the process, submit themselves to various forms of scrutiny, it is no great surprise that autofiction has been ascendant for the last decade or so (including, in the Anglo-American sphere, writers such as Rachel Cusk, Sheila Heti, Ben Lerner, and, more recently in the Russophone sphere, Dmitry Danilov, Alexander Stessin, and Oksana Vasyakina). While what constitutes the new genre of autofiction (and what separates it from autobiography or the autobiographical novel) remains somewhat ill defined, a core element is an intentional blurring of the boundaries between autobiography and fiction. The verifiable truth claims typical of the autobiographical pact are thrown into deliberate confusion. It is worth noting that Nabokov conceived of his own autobiography as something wholly new, in similar terms. In 1946, he wrote to an editor at Doubleday that it would be "a new kind of autobiography, or rather a new hybrid between that and a novel."[3] Lest we forget, "Mademoiselle O"—which Nabokov later called the "cornerstone" of his autobiography—was first published as a short story.[4]

All of which is to say that, from certain perspectives, Nabokov could be seen as standing at the beginning of a literary period that is still unfolding, rather than the end of a previous one. Drawing out the connections between Nabokov's autobiographical project and contemporary forms of self-representation recognizable to our students can make for a productive framework. To be clear, I am not suggesting that these forms are identical, nor that my approach to teaching Nabokov (or any author, for that matter) consists solely of foregrounding what is shared or familiar and papering over difference. I offer this comparative approach as a strategy for helping students understand what the text shares with other examples of self-narrative, thus also sharpening our sense of what is distinctive about Nabokov's autobiography.

In courses on "Picturing the Self" and "Photography and Narration," I usually teach Nabokov's autobiography broadly conceived, including not only the self-narrative *Speak, Memory* but also the attendant forms that Nabokov utilized to project his authorial persona and assert control over the text's reception. While working on the autobiography in 1947, Nabokov wrote to Edmund Wilson that it would be "a scientific attempt to unravel and trace back all the tangled threads of one's personality."[5] There are undoubtedly many ways to untangle these threads and help students find the hidden pattern woven in the carpet, but I have found that one productive way to encourage this process is through an investigation of the relationship between the primary text and the paratextual elements. In Nabokov's foreword, the hand-drawn map of his childhood estate, the playful index, and his (unpublished) fictional review "On *Conclusive Evidence*," we can see quite vividly how Nabokov tries to train us to read in a particular fashion, to find the thematic patterns embedded in the text. Whereas exploring the role of paratexts that Nabokov did not himself create, such as the book cover and photographs, can also reveal the ways in which the material book is a product of collaboration rather than singular control.

Part of what motivates my focus on the paratexts when teaching Nabokov's autobiography is that these elements are new additions that distinguish *Speak,*

Memory from its predecessors. Indeed, one thing to acknowledge at the outset of teaching this text is that there are multiple versions of it. Like its author's migratory path, the autobiography had its own circuitous and multilingual journey. As mentioned above, the chapter "Mademoiselle O," originally written in French, was first published as a short story in the French literary journal *Mesures* in 1936. After his arrival in America in 1940, Nabokov published the story in English (translated by Hilda Ward and revised by Nabokov) in *The Atlantic Monthly* in 1943; a different version was published in his short story collection *Nine Stories* (1947). During this period, Nabokov also published a series of autobiographical pieces for *The New Yorker* that, together with the latest version of "Mademoiselle O," would go on to comprise the book-length memoir *Conclusive Evidence* (1951).[6] In 1954, Nabokov translated his memoir into Russian and expanded it, giving it the title *Drugie berega* (Other shores). To conclude this exercise in autobiographical self-translation, in 1966 he published *Speak, Memory: An Autobiography Revisited*. As he put it, this version was a "re-Englishing of a Russian re-version of what had been an English retelling of Russian memories in the first place."[7] He intended to write a second volume of memoirs (possible titles included *Speak On, Memory* and *Speak, America*), but it never materialized.

What does it suggest that Nabokov continually worked on his self-narrative, across different languages and forms, over several decades? Looking at the text's publication history with students can open up preliminary discussions about autobiography as a genre and how such generic expectations might be confounded by this text. One aspect of *Speak, Memory* that students may find surprising is that the autobiography does not proceed in chronological fashion, nor does it focus on the biographical or historical events that one might expect. Nabokov maintained that the "true purpose of autobiography" is following the "thematic designs" of one's life.[8] Each chapter is roughly organized around a theme. Within each chapter our author moves around freely in time, and across the chapters various patterns recur. The autobiography focuses primarily on his inner life, the workings of memory, and his development as an artist.

In our first session on *Speak, Memory*, we also spend some time thinking about how the map at the beginning of the text prepares us for Nabokov's autobiography. The map introduces the reader to Nabokov's visual poetics as well as his subtle sleights of hand. Drawn by Nabokov, the map pictures the Vyra, Rozhdestveno, and Batovo estates where he spent his childhood. Why include a map? I share with them that Nabokov, as a university professor, often drew maps and diagrams to help his undergraduate students properly visualize the kinds of details that "yield the sensual spark without which a book is dead."[9] As part of his lectures, he supplied his students with, for example, a hand-drawn chart of Leopold Bloom and Stephen Dedalus's itineraries through Dublin in *Ulysses*. In a more student-centered classroom, we might invite our students to create such maps and diagrams themselves as a creative exercise in close reading. Indeed, I like to encourage the students to annotate Nabokov's map as they read *Speak, Memory* to visually track the locations of key events and thus to be able to see the density of patterns and coincidences that mark his childhood landscape. To take one location identified on the map as an example: the *chemin du Pendu* ("the path of the hanged") on the Batovo estate. In Chapter 3, Nabokov shares with the reader his hypothesis that Pushkin fought a duel with the Decembrist Kondraty Fyodorovich Ryleev on the grounds of the Batovo estate in 1820. The path, beloved by Ryleev, acquired its name when he was later executed. Marking this duel on our map, we can better appreciate the detail in Chapter 10 that Nabokov and his cousin Yuri would fight mock duels as children "in a green avenue where a duel was rumored to have been fought many dim years ago."[10] While here Nabokov draws connections to a literary father figure, he also relives an event that his own father experienced on the same path. In 1907 on the chemin du Pendu Nabokov found two Amur hawkmoths, rare for that region; twenty-five years earlier on the same spot his father netted a Peacock butterfly, also scarcely encountered in those parts.[11] Such repetitions, scattered throughout the text, can be profitably charted on the map itself.

Given the pedagogical significance Nabokov placed on such diagrams, I find it worthwhile to dwell on this prefatory map in my own classroom. Several of the threads that will structure our sessions on *Speak, Memory* can be spun out of this seemingly straightforward image. The sketch of the butterfly, after all, invites us to read the map beyond its utilitarian purpose, and instead as an artistic image to be interpreted. This is the *Parnassius mnemosyne* butterfly that Nabokov will later pursue in Vyra, on the banks of the Oredezh River.[12] With its reference to both poetry (Mount Parnassus) and the goddess of memory (Mnemosyne), the butterfly conjures up the themes of memory, metamorphosis, and artistic creation that will run throughout the text. Given that the autobiography is organized around thematic patterns, it is useful to get students to track recurring themes or images as they read so that they can see the pattern emerge for themselves. The butterfly on the map is a good springboard for this kind of approach; one can ask students to create a list of other moments in the text where butterflies (and associated themes of metamorphosis, migration, etc.) appear.

A consideration of the map's relation to the text can also lead to a discussion of Nabokov's strong visual memory, cultivated from an early age by his mother. In the second chapter, he describes his mother's injunction to remember beloved visual details of their Vyra estate: *vot zapomni*. Thus, he "inherited an exquisite simulacrum" of the past that protected against later physical losses.[13] But before the more final separation occasioned by revolution and emigration, he experiences his first aches of nostalgia for home while away in the Adriatic for the summer as a child. His response is to draw on his pillow a map of the estate, similar perhaps to the one at the beginning of our text.[14] Early on, the idea that one can only return through art begins to take shape. We see this as well with a painting of a beechwood forest that Nabokov, as a child, imagines "climbing into."[15] He manages this magical feat by the chapter's end, as we see him walking through a beech forest with the artist Mstislav Dobuzhinsky, who taught him about the "precision of linear expression," a technique that has helped him with the "camera-lucida needs of literary composition."[16]

Or we might compare the map with another prefatory visual image: the photograph of the Nabokovs' St. Petersburg home that ushers us into the first chapter. In an extensive caption, Nabokov amends this photograph (taken in 1955, long after his departure) to reveal the ways in which this image fails to capture the space as he remembers it. The lindens on the street were not there before and now obscure our view of the window of the room where he was born. The street and city have changed their names. The house has taken on new identities; after the Nabokovs fled, it became the Danish mission and then a school of architecture. Through his own verbal portrait, we begin to see the house as it was and are allowed to enter. Whether stepping into a carefully detailed painting, revisiting old haunts through a map, or infusing the mechanical medium of photography with memory, he is able to escape the "prison of time" through his painterly recreation of the past.[17]

The map acts as a threshold to the text, inviting us to step back into this lost realm. But what kind of entryway is it? Inevitably, at least one student notices that the traditional compass points have been inverted: South is at the top, North at the bottom. The map literally disorients you. Is there a jolt of pleasure once we realize we have been looking at it the wrong way around? Or frustration with having been made to stumble before reaching the first page? Why disorient us in this way? With this subtle shift, Nabokov estranges our perspective. The inversion of the map seems to concede, once again, that he cannot return by a regular route; we are encouraged to see this as imagined geography, one that only he can grant us access to.[18] The map also offers a foretaste of the kind of deception that Nabokov prizes in art and nature: "Let visitors trip."[19]

I ask the class to look out for other moments of artistic deception as they continue to read. For, if we don't read carefully, we are certainly in danger of tripping during one particularly vertiginous passage as Nabokov seamlessly leaps from a bog in Russia around 1910 to Longs Peak, Colorado, in 1943 on a hunt for butterflies.[20] Indeed, it is the natural world, with its "mysteries of mimicry," that offers a model for art. He finds a "game of intricate enchantment and deception" in the way a type of butterfly resembles a leaf and experiences a "stab of wonder" when a disguised insect or bird suddenly becomes visible within a "tangle of twigs."[21]

We see something akin to this game of mimicry in a photograph of Nabokov, taken by his wife Véra, included in the autobiography. Given our students' familiarity with creating self-portraits through photographs and captions on social media, it is generally worth lingering over how Nabokov treats these images. Photography and autobiography have in common that they claim to represent a real-life referent. How do the authorial photographs included help to support Nabokov's self-narrative? We discuss the tension between seeing photographs as evidentiary documents due to the indexical trace and as constructed images that are not necessarily more reliable than other forms of representation. Students are attentive to how a photograph's meaning can be shaped by the context it is placed in, especially if there is a caption. They note that while the caption often seems neutral, simply a written transcription of what is visible, it can produce an entirely new narrative. In this context, students often point to the length of Nabokov's captions, and we discuss the ways that the author tries to shape our readings of these images through textual mediation. What kind of narrative does he spin out of these images? The caption accompanying Véra's snapshot of Nabokov in profile at his desk, for example, give us an opportunity to see how Nabokov reads himself. In the caption, Nabokov informs us that he is writing *The Luzhin Defense* (*Zashchita Luzhina*, 1929). He draws our attention the tablecloth's checkerboard pattern, highly appropriate for this novel about chess. Not only does Nabokov point to how the photograph's elements draw together many of the thematic threads of his life ("Seldom does a casual snapshot compendiate a life so precisely"), but the image itself is teeming with patterns on the tablecloth, the wallpaper, and Nabokov's sweater.[22] It is as if he, like the butterfly, can mimetically blend into his densely patterned surroundings.

Discerning the pattern within the disordered jumble is, for Nabokov, "the closest reproduction of the mind's birth."[23] This is the "blissful shock" that his son Dmitri will have in the final passage of the autobiography once he finds "what the sailor has hidden" in the "scrambled picture" of the harbor, a shock that mirrors our own aesthetic appreciation of seeing the patterns emerge.[24] But if, upon reaching the end, the student has not found what the author has hidden, Nabokov is ready with more clues. As we know, for Nabokov there are only re-readers. It is only now, once we have read to the end, that we can hold the entire picture in our mind's eye and begin to inspect it more closely. Here it can be useful to spend time on the index, an element that seems perfunctory at first glance but is given pride of place in the poem that concludes the Foreword: "Through the window of that index / Climbs a rose / And sometimes a gentle wind *ex / Ponto* blows."[25] As a class, we consider what an index does and why Nabokov might engage the index at all.[26] (It can also be compared with the index in *Pale Fire*, if one is teaching this text as well.) The index is not often thought of as a constitutive part of the artwork, which makes Nabokov's unorthodox use of it deserving of our attention. It offers yet another example of the extent of Nabokov's control over the various parts of the material book. No element is too small. I suggest to my students that the index stages a game of cross-referencing that illuminates the connection between different themes in the text.[27] The list, after all, is one of Nabokov's preferred genres; the spatial organization of the list allows him to collapse time and "superimpose one part of the pattern upon another," as he does with his "magic carpet."[28] One can use the index to send students back into the text, as they follow any cross-referenced entries that seem significant. A new picture emerges. For example, the entry for "Colored hearing" lists a page reference (34–36) and then instructs us to also see "Stained glass." If we turn to the "Stained glass" entry, we are given another page number (105) and directed on to the entries for "Jewels" and "Pavilion." *Jewels* gives us more page references (36, 81, 111, 143, 188, 252), as does *Pavilion* (215–216, 230). In small groups, students can revisit these passages and discuss what binds these themes together. One might even take a cue from Nabokov's own pedagogical practice and ask students to visually map out how these themes intersect, as he does in his lecture notes for *Bleak House*.[29] Although, rather than have the instructor provide such a diagram to the students, it seems more valuable for the students to produce it themselves. Following the scavenger hunt through the index grants insight into Nabokov's sense of the autobiography's internal structure, but the work of interpretation and analysis still falls to them as readers.

Once we have finished the autobiography, as the culmination of our focus on paratextual elements, I ask students to design their own book cover for *Speak, Memory*.[30] Thinking about the book cover as what Gérard Genette calls "a *threshold*," we briefly look at various existing book covers of *Speak, Memory* to consider how they visually represent, interpret, and prepare the reader for the text.[31] While we have explored how the other paratextual elements helped Nabokov direct readers' interpretations, the book cover is one aspect of the material book that threatens to elude his grasp.[32] Recognizing the power of the book cover to shape a reader's interpretation of the text, Nabokov often provided specific directives to his publishers about his covers. In 1950, for example, he wrote to John Fischer concerning the cover for *Conclusive Evidence*: "Who is designing the jacket? I trust there is no 'Russian' stuff—churches, pagodas, samovars—being considered. I am raising this question only because I have had something of the sort inflicted upon me by an English publisher."[33] Noting the abundance of letters dedicated to the details of book cover design in Nabokov's correspondence with his publishers, John M. Kopper has suggested that Nabokov "saw the book cover not as a marketing device but as an interpretive statement controlling a reader's entry into the work."[34] While this may be how Nabokov saw it, my students have been quick to point out that the cover *is* a central part of advertising a book. The cover attracts the reader, who then advertises it to the public as they hold it in their hands at a café, on the subway, or—increasingly—on social media. In recent years, it has been noted how online retail and social media, Instagram in particular, are shaping book cover design.[35] What catches the eye while scrolling on a small screen? Awash in targeted ads, content generated by algorithms, and posts by "influencers," my students are, unsurprisingly, interested in the dynamics of consumer culture. But they tend to see the works we read in the literature classroom as divorced from the marketplace, a view no doubt encouraged by Nabokov and other modernist writers. Dwelling on Nabokov's involvement with his publishers over aspects of the book's design and promotion provides a way for students to think further about how the writer navigated the uneasy relationship between art and commerce.[36]

Given our focus on the visuality of Nabokov's text, students are by this point well primed to think about questions of representation. Designing a book cover is an act of interpretation on the part of the reader. What should go on the cover? How would the various elements be arranged and why? What aspects of the text elude or frustrate visual representation? Students often produce covers that feature elements we typically associate with Nabokov: chess, butterflies, patterns, spiral structures. I also ask students to reflect on their choices in a short "Artist's Statement" that accompanies their cover. This creative assignment invites students to consider the book as a whole, drawing together the various threads and interconnected strands to create their own image that attempts to encapsulate the text. It offers students an alternative form of analysis that helps prepare them for writing more traditional papers, as they are able to test out and explore ideas in a low-stakes, creative format.

No definitive version of the book's cover can be said to exist. In teaching Nabokov, I find this fact a helpful counterweight to the idea of Nabokov as authorial tyrant. It gives license to students' interpretations; their role as a reader (or a book cover designer) helps to make the book, too. It is a moment of collaboration between the reader and Nabokov—one that can be compared to the sweaty embrace between author and reader atop a mountain imagined by the author in his programmatic essay "Good Readers and Good Writers."[37] This assignment thus offers an opportunity for students to think critically about Nabokov's approach to the author-reader relationship—as well as their own. They might, after all, have a different theory of how this dynamic operates. Some resist the readerly position of following all the clues or solving the puzzles to be rewarded with an embrace from the controlling author, while others want to read Nabokov on terms that the author expressly denies. For that matter, the implications of the author-reader embrace may feel different when the work in question is, say, *Lolita* rather than *Speak, Memory*.[38]

On the subject of Nabokov's imagined reader, there is one final paratextual element that one might introduce when teaching the autobiography. Nabokov initially considered publishing an additional chapter to conclude the text: "'Chapter Sixteen' or 'On *Conclusive Evidence*,'" in which he poses as the book's reviewer. In a letter to his editor at *The New Yorker*, Nabokov wrote that this final chapter is

> the most important one of the series (indeed, the whole book was written with this conclusion and summit in view) since therein are carefully

gathered and analyzed (by a fictitious reviewer) the various themes running throughout the book—all the intricate threads that I have been at pains to follow through each piece.[39]

Nabokov's mock reader here bears no similarity to the invented John Ray, Jr., whose foreword to Humbert's manuscript attempts to frame the text as a psychiatric "case history" with a "general lesson" about "general trends," nor to Charles Kinbote, whose commentary engulfs John Shade's poem in *Pale Fire*.[40] Much can be done with the fact that Nabokov's ideal reader is, simply, himself. As he put it in an interview, the author "clashes with readerdom because he is his own ideal reader and those other readers are so very often mere lip-moving ghosts and amnesiacs."[41] However, after casting aspersions on the general reader, he goes on to offer a qualification: the good reader will "make fierce efforts when wrestling with a difficult author," for which they will ultimately be rewarded.[42] Ascending a mountain differs from being locked in battle, but both visions of the author-reader relationship involve a level of physical exertion on the part of the reader.

Thus, it is no surprise that Nabokov ultimately left out the review at the end of his autobiography—it resolves too neatly all the puzzles and patterns that readers are supposed to struggle through themselves. Nonetheless, the review offers insight into how Nabokov would like to be read and can be a useful example for students in this regard, but it is also important to remind them of their own agency as readers. To reinforce this, one could ask students to write their own reviews, either mimicking the style of Nabokov's or experimenting with different interpretive approaches.

My emphasis here has largely been on the paratextual elements, for these are parts of the book where the relationship between author, reader, and text comes into sharp focus. As the paratexts frame the text proper, they provide a meeting point between author and reader. The autobiography, as a work of authorial self-fashioning, heightens the stakes of being misread or misinterpreted. Thus, we see how Nabokov attempts to shape the reader's interpretation of the text through a host of paratextual elements, but there remain moments where that control potentially slips away. Engaging with Nabokov's vision of the author-reader relationship can help students become more cognizant of how that relationship structures his text, their own implied position as readers, as well as the different modes of reading available to them. By understanding the rules of the game, readers can also choose to play it differently.

Notes

1 Vladimir Nabokov, *Strong Opinions* (New York: McGraw-Hill, 1973), 69.
2 For more on this topic, see Duncan White, *Nabokov and His Books: Between Late Modernism and the Literary Marketplace* (Oxford: Oxford UP, 2017).
3 Vladimir Nabokov, *Vladimir Nabokov: Selected Letters, 1940–1977*, ed. Dmitri Nabokov and Matthew J. Bruccoli (San Diego: Harcourt Brace Jovanovich, 1989), 69.
4 Vladimir Nabokov, *Speak, Memory: An Autobiography Revisited* (New York: Vintage International, 1989), 11.
5 Vladimir Vladimirovich Nabokov and Edmund Wilson, *Dear Bunny, Dear Volodya: The Nabokov–Wilson Letters, 1940–1971*, ed. Simon Karlinsky, revised and expanded edition (Berkeley: U of California P, 2001), 215.
6 For more on the variants of "Mademoiselle O," see chapter six of John Burt Foster, *Nabokov's Art of Memory and European Modernism* (Princeton, NJ: Princeton UP, 1993).
7 Nabokov, *Speak, Memory*, 12.
8 Ibid., 27.
9 Nabokov, *Strong Opinions*, 156–157.
10 Nabokov, *Speak, Memory*, 197.
11 Ibid., 156, 12, 75.
12 Ibid., 210.
13 Ibid., 40.
14 Ibid., 76.
15 Ibid., 86.
16 Ibid., 92.
17 Ibid., 20.
18 Incidentally, Brian Boyd has pointed out that the map contains inaccuracies. See Boyd, *Stalking Nabokov: Selected Essays* (New York: Columbia UP, 2011), 299–300.
19 Nabokov, *Speak, Memory*, 139.
20 Ibid., 137–139.
21 Ibid., 124–125, 298.
22 Ibid., 257.
23 Ibid., 298.
24 Ibid., 309–310.
25 Ibid., 16.
26 This exercise also has a practical function: it alerts students to the value of an index in general, an often-overlooked tool they can use in their research to get a quick overview of what a scholarly book contains.
27 See Dabney Stuart, "The Novelist's Composure: *Speak, Memory* as Fiction," *Modern Language Quarterly* 36, no. 2 (1975): 177–192; Michael Nieto Garcia, "Nabokov's Index Puzzle: Life and Art Transcendent in *Speak, Memory*," *Nabokov Studies* 13, no. 1 (2014/2015): 167–191.

28 Nabokov, *Speak, Memory*, 139.
29 Vladimir Nabokov, *Lectures on Literature*, ed. Fredson Bowers (San Diego: Harcourt Brace Jovanovich, 1980), 71.
30 In my experience, I have found it easiest to ask students to draw their design on a piece of paper. While today's students are often presumed to be "digital natives," using design programs like InDesign or Photoshop still involves a learning curve. If going this route, instructors should make sure that a suitable program is freely accessible to students and be prepared to provide a tutorial.
31 Gérard Genette, *Paratexts: Thresholds of Interpretation*, trans. Jane E. Lewin (New York: Cambridge UP, 1997), 2.
32 For more on Nabokov and book covers, see John Bertram and Yuri Leving, *Lolita: The Story of a Cover Girl: Vladimir Nabokov's Novel in Art and Design* (Blue Ash, OH: Print Books, 2013).
33 Nabokov, *Selected Letters*, 107.
34 John M. Kopper, "Correspondence," in *The Garland Companion to Vladimir Nabokov*, ed. Vladimir E. Alexandrov (New York: Garland, 1995), 62.
35 See, for example, Ellie Violet Bramley, "In the Instagram Age, You Actually Can Judge a Book by Its Cover," *The Guardian*, April 18, 2021, www.theguardian.com/books/2021/apr/18/in-the-instagram-age-you-actually-can-judge-a-book-by-its-cover; Margot Boyer-Dry, "Welcome to the Bold and Blocky Instagram Era of Book Covers," *Vulture*, January 31, 2019, www.vulture.com/2019/01/dazzling-blocky-book-covers-designed-for-amazon-instagram.html; Holly Connolly, "Is Social Media Influencing Book Cover Design?" *The Guardian*, August 28, 2018, www.theguardian.com/books/2018/aug/28/is-social-media-influencing-book-cover-design.
36 For useful background on Nabokov and his publishers, see chapter 4, "Publication," in White, *Nabokov and His Books*.
37 Nabokov, *Lectures on Literature*, 2.
38 For a discussion of this relationship in the context of the #MeToo movement, see Eric Naiman, "Nabokov and #MeToo: Consent, Close Reading, and the Sexualized Workplace," in *Teaching Nabokov's Lolita in the #MeToo Era*, ed. Elena Rakhimova-Sommers (Lanham, MD: Lexington Books, 2021), 145–146.
39 Nabokov, *Selected Letters*, 95.
40 Vladimir Nabokov, *The Annotated Lolita*, ed. Alfred Appel Jr. (New York: Vintage, 1991), 5.
41 Nabokov, *Strong Opinions*, 183.
42 Ibid., 183.

Vulnerability, Discipline, Perseverance, Mercy: On Teaching Nabokov's Short Stories

Olga Voronina

Nabokov is a magnet. No matter how fast the lathe of academia turns, in what direction it moves, and how alluring or pointless students think Literature is as a major, there are always undergraduates willing to read his books and professors willing to teach them. At Bard College, where I have been a member of the Languages and Literatures division for eleven years, three or four faculty list Nabokov's works on their syllabi each semester. A couple of short stories assigned in a creative writing course. *Speak, Memory*, appearing in a seminar on autobiography and the poetics of selfhood. *Bend Sinister*, offered in a class that explores dystopian narratives. The commentary to *Eugene Onegin* and "The Art of Translation" discussed in a translation workshop. The complexity of Nabokov's storytelling, the idiosyncrasy of his metaphysical ideas, the themes of pedophilia and incest around which *Lolita* and *Ada or Ardor: A Family Chronicle* coagulate, and his professed lack of interest in politics do not impede the magnetism. There is the sheer force of talent to consider, the pull of the author whose style, as Michael Wood explains, "is so subtle that it reflects not a meticulous control of a fictional world but a disciplined vulnerability to the shocks of a historical one."[1] I would add to this, "not *only* a meticulous control," for in the Nabokovian pairing of discipline and vulnerability the former definitely prevails. It is Nabokov's self-discipline—and the disciplining reading strategies embedded in his texts—that promise the figure of authority both to confront and venerate to those who read much less fiction than their parents and grandparents did, who condemn sexual taboo as a literary subject, and who embrace political activism as a new way of life. They start a Nabokov class to "check him out" and leave smitten, deeply engaged. As one of my students recently said, "If we do cancel the canon, I want this 'dead white male' to stay alive."

Cultivating this reluctance to throw Nabokov off the steamboat of modernity is one of the joys and privileges of my job. Every other year I teach "Nabokov's Shorts: The Art of Conclusive Writing," in which students are invited to learn not only about Nabokov but also from him. The course offers an introduction to upper-college level of literary criticism through the exploration of narrative structures in Nabokov's short stories and the works he initially wrote for magazines in chapter-length installments, called "stories" at the time of publication, specifically, *Speak, Memory* and *Pnin*. The first page of my syllabus features the famous 1975 photograph by Horst Tappe, in which the writer-lepidopterist, clad in shorts, marches through an Alpine landscape in search of a rare and, if he is lucky, yet unnamed butterfly. Although the pun is intended, the premise of the course has little to do with elusive lepidoptera and Nabokov's choice of outfits for hunting expeditions. At its core lies the idea that short stories were, for him, a magic portal to two successive—and successful—professional careers: first, the career of an émigré Russian writer finding his footing in prose in the 1920s and '30s, and then the "American" career culminating in the conquest of the global literary market. The latter began in the 1940s with Nabokov's publication of concise works of fiction in the English language in *The Atlantic* and *The New Yorker*. "[T]he short story as genre is the ultimate test of a writer's perfection," Maxim Shrayer writes in his seminal *The World of Nabokov Stories*, and it is the Nabokovian version of this excellence that we explore in the course.[2] The only reason why I refrain from citing the "art of perfection" in its title is because my main goal as a teacher is to translate Nabokov's short-prose writing—the structural soundness, thematic intensity, and deep psychological saturation of his "shorts"—into an inspiration for Bard undergraduates' own convincing and lucid (critical) prose.

I offer "Nabokov Shorts" as a Junior Seminar and, therefore, gear it to the needs of Literature majors committed to writing their qualifying theses—"senior projects," in Bard's parlance—on a particular author, literary movement, or series of novels or plays. We meet for two hours and twenty minutes once a week and read two dozen critical essays in addition to twenty-two stories, the autobiography, and *Pnin*. Due to more than a hundred pages of concentrated reading assigned per session, the class has earned a degree of notoriety among Bard's already overwhelmed juniors and seniors, who pick up this load with a heavy sigh. Nevertheless, the interest in "Nabokov's Shorts" has been steady. I credit it, first and foremost, to the literary works themselves: their energy and verbal plasticity, their puzzles and revelations, their exquisite craftsmanship—all the qualities, which Edgar Allan Poe, whom Nabokov so exuberantly parodied in *Lolita*, once pronounced the "deliberate care" of composition capable of leaving the reader with "a sense of the fullest satisfaction."[3]

But there is another draw as well: the reading method which Nabokov taught his students at Wellesley and Cornell and which I encourage my students to embrace. We start with the introductory essay to *Lectures on Literature*, with its requirement that "a good reader, a major reader, an active and creative reader is a re-reader"[4] and from there move on to other Nabokov's "strong opinions":

"Art is difficult."[5]

The intricacy of individual fate is way more complex and thought-provoking than a cultural cliché or political platitude.[6]

And accumulating the recurring motifs in a story is just as important as remembering where they come from, how they connect to other thematic arrangements, and what greater artistic function they perform.[7]

"All communication is a code, poetry being simply the most complex, integrated ordering of encoded elements," Robert Alter says apropos *Pale Fire*.[8] My decision to structure every class around close reading assignments originates from the poetic density and semiotic intricacy of the stories we read together: "La Veneziana," "Christmas," "The Return of Chorb," "A Guide to Berlin," "A Nursery Tale," "The Potato Elf," "The Aurelian," "The Visit to the Museum," "Lips to Lips," "Terra Incognita," "Perfection," "The Leonardo," "Breaking the News," "Recruiting," "Spring in Fialta," "Cloud, Castle, Lake," "Vasiliy Shishkov," "Ultima Thule," "Solus Rex," "Signs and Symbols," "The Vane Sisters," and "Lance." The students' admiration for Nabokovian plots, with their speedy plunge into narrative action and provocative endings, settles in right away, and almost everyone becomes captivated by Nabokov's rhetorical prowess and stylistic virtuosity. That said, becoming a Nabokophile does not immediately turn one into a Nabokovian, namely, the commentator who can decode Nabokov's texts without donning, willingly or unwittingly, the mantle of King Kinbote. To teach my students how to decipher both the "main" and "semitransparent" layers of Nabokov's short stories, another bit of advice from the author himself comes in handy: the teacher's job is to demonstrate "how a writer continually builds up his story by packing in detail, detail, detail."[9]

Following this recommendation, I impel the class to move through the narrative landscape slowly, one image, word, letter, and, sometimes, grapheme at a time. Nabokov insisted that a "good reader" collects "sunny trifles" of the story before indulging in the "moonshine of generalizations," but, unavoidably, the moonshine beckons, while the tiny particulars—"a smear on the platform, a cherry stone, a cigarette butt"—are easy to overlook.[10] In the beginning of "Nabokov's Shorts," students tend to switch from the work of sleuthing for narrative clues to discussing the issues of class and gender, race, and power, as well as Nabokov's politics, philosophy, and poetics, without backing up their conclusions with much textual evidence. These broad conversations endow each class with vigor and sparkle, but I encourage them on the condition that every sweeping statement sweeps in the direction of Nabokovian precision. Instead of judging the author from his biography (which, in the beginning of the course, Bard juniors and seniors are not likely to know in detail anyway), I recommend that they address the works themselves. For example, it might be tempting for high-minded beginners to slate Nabokov as an aristocrat and a snob after reading *Speak, Memory*, unless they are able to trace the motif of genteel poverty in "A Guide to Berlin," "Perfection," and "Recruiting"; discover exile-provoked patterns of grief and anxiety in "The Visit to the Museum," "Breaking the News," "Vasily Shishkov," and "Signs and Symbols"; or notice emblematic details of this "elitist's" stubborn advocacy for the underdogs of history and fortune in "Leonardo," "Cloud, Castle, Lake," "The Vane Sisters," and *Pnin*.

"He comes across as this snorting wizard of *hauteur*, but he is the dream host, always giving us on our visits his best chair and his best wine," Martin Amis writes.[11] After learning how to recognize the persistent theme of compassion in Nabokov's oeuvre, my class begins to feel more at home in this fictional world. In their conversations and papers, the Nabokovian dictum, "Beauty plus pity…is the closest we can get to a definition of art," starts coming to the fore.[12] Such research topics as "From the Rags of Exile to Artistic Riches: The Portrait of the Artist as a Young Man in 'A Guide to Berlin' and

'Vasiliy Shishkov'" or "The Motif of Benevolence in Nabokov's Short Stories" begin taking precedence over the view of Nabokov as an elitist writer prone to snobbery that less attentive readers might embrace.

Our discussion of the dystopian "Cloud, Castle, Lake" illustrates how close reading helps define the ethical and aesthetic nucleus of this course. The failed attempt of the protagonist, a Russian émigré in Berlin, to flee a cohort of monstrous tourists ends in his losing "strength to belong to mankind any longer."[13] Students immediately grasp the anti-totalitarian point of the story and express sympathy for Vasily Ivanovich's self-elimination by eagerly drawing parallels between the hero's plight and that of countless victims of the Nazi regime. But what they need help with realizing is the broader scope of Nabokov's indictment of totalitarianism as well as the potency of the escape narrative built into "Cloud, Castle, Lake" by means of several subtle allusions. The realization happens after we start investigating the dactylic rhythm of the story, reiterated in the tripartite list of the seemingly accidental objects observed by Vasiliy Ivanovich from a train car window.[14] As Alexander Dolinin points out, both the humble catalogue ("a smear on the platform, a cherry stone, a cigarette butt") and Vasiliy Ivanovich's parting words addressed to his torturers ("We can't travel together any longer [*Mne bol'she s vami ne po puti*]") contain a reference to Yuri Olesha, who was labeled a "fellow traveler [*poputchik*]" due to his refusal to fully embrace the Communist ideology.[15] The narrator of Olesha's short story, "The Cherry Stone," contemplates planting a cherry tree in the middle of a bare place, where a giant Soviet building is to be erected, in order to avoid a commitment both to the bourgeois past (the vacant lot) and the Communist future (the new edifice). He is a writer, unlike Vasiliy Ivanovich, but like Nabokov's hero, he cannot belong to a coterie of ideological conformists tottering on the brink of becoming political fanatics. For Olesha, the cherry tree seems to metonymically represent the Chekhovian cherry orchard—the place of nostalgia as well as the realm of artistic freedom.

Whereas Vasiliy Ivanovich tries to abscond from the brainwashing trip to a rented room above the lake graced with a castle and a cloud—that epitome of the Nabokovian "otherworld" with its "help, promise, and consolation"—the goal of Olesha's narrator is to find a "third way" for a captive Soviet artist to follow.[16] The path leads to an "invisible land in the land of observation and imagination," where he may, "in spite of everything, contrary to all established order and the society, create within [himself] a world emancipated of all laws except the transparent laws of [his] own personal impressions."[17] Nabokov, who taught "The Cherry Stone" at Wellesley, finds "a magnificently illustrated idea of a real true writer's temperament" as well as an ingenious alternative to Soviet "party literature" in this short work of fiction.[18] Throughout our discussion of this subtext, students begin to see that, due to the translocation of Olesha's "invisible land" to "Cloud, Castle, Lake," the totalitarian context of the short story expands from Nazi Germany to the Stalinist Soviet Union and beyond, while Vasiliy Ivanovich's liberation acquires a creative dimension and thus, a meaning that complements the notion of transcendence embedded in the story's last line: "Of course, I let him go."[19] In other words, the method of approaching one text through the other teaches students how to add depth and complexity to their interpretations of the Nabokovian oeuvre. While the history Nabokov references in "Cloud, Castle, Lake" is tragic, the "artistic reality" he shapes out of these grim circumstances does not fail to surprise and satisfy.[20]

To make the class realize that a meaningful act of literary scrutiny is a precondition for a lively dialogue with an inspiring outcome, I preface the study of each work of fiction with questions that both reveal a fragment of Nabokov's pattern and stimulate students' interest in character arcs, psychological nuances of the story's conflict, and the role of the narrator in controlling our response to it. This kind of guidance helps advance their comprehension of the "shorts," such as "The Potato Elf," assigned early in the course. After discussing the fabula of the story and the circumstances of its title character's existence, I alert my critics-in-training to Nora's emotional reaction to the tiny, injured Fred Dobson, who arrives in the house in the arms of her conjuror husband ("Child. Lost. Found. Her dark eyes grew moist") and invite them to think about how the image of a hurt foundling echoes the heroine's destiny—getting pregnant by the dwarf, becoming a mother to a long-desired child, and then losing *her* boy to an illness.[21] Is Nora cold-hearted and licentious or a victim of Shock's endless joking around? Is the death of the child one of Nabokov's brutal catastrophes of the kind Zoran Kuzmanovich suggests "cannot make sense in the world,"[22] or does it serve as authorial punishment for Nora's solipsism—the unwillingness to comprehend her husband's rare talent as well as Fred's loneliness, neediness, and naiveté? And, conversely, why does Fred, who reminds Nora of her son, die at the moment of supreme bliss, after having learned that he fathered a healthy and handsome human being, but before finding out that the boy is dead? Although

Nabokov confessed that "The Potato Elf" was, "all in all" not his "favorite piece," he also found its "artificial brightness...none too displeasing."[23] The questions and reading prompts send the students zigzagging through the text to eventually discover that, whereas Fred's existence appears to be brightly lit, the predicament of Nora lingers in the story's shadows. By juxtaposing the life trajectories of the two characters, they are able to follow the Nabokovian themes of "tenderness and pain," "horror and pity," as well as the trope of conjuring as psychological and fatidic manipulation.[24]

The chronological trajectory of the course makes us sharply turn from reading Nabokov's stories in translation to exploring his fiction written in English. Our comparison of "Breaking the News" and "Signs and Symbols" opens a passageway for the discussion of Nabokov's Russian works as a backdrop for his American "shorts." Nabokov himself pointed out the affinity in "milieu and the theme" between the two in a remark included in *A Russian Beauty and Other Stories*.[25] Both narratives pivot around the yet unannounced demises of young men who are the sole meaning of their parents' existence. In both of them, Nabokov keeps the elderly characters in the state of anxious suspense about the fate of their doomed sons, thus never actually destroying them with the devastating news. Instead, the task of collecting warning signals about the tragedies falls to the reader. In "Signs and Symbols," our registering every detail of the Jewish couple's journey to their son's mental hospital and back, as well as the labels of jelly jars in their undelivered gift basket, increasing in astringency from apricot to quince, transforms the reading experience into a prolonged, excruciating, catharsis.[26] Nevertheless, it is essential to read "Signs and Symbols" as the story that delivers the promise of survival after death both to the young man and to his kin: the mother and father, still alive, along with Aunt Rosa and other relatives who perished in the Holocaust.[27] Ingrained in the story's imagery, the metaphysical hope turns the readers' search for auspicious clues—communications from the otherworld—into a mission to absolve Nabokov's characters of their pain. As Dolinin writes, "Having broken the code, we can be certain that in the fictional universe where Nabokov is God, they too will be allowed to pass through and meet the sender of the secret message."[28]

Written thirteen years prior to "Signs and Symbols," "Breaking the News" challenges the reader in the same way. Although we learn at once about the death of Misha, the only son of the old and almost entirely deaf Evgenia Isakovna Mintz, the "complex, integrated ordering of encoded elements" in the story forces us to collect subtle warnings of disaster and impending grief, which someone—the author, but also possibly the boy's solicitous ghost—sends to the Russian-Jewish émigré as she runs chores in preparation for a small gathering in her apartment later that day. One of these signs is the postcard slipped under her door that morning. It contains Misha's words, "I literally fall off my feet" (in fact, he fell into an elevator shaft of a factory office in Paris).[29] Another sign is the resemblance between an accidental passerby in the street and one Vladimir Markovich Vilner, who, as Mrs. Mintz remembers, "died alone."[30] The sad association is echoed by a chance encounter with another miserable person. Likewise, the words of a watchmaker who is supposed to fix Misha's watch "jumped at her with a crash," while a meeting with a Madame Shuf by a clothing store and the latter's question about news from Paris interrupts Evgenia Isakovna's contemplation of "a display of men's shirts," none of which will be of any use to her son any longer.[31] These spectral messages are both portents of the disaster and markers of the possibility of transcendence. Whereas the friends of Mrs. Mintz believe that the news will kill her and, therefore, fumble for the words with which to approach the poor woman, the warning signs that surround Nabokov's heroine alert the reader to the "gradual preparation" that has already started on a less grotesque wavelength, and not only for the pronouncement about death, but for death itself. It is not accidental that the names of two central characters in the story, Chernobylski (from *chernobyl'nik,* also known in Russian as *polyn'*) and Mintz (partially homophonous with German "*Minze*"), refer to potent herbs, mugwort and mint. In folklore and poetry, they symbolize passing, mourning, Lethean obliviousness, and the non-finite nature of death.[32]

The argument that emerges when I encourage my students to place "Breaking the News" and "Signs and Symbols" side by side takes us to the problem of "cruelty" of Nabokov's narrative choices and, from there, to pondering the writer's responsibility in portraying loss and grief, pain and injustice, individual suffering and mass atrocities.[33] Joanna Trzeciak convincingly suggests that our attention in reading both stories should be directed toward the parents, rather than the young protagonists, and argues that the "emotional content of silence" in them is comparable as well as fundamental.[34] Nevertheless, two questions about "Breaking the News" and the artistic rendering of its themes in "Signs and Symbols" would remain open unless we probe Nabokov's narrative structures with further emphasis on textual details. One of them has to do with the stories' response to history. Trzeciak calls "Signs and Symbols" a "post-Holocaust reprise of 'Breaking the News,'" but the latter story, published on April 8, 1934, and later marked by the author as written in 1935,[35] may already contain a denouncement of the brutality of Hitler's regime, such as the 1933–35 laws banning Jewish citizens from working in their professions.[36] By asking the class why Boris Lvovich Chernobylski has to help Misha Mintz find a job in Paris, or, rather, why Misha leaves Berlin where his "darling Moolik" lives, I attempt to re-actualize this historical context.[37] Eventually we reach the conclusion that the deprivation of Jewish professionals of their rightful employment in Germany and Misha's diminishing chances to attain success in life in spite of his being "plunged up to the neck in work" intimates his dying by suicide. The words of the Chernobylskis' lodger emphasize this tragic plot twist: "I must say, incidentally, that I don't understand how he could fall. You understand how?"[38] Since the hero's implied death in "Signs and Symbols" is definitely by suicide, Nabokov's admission that the story shares the "milieu and the theme" with "Breaking the News" reinforces the possibility of Misha's taking his own life. From there, my students find it much easier to make the connection between the deaths of these two young protagonists and the Nabokovian theme of "endless waves of pain" that afflicted the Jewish people before and after the war.[39] The close reading also gets the class prepared for reading *Pnin*. Its hero's own expression of the Holocaust theme initially seems deeply buried under the surface of the novel but becomes all-pervasive after several re-readings.[40]

The watershed of World War II separates "Breaking the News" and "Signs and Symbols," and yet it is not history alone that Nabokov rescues his sufferers from. Another question that emerges from the comparison between the two stories has to do with his benevolence as a creator of fictional worlds that echo the pain of the world outside and beyond fiction, the "reality" of here and now. I tell the class how Harold Ross, editor-in-chief of *The New Yorker*, once spoke of "Signs and Symbols" as "a very good picture of hopeless misery," and they agree that human misery is one of Nabokov's most essential thematic foci.[41] Our goal, then, is to establish that hopelessness, on the contrary, is not what the writer professed. We discuss how the intimation of transcendence with which Nabokov surrounds the elder heroes of "Breaking the News" and "Signs and Symbols" warrants what Leona Toker calls "the survival of conscience in the postcataclysmic world," and we also look into the manifestation of authorial benevolence through the motif of nonverbal or "silent" communication.[42] Nabokov welcomed silence or, rather, noiselessness; when once asked by a journalist, "What do you detest most in the world," he responded: "Brutality, stupidity, noise."⁴³ It becomes a revelation for my students that Evgenia Isakovna's blissful deafness and the endless pause after the last phone call granted to the mental patient's parents may thus be seen as acts of mercy. They who reluctantly remove their earbuds and plug them back in right after class eagerly discuss how silence equals benevolence in "Breaking the News" as well as in "Signs and Symbols," because the real news is not in the message but in its being sent and delivered: "He who has ears, let him hear."⁴⁴

In her otherwise very compelling analysis of "Breaking the News" and "Signs and Symbols," Trzeciak connects Nabokov's "silentology" to "the path of signs and symbols" which "leads nowhere" and is, therefore, "an act of cruelty toward the reader."⁴⁵ The reading strategy I introduce in my course negates this interpretation. Our textual, biographical, and historical scrutiny of both tales allows students to understand that the trope of silence in them not only indicates the writer's concern for his characters but also demonstrates the generosity and trust with which he treats his audience. By inviting the readers to decode his complex textual and contextual puzzles, Nabokov teaches them how to fuse aesthetic appreciation and compassion. He also makes the readers privy to the mystery central to his oeuvre in general, summarized by Vladimir Alexandrov as the "faith in the apparent existence of a transcendent, nonmaterial, timeless, and beneficial ordering and ordered realm of being that seems to provide for personal immortality and that affects everything that exists in the mundane world."⁴⁶ One semester is not enough for my cohort of Nabokovians to experience the functioning of these two principles in many other works by Nabokov, such as *Glory*, *Bend Sinister*, *Lolita*, and *Pale Fire*. We do, nevertheless, get to solve a number of narrative riddles and trace patterns of individual fate in *Speak, Memory* as well as discuss how these patterns, along with the narrator's obliviousness to the importance of personal (and textual) detail, leads to the catastrophic dissonance between the life lived and the story told in *Pnin*. Most importantly, the reading of the autobiography and the novel after the scrupulous investigation of Nabokov's "shorts" allows us to concentrate on the specifically Nabokovian figure of transcendent space-time—the otherworldly chronotope that, when the author deems it necessary, can provide an asylum for victims of predetermined violence and accidental doom.

Whereas the first half of "Nabokov's Shorts" is dedicated to the exploration of short stories with the help of Nabokov's own reading method (we read three stories per class, in a seven-week marathon) and culminates in a midterm paper of five to seven pages dedicated to one of the tales, the second half of the course allows the students to make their way through *Speak, Memory* (three weeks, five chapters at a time) and *Pnin* (four weeks, two chapters per class, and one session that is dedicated to Chapter 7 and a re-reading) while working on the draft and revisions of their final papers, the focus of which is not only on an individual text but also on the broader questions of Nabokov's poetics, aesthetics, ethics, and metaphysics. In between these two halves of the course, we hold a writing workshop, prior to which every class participant is given two papers by other students to read and review. When we come together to share the essays and deliberate on writing strategies for further critical exploration of Nabokov's works, I ask students to present their argument in a two-minute report, which is then followed by one main reviewer's in-depth analysis and two secondary reviewers' remarks. Needless to say, I also read the papers and provide copious written commentary on them. The workshop, coupled with my written feedback, motivates course participants to complete their second essay of twelve to fifteen pages. They submit the paper draft in the eleventh week of class and expand it into a fifteen-to-twenty-page final version by the end of its fifteenth week. All in all, in addition to being a bootcamp in close reading and meticulous literary analysis, "Nabokov's Shorts" also serves as a structured introduction to intensive writing on the author whose works are famous for their thematic intricacy and narrative impenetrability. It succeeds, because our conversations about Nabokov's welcoming "good readers" and opening his codes and puzzles to them endows my students with the agency of "confronting" him as literary critics.

Bard juniors are a dynamic cohort trained to combine classroom learning with hands-on exploration of their subject in science labs, art and film studios, concert halls, and through engagement with local businesses and NGOs. For them, literary criticism is not only a way of in-depth reading or a rewarding genre of writing but also a potential future profession, the institutional, technical, and legal features of which they are eager to absorb. Since I conduct my own research on Nabokov in the archives at the New York Public Library and the Library of Congress, sharing this aspect of my work with the class seems not only natural but also pedagogically rewarding. This is why several sessions of "Nabokov's Shorts" are dedicated to our perusal of copies of his manuscripts, which, to avoid copyright violation, I share with the class on a large screen—one densely crossed-out and scribbled-all-over page at a time. During these sessions I explain how one approaches an archive with a research request, in what manner to handle rare books and manuscripts, and why organizing one's archival copies and notes is a researcher's most essential skill. After class, students often stay behind to tell me that they find our "practicums" most useful. Having never before drawn a happy parallel between modern literary studies and the concept of an archive, they begin to find archival sleuthing a worthy and fascinating occupation.

Both in personal conversations and during group discussions, some course participants also indicate that our examinations allow them to comprehend the notion of Nabokov's "disciplined vulnerability" identified by Wood.[47] The writer's correspondence with editors, in particular, helps undergraduates understand the challenges of Nabokov's transition from Europe, where his Russian works were appreciated by a small but intellectually and culturally cohesive group of émigré readers, to the United States, where the new literary market, the more diverse audience, and the different idiom and diction required a dramatic and often painful literary makeover. My students are taken aback by the fact that Nabokov went through a period of intensive, albeit grudging, linguistic apprenticeship and that his interactions with *The Atlantic*'s Edward Weeks and *The New Yorker*'s Katharine White included not only praise given and received but also exhaustive editorial back-and-forth, including the editors' corrections of his word choices, syntax, and intonation. We look at his reluctant acceptance or adroit dodging of demands for structural revisions from his editors by studying their correspondence.[48] We also marvel at how Nabokov, who went to Cambridge and claimed that he grew up as a "perfectly normal trilingual child" in a family of Anglophiles, accepted stylistic feedback from Weeks and White.[49] Students find it hard to believe that the English of the author of *Lolita* and *Pale Fire* required polishing during Nabokov's first ten years in America, but the galley proofs of "Signs and Symbols," "The Vane Sisters," "Lance," *Speak, Memory*, and *Pnin* reveal this well-hidden side of his artistic personality. Even the staunchest of my rebels find it inspiring. As reported in course evaluations, the lessons they learn are not only that reading has to be close and literary analysis, meticulous, text-oriented, and sometimes supported with archival research but also that perfection in writing is a process and editorial guidance, a boon.

Notes

1 Michael Wood, *The Magician's Doubts: Nabokov and the Risks of Fiction* (Princeton, NJ: Princeton UP, 1994), 27.
2 Maxim D. Shrayer, *The World of Nabokov's Stories* (Austin: U of Texas P, 1999), 4.
3 Edgar Allan Poe, "Twice-Told Tales, By Nathaniel Hawthorne: A Review," in *The Works of Edgar Allan Poe*, ed. Edmund Clarence Stedman and George Edward Woodbury (New York: Charles Scribner's Sons, 1927), 32.
4 Vladimir Nabokov, *Lectures on Literature*, ed. Fredson Bowers (New York: Harcourt Brace Jovanovich, 1980), 3.
5 Vladimir Nabokov, *Strong Opinions* (New York: Vintage International, 1990), 115.
6 Ibid., 128–129; Nabokov, *Lectures*, 64–65.
7 Ibid., 3–5.
8 Robert Alter, *Nabokov and the Real World: Between Appreciation and Defense* (Princeton, NJ: Princeton UP, 2021), 65.
9 Vladimir Nabokov, *Selected Letters: 1940–1977*, ed. Dmitri Nabokov and Matthew J. Bruccoli (New York: Harcourt, 1989), 117; Vladimir Nabokov, *Think, Write, Speak: Uncollected Essays, Reviews, Interviews, and Letters to the Editor*, ed. Brian Boyd and Anastasia Tolstoy (New York: Alfred A. Knopf, 2019), 254.
10 Nabokov, *Lectures*, 1; Vladimir Nabokov, *The Stories of Vladimir Nabokov* (New York: Vintage International, 2008), 432.
11 Martin Amis, "Nabokov and Literary Greatness: Remarks in Honor of the One Hundredth Anniversary of the Birth of Vladimir Nabokov," PEN American Center, April 15, 1999, https://martinamisweb.com/pre_2006/amisnabokov.htm. Last accessed May 12, 2022.
12 Nabokov, *Lectures*, 251.
13 Nabokov, *Stories*, 437.
14 Shrayer, *World of Nabokov's Stories*, 134–161.
15 Alexander Dolinin, *Istinnaia zhizn' pisatelia Sirina. Raboty o Nabokove* (St. Petersburg: Izdatel'stvo Akademicheskii Proekt, 2004), 192–193.
16 Nabokov, *Stories*, 436; Iurii Olesha, *Izbrannie sochineniia* (Moscow: Gosudarstvennoe izdatel'stvo khudozhestvennoi literatury, 1956), 263.
17 The cited translation is Nabokov's own. It is included in his lecture "Soviet Short Story," currently in the Henry W. and Albert A. Berg Collection of English and American Literature of the New York Public Library. Vladimir Nabokov Papers, 1918-1987, n.d., ms. box. I am grateful to Andrei Babikov for a copy of the English text of the manuscript, from which this and other citations derive.
18 "Soviet Short Story," cited in Andrei Babikov, *Prochtenie Nabokova. Izyskaniia i Materiialy* (St. Petersburg: Izdatel'stvo Ivana Limbakha, 2019), 225–226, 276–277.
19 Nabokov, *Stories*, 437.
20 This reading goes against Dolinin's suggestion that Olesha's "creative death" prompted Nabokov to write "Cloud, Castle, Lake." Dolinin, *Istinnaia Zhizn'*, 193.

Referring to Olesha's speech at the First Congress of Soviet Writers (1934), in which he sees an admission of defeat before "forces of history," Dolinin writes: "According to Nabokov, the capitulation of an artist before history, his giving up his own 'invisible land,' and the attempt to find a compromise with the 'Bureau of Pleasantries' are tantamount to 'an invitation to a beheading' and can lead only to the loss of creative powers, self-destruction, and death." Dolinin, *Istinnaia zhizn'*, 194. Nabokov's own lecture on Olesha contradicts this statement. It focuses on the writer's ability to resist the regime's infringement on his creative freedom and asserts that "The Cherry Stone" is "the description of an artist's exploration of an invisible land which is the free personal region where the Five year's plan has no sway." "Soviet Short Story," cited, in Russian, in Babikov, *Prochteniia*, 276. The English original is in the Berg Collection; see note 18.

21 Nabokov, *Stories*, 232.
22 Zoran Kuzmanovich, "Suffer the Little Children," in *Nabokov at Cornell*, ed. Gavriel Shapiro (Ithaca, NY: Cornell UP, 2003), 57.
23 Nabokov, *Stories*, 672.
24 Nabokov, *Stories*, 240.
25 Vladimir Nabokov, *A Russian Beauty and Other Stories* (New York: McGraw-Hill, 1973).
26 Nabokov, *Stories*, 598–599, 603; Gennady Barabtarlo, "Five Missing Jars," in *Anatomy of a Short Story: Nabokov's Puzzles, Codes, "Signs and Symbols,"* ed. Yuri Leving (New York: Continuum, 2012), 141; Alexander Dolinin, "The Signs and Symbols in Nabokov's 'Signs and Symbols,'" in *Anatomy of a Short Story*, 263.
27 Nabokov, *Stories*, 601.
28 Dolinin, "Signs and Symbols," 269.
29 Nabokov, *Stories*, 391; Joanna Trzeciak, "'Breaking the News' and 'Signs and Symbols': Silentology," in *Anatomy of a Short Story*, 218.
30 Nabokov, *Stories*, 392.
31 Nabokov, *Stories*, 392–393; Trzeciak, "'Breaking the News,'" 218.
32 *Polyn'* (mugwort) as an herb associated with bitterness, obliviousness, and death appears in Russian folklore and poetry, from Konstantin Batiushkov (*"Bez smerti zhizn' ne zhizn'. I chto ona? | Sosud, gde kaplia miodu sred' polyni..."* 1883) to Maximilian Voloshin ("Polyn'," 1907). Mint is linked to death through the myth of Demeter and Persephone. The former had to partake of a mixture of mint, barley flour, and water to survive in the otherworld, and the latter transformed the lover of her husband Hades, the nymph Mentha, into a mint plant. See Philip Mayerson, *Classical Mythology in Literature, Art, and Music* (Newburyport, MA: Focus, 2001), 108–110, 230.
33 I assign an excerpt from Richard Rorty's seminal study of the theme of cruelty in Nabokov's oeuvre as well Michael Wood's essay on this subject before this class. See Richard Rorty, *Contingency, Irony, and Solidarity* (New York: Cambridge UP, 1989), 141–168; Wood, *Magician's Doubts*, 55–82.
34 Trzeciak, "'Breaking the News,'" 216–217.

35 Dmitri Nabokov inserted "1935" in the text of his translation of "Breaking the News," most likely with his father's direct approval. Thus, in English, the story is set in March 1935. See Nabokov, *Stories*, 390.

36 In 1933, the legislation to force Jewish citizens out of German workforce was introduced. 1934, the year of publication of "Breaking the News," was the time of "barring non-Aryans from a rather broad range of occupational areas.... Young non-Aryans can no longer able to pursue their vocations in these fields." Wolfgang Gruner, *Jewish Forced Labor under the Nazis: Economic Needs and Racial Aims (1938–1944)* (New York: Cambridge UP, 2008), 340; see also Konrad H. Jarausch, "The Conundrum of Complicity: German Professionals and the Final Solution," in *The Law in Nazi Germany. Ideology, Opportunism, and Perversion of Justice*, ed. Alan E. Steinweis and Robert D. Rachlin (New York: Berghahn Books, 2013), 22. The notorious Nuremberg laws of 1935, to which Trzeciak alludes, were adopted in September of 1935, i.e., several months after the death of Misha Mintz even in the corrected, English, version of the story. Nevertheless, the emphasis on Chernobylski's effort to provide an employment recommendation for Misha ("it was I who helped him, found him a job") and the repeated references to Paris in the story place Nabokov's hero among Jewish professionals who desperately fled to France in 1933, "at a rate of 1,500 per month between April and August," or in 1934, when the immigration became less numerous, but remained steady. Nabokov, *Stories*, 391; Walter F. Peterson, *The Berlin Liberal Press in Exile: A History of the Parizer Tagesblatt – Parizer Tageszeitung, 1933–1940* (Tübingen: Niemeyer, 1987), 54–55.

37 Nabokov, *Stories*, 391.

38 Ibid.

39 Ibid., 601.

40 Leonid Livak, "Jewishness as Literary Device in Nabokov's Fiction," in *Vladimir Nabokov in Context*, ed. David M. Bethea and Siggy Frank (Cambridge and New York: Cambridge UP, 2018), 235–237; Will Norman, *Nabokov, History, and the Texture of Time* (New York: Routledge, 2012), 104–129.

41 Olga Voronina, "Vladimir Nabokov's Correspondence with the New Yorker regarding 'Signs and Symbols,' 1946–8," in *Anatomy of a Short Story*, 53.

42 Leona Toker, *Nabokov: The Mystery of Literary Structures* (Ithaca, NY: Cornell UP, 1989), 13.

43 Nabokov, *Think, Write, Speak*, 502.

44 *Matthew* 13:43.

45 Trzeciak, "'Breaking the News,'" 223.

46 Vladimir Alexandrov, *Nabokov's Otherworld* (Princeton, NJ: Princeton UP, 1991), 5.

47 Wood, *Magician's Doubts*, 3.

48 I feel lucky to be able to share with my students excerpts of Nabokov's correspondence with White and Weeks, which exists in manuscript form at the Berg Collection, the NYPL, but even when these materials are not available, Nabokov's already

published letters to editors suffice to demonstrate how sharp the writer's learning curve was in the 1940s and 50s. See Nabokov, *Selected Letters*, 76–77, 89–90, 98–99, 115–118, as well as Vladimir Vladimirovich Nabokov, "Outgoing Correspondence. *The New Yorker*. June 18, 1942–February 6, 1970" and "Outgoing Correspondence. *The Atlantic Monthly*, February 2, 1946–May 21, 1952," Vladimir Nabokov Papers, 1918–1987, ms. box. Both sets of folders contain editors' letters to Nabokov as well.

49 Nabokov, *Strong Opinions*, 43; Voronina, "Vladimir Nabokov's Correspondence," 42–60.

The Original of Laura and the Archival Nabokov

Lisa Ryoko Wakamiya

The Original of Laura introduces students to an unfamiliar Nabokov. Having contended with a Nabokov who tightly controlled his reception, my students approached this posthumously published work with the understanding that it was never intended for publication, was never finished, and some familiar echoes aside, resembled no other work by Nabokov that we had encountered before. Indeed, The Original of Laura likely resembled no other published work of literature my students had ever encountered. The hardcover 2009 Knopf edition of The Original of Laura photographically reproduces 138 handwritten index cards that make up a significant part of the extant manuscript. Below the image of each card is a typescript of the text. The photographic reproductions of the cards are perforated to allow readers, if they wish, to punch them out and recreate the stack of cards from which the edition was produced.

The appearance of The Original of Laura in print positioned it within conversations about literary history, stewardship, and the institution of authorship. These debates primarily focused on Dmitri Nabokov's controversial decision to publish the manuscript despite his father's injunction to destroy it if it remained unfinished at the time of his death, as well as the manuscript's mixed reception.[1] Rather than ask my students to engage with the moot question of whether the manuscript should have been published or with others' reception of the manuscript, I asked them to generate detailed annotations of its material form. The perforated photographic reproductions of Nabokov's index cards have been dismissed as "gimmicky," but this overlooks the potential for viewing *The Original of Laura* as an archival document, and the opportunities this presents for understanding methods of textual criticism and the various processes by which archival material can make new interpretations of literature possible.

When I teach a seminar devoted entirely to Nabokov's work, I familiarize my advanced undergraduate and graduate students with the finding aids for the Vladimir Nabokov Papers at the Library of Congress and the Berg Collection of the New York Public Library early in the semester. There, we look up the assigned readings for the course to see what types of archival materials are available for each (holograph and typescript drafts, notes, unpublished fragments, and so on). We revisit the finding aids throughout the semester as we encounter scholarship that draws from Nabokov's archives and consider possible future research directions. Toward the end of the semester, I introduce *The Original of Laura* by asking my students to participate in "The Nabokov Prose-Alike Centennial Contest."[2] In 1999, the journal *The Nabokovian* invited readers to discern two previously unpublished excerpts from *The Original of Laura* from among five short prose passages (the other three were chosen from solicited excerpts written by readers who were instructed to imitate "VN's style as closely as possible—earnest, not jocular—not an obvious parody or pastiche").[3] I ask the students to read the passages at home and comment on them using annotation software to mark up the pages with their observations. We follow this up with an in-class discussion.

The most recent time I asked my students to take their best guesses, it was linguistic play and a familiar theme that led the students to identify one of the passages from *Laura*: the "mobile omoplates" and "narrow nates" of one excerpt attracted nearly unanimous attention for their assonance, obscurity, and association with a nubile body. The phrase "asparagus instead of aspirin" in the other passage from *Laura* was noted by only one student. "Not Nabokovian" style—a reference to a duck "squealing like a piglet" and a description of a character's name as "Hegelian"—led several students to reject one entry outright.[4] One passage, disguised as an unpublished excerpt from *Pnin*, prompted a student to consult the finding aids for the Vladimir Nabokov Papers at the Library of Congress and the Berg Collection. She found undated notes related to *Pnin* but no unpublished manuscript drafts. Another student compared the experience of reading a solicited entry to viewing a skillful forgery of an old master's painting; it reproduced the original's brushstrokes in scrupulous detail but lacked its indefinable magic.

The "prose-alike" contest asks readers to pull from their inventory of what they find familiar in Nabokov's writing to identify an unfamiliar work. This drew my students' attention to examples of Nabokov's "signature," what Michael Wood identifies as "the visible shorthand for a literary person...their habit and their practice, their mark."[5] Nabokov's active involvement in the published forms of his work had come up earlier in the semester: the register of the prefaces written after Nabokov's emigration to the United States and appended to the translations of his early Russian writings; his attention to Pnin's appearance on the eponymous novel's cover; the playful, illustrative index to *Speak, Memory*; the proposition that one could read *Pale Fire* from cover to cover, or by jogging between Shade's poem and Kinbote's notes, or some other way. *Pale Fire* is at once a poem by John Shade and a novel by Nabokov, and we never doubt that Nabokov himself orchestrated this doubling. *Nikolai Gogol* effaces the ostensible subject of the book, merging literary criticism with an exploration of the institution of authorship. Nabokov's translation of *Eugene Onegin* begs the question: Are we really reading Pushkin? As we tackled these works, there was an understanding that the versions we were reading, published during Nabokov's lifetime, were shaped to some degree by authorial intention.

While our discussions of intention never centered on whether the author's texts alone dictated a "correct" way to read them, *The Original of Laura* foregrounds how multiple intentions—those of the author, his editors, heir, or others—shape our expectations. The book's photographic reproductions of Nabokov's notecards and typed transcriptions of them, idiosyncratic spellings and notes to himself intact, present *The Original of Laura* as the work of a single author, but the preface written by Dmitri Nabokov, the editorial decisions that organized the notecards, and the book's elaborate design by Chip Kidd all reveal *The Original of Laura* to be a collaborative effort. The tension between the unfinished manuscript and the format of the published book challenged our perceptions of Nabokov's carefully crafted conception of authorship in a way previous works had not. We do not question that we are reading Nabokov when we read *The Original of Laura*, but we are reading him as others wanted him to be read.

By way of comparison, I shared Mario Maurin's letter to the editor of *The New Review* in response to Robert Alter's review of the posthumously published *Lectures on Literature*, in which Maurin refers to the "so-called *Lectures on Literature*" as "essentially a fraudulent publication."[6] Despite the "numerous photographic reproductions of VN's annotated copies" of the novels he taught at Cornell, and the editor Fredson Bowers's scrupulous list of "the various kinds of manipulation to which he has had to resort in order to produce a readable text," Maurin argues that the "sad, simple truth is that there are no Nabokovian Lectures on Literature."[7] After considering revising his lecture notes for publication in 1972, Nabokov himself avowed, "My university lectures (Tolstoy, Kafka, Flaubert, Cervantes, etc. etc.) are chaotic and sloppy and must never be published. None of them!"[8] And yet we have them, and their published versions offer insight into how Nabokov taught and read and, by extension, insight into how he wanted to be taught and read. I assign the essay "Good Readers and Good Writers" from *Lectures on Literature* in the first week in the semester for precisely this reason. Later in the semester, as we read *The Original of Laura*, we return to "Good Readers and Good Writers" with the understanding that Bowers reconstructed it "from parts of [Nabokov's] untitled written-out opening lecture to the class before the exposition began of *Mansfield Park*, the first book of the semester,"[9] and appreciate not only what we have of the essay but the possibilities that greater access to Nabokov's unfinished writing brings.

Reading Maurin's letter together with Bowers's introduction to the *Lectures on Literature* points to how reading Nabokov's posthumously published work relates to textual criticism. As the conversation moves toward scholarly editing, an appreciation of textual criticism and its contributions to our understanding of Nabokov's work becomes foregrounded. Editors regularly alter manuscript texts as Bowers did, and in doing so "are no longer presenting the text of the document but are focusing on the text of the work or statement that in their opinion was intended by someone in the past or is more desirable in the present."[10] In the case of *Lectures on Literature*, much of what Bowers has reconstructed was delivered orally and was written in a form intended exclusively for Nabokov's eyes, not the reader's. G. Thomas Tanselle's discussion of textual reconstruction enumerates some of the considerations that scholars must bear in mind:

> The way one threads a path through these uncertainties to arrive at a defensible reconstruction of the text of a work of literature depends on the position one takes regarding two questions: what agency is responsible

for the production of a work, and what point is the most significant in its history. On the former question, one may feel that the author has sole responsibility for a work and that a text reflecting the author's intention (and purged of elements contributed by others) best represents the work; or one may believe that literature is a social art, the collaborative product of a number of people....On the second matter, one may decide that the form of a work most worth focusing on is the one that existed at the moment when the work was regarded as finished by those responsible for it (whether the author alone or the author in conjunction with others), a moment that may be deemed to have brought to fruition the efforts of a period of creativity; or one may prefer the last version of a work overseen by whoever is considered to have had charge of it.[11]

As Bowers makes clear in his introduction, the lectures "exist in very different states of preparation and polish, and even of completed structure," rendering it "impractical to offer these manuscripts to the reading public in verbatim form, either structurally or stylistically."[12] One of Bowers's guiding principles in producing his edition of the lectures is that "the reader may participate in the discourse as if he were present as a listener,"[13] and toward that end he inserted text found among the lecture notes "at appropriate places," including some quotations from the literary texts Bowers selected himself "when the occasion seemed to require illustration of a point that Nabokov was making."[14] "On the other hand," Bowers notes elsewhere, "some of Nabokov's comments directed exclusively to his students and often on pedagogical subjects have been omitted as inconsistent with the aims of a reading edition." These include "admonitions to use a dictionary to look up unfamiliar words, and similar comments suitable only for students' ears and not for the printed page."[15] In producing *Lectures on Literature,* Bowers fulfilled the task of producing a text that is at once readable and a reasonable semblance of what Nabokov wished to convey in his lectures. His decision to retain "various addresses to the class as *you*" in some instances, and to change them "to a more neutral form of address" in others is indicative of the shift in the lectures' audience, from real students listening to Nabokov deliver his lectures in real time to an idealized reader who can pick up the published *Lectures on Literature* at any given time.[16]

Having recognized some of the challenges Bowers faced and with appreciation for the reading edition he produced, one could—with training and experience in the practice of textual criticism and an understanding of its possibilities—visit the NYPL's Berg Collection and Library of Congress to reconstruct another edition of Nabokov's teaching materials from his annotated books, handwritten notes, and typescripts according to different editorial principles. An edition consisting of photographic reproductions of Nabokov's teaching materials accompanied by annotated transcriptions would form a companion to Bowers's edition. Indeed, one of the possibilities enabled by Bowers's edition is the production of an edition that presents archival materials as artifacts.[17] Such an edition would find another audience, not the idealized reader who could imagine himself a listener in Nabokov's lecture hall but an interpreter for whom the characteristics of manuscript texts—their incompleteness, variations in legibility, and disorganization—potentially convey meaning.

The photographic reproduction of the manuscript of *The Original of Laura* is productively situated within conversations about the tradition of textual criticism. Its ideal reader is not the reader who expects to encounter a novel, not even "a novel in fragments" as the front dust jacket proclaims it to be. Such a reader, as the numerous critical responses to *The Original of Laura* have shown, may regard the fragments as a curiosity at best, a betrayal of the author at worst. But as a reproduction of an archival document, *The Original of Laura* opens up the possibility for discussing the philological processes involved in ordering the index cards, producing their typographic transcription, and, more generally, working with a writer's unpublished archival materials.

Considering the fragments as archival material brings with it a new set of questions and priorities. What would an ideal editor's preface to *The Original of Laura* look like? Dmitri Nabokov describes "ordering and preparing, and then dictating, a preliminary transcript," but we do not know, beyond those few index cards on which the author himself suggested an order, what principles Dmitri Nabokov used to organize them or how others were involved in the process.[18] My students wanted to know what decisions determined the final ordering of the cards and how these cards, in their incompleteness and varying degrees of legibility, compare with other sets of index cards for other works that exist in the archives. They wanted to know about the "X" that appears on the verso of some cards and not on others. They were curious about the cards that reveal traces of erased handwriting that remain somewhat legible (as on the card titled "D o" on page 243). Was the erased handwriting more legible on the original cards, and could it be reconstructed? If one wanted to see the original cards, how would one go about doing this?

The revelation that Brian Boyd had subsequently identified twenty-one additional index cards as part of *The Original of Laura* led to additional discussion about whether an entirely new edition should be produced, and what principles would determine the placement and integration of the more recently identified cards within the existing order.[19]

The questions raised in such discussions allow for consideration of existing research on the archival Nabokov, such as Gennady Barabtarlo's *Insomniac Dreams*, which photographically reproduces the notecards on which Nabokov wrote down his dreams for eighty days, beginning in October 1964.[20] Barabtarlo compares the dream-notes with extracts from Nabokov's fiction, revealing similarities between them. As a way of approaching *The Original of Laura*, we might take a cue from John Lanchester's review of *Insomniac Dreams*, in which he remarks on the *differences* between the dream-notes and the fiction: "The dreams are quite difficult to read, not through any density of prose or complication of thought, but because they are not really written—they are not finished prose. Comparison with the inevitably dazzling extracts from Nabokov's fiction make this point. The dreams are not so much fragments of writing as fragments of not-writing or near-writing or pre-writing."[21] Of the dream experiment, Barabtarlo writes, "It is very likely that Nabokov meant to mold his later dream experiment into a literary form as well, perhaps with a view to incorporating excerpts into his second book of autobiography."[22] This observation, together with Lanchester's, suggests an approach to Nabokov's unfinished "pre-writing" in *The Original of Laura*. Rather than compare *The Original of Laura* with Nabokov's finished works, as many scholars and writers have, we should compare it with other examples of Nabokov's unfinished work. The goal would not be to speculate about what *The Original of Laura* could have been but to understand more about Nabokov's writings intended exclusively for himself.

I regularly ask students whether *The Original of Laura* belongs in the seminar on Nabokov's work, and if so, where and how? The answers have been thoughtful and surprising, ranging from remorse at having encountered a Nabokov who did not wish to be read to an awakened interest in the unfinished Nabokov who resides in the archives. Rather than make the reception of *The Original of Laura* the focal point of our conversations, an approach that integrates archival finding aids, research practices, and materials into the course emphasizes textual criticism and production, and how new editions of Nabokov's work and new scholarship about them might eventually be published.

Notes

1 For an overview of writers', critics', and scholars' responses to *The Original of Laura*, see *Shades of Laura*, ed. Yuri Leving (Montreal: McGill-Queens UP, 2013), 157–216.
2 The "Nabokov Prose-Alike Centennial Contest" by the International Vladimir Nabokov Society appears in *The Nabokovian* 42 (1999), 32–37.
3 Ibid. 32.
4 The seminar was taught most recently in Spring 2021.
5 Michael Wood, *The Magician's Doubts: Nabokov and the Risks of Fiction* (Princeton, NJ: Princeton UP, 1994), 23.
6 Mario Maurin, "Annotated Nabokov," *The New Review* (November 15, 1980), 7.
7 Ibid.
8 Brian Boyd, *Vladimir Nabokov: The American Years* (Princeton, NJ: Princeton UP, 1991), 602.
9 Fredson Bowers, "Editor's Foreword," in Vladimir Nabokov, *Lectures on Literature* (New York: Harcourt Brace Jovanovich, 1980), xiv–xv.
10 G. Thomas Tanselle, *A Rationale of Textual Criticism* (Philadelphia: U of Pennsylvania P, 1992), 57–58.
11 Ibid., 73–74.
12 Bowers, "Editor's Foreword," ix.
13 Ibid., xi.
14 Ibid., x.
15 Ibid., xiii.
16 Ibid.
17 As Olga Voronina observes, "A new volume of painstakingly prepared and more complete Nabokoviana will not necessarily cancel the earlier editions, which have already earned a reputation as canonical texts." Galya Diment et al., "Publishing *Laura*," in *Shades of Laura*, 27.
18 Dmitri Nabokov, "Introduction," in Vladimir Nabokov, *The Original of Laura* (New York: Knopf, 2009), xvii. Yuri Leving writes that "Nabokov's manuscript existed as a series of index cards in no obvious order." Yuri Leving, "Introduction: Nabokov's 'Swan Song,'" in *Shades of Laura*, 16. Gennady Barabtarlo writes that the cards "are numbered, presumably, in the order in which they were found, and since the incremental numeration is not by Nabokov's hand, that order in many instances does not establish the position of this or that episode in the novel." Gennady Barabtarlo, "Terminating the Sequence," in *Shades of Laura*, 66. Maurice Couturier expresses doubt that the cards have been preserved in their original order. See *Shades of Laura*, 166.
19 To date, these cards, discovered one year and three months after the release of *The Original of Laura* in book form, have not been published. Brian Boyd and Yuri Leving, "Chronology of the Novel in Fragments: Composition, Publication, Reception," in *Shades of Laura*, 26. Elsewhere in *Shades of Laura*, Brian Boyd writes that he found 20

cards, rather than 21. Brian Boyd, "The Last Word—Or Not? On Some Cards Named *Laura*," in *Shades of Laura*, 257.
20 Gennady Barabtarlo, *Insomniac Dreams: Experiments with Time by Vladimir Nabokov*. Compiled, edited, and with commentaries by Gennady Barabtarlo (Princeton, NJ: Princeton UP, 2018).
21 John Lanchester, "Nabokov's Dreams," *London Review of Books* 40, no. 9 (2018): 18.
22 Barabtarlo, *Insomniac Dreams*, 5.

Bibliography

"About Scalar." *Scalar*. https://scalar.me/anvc/scalar/. Last accessed May 12, 2022.

Adams, Rachel. "Disability." In *Keywords for Disability Studies*, ed. Rachel Adams, Benjamin Reiss, and David Serlin, 30–44. New York: New York UP, 2015.

Alexandrov, Vladimir. *Nabokov's Otherworld*. Princeton, NJ: Princeton UP, 1991.

Alter, Robert. *Nabokov and the Real World: Between Appreciation and Defense*. Princeton, NJ: Princeton UP, 2021.

Amis, Martin. *Experience: A Memoir*. New York: Vintage, 2001.

———. "Nabokov and Literary Greatness: Remarks in Honor of the One Hundredth Anniversary of the Birth of Vladimir Nabokov." PEN American Center, April 15, 1999. https://martinamisweb.com/pre_2006/amisnabokov.htm. Last accessed May 12, 2022.

"And Now, Poshlost." *Time* (December 1, 1967): 118. https://content.time.com/time/subscriber/article/0,33009,712044,00.html. Last accessed May 12, 2022.

Appel, Alfred, Jr. *Nabokov's Dark Cinema*. New York: Oxford UP, 1974.

Apter, Emily, and Elaine Freedgood. "Afterword." *Representations* 108, no. 1 (2009): 139–146.

Arnold, Matthew. *Culture and Anarchy*. Edited by J. Dover Wilson. Cambridge: Cambridge UP, 1966.

Babikov, Andrei. *Prochtenie Nabokova. Izyskaniia i materiialy*. St. Petersburg: Izdatel'stvo Ivana Limbakha, 2019.

Baldwin, James. *The Price of the Ticket: Collected Nonfiction 1948–1985*. Boston: Beacon Press, 2021.

Balint, Benjamin. *Running Commentary: The Contentious Magazine That Transformed the Jewish Left into the Neoconservative Right*. New York: Public Affairs, 2010.

Barabtarlo, Gennady. "Five Missing Jars." In *Anatomy of a Short Story: Nabokov's Puzzles, Codes, "Signs and Symbols,"* ed. Yuri Leving, 140–143. New York: Continuum, 2012.

———. *Insomniac Dreams: Experiments with Time by Vladimir Nabokov*. Compiled, edited, and with commentaries by Gennady Barabtarlo. Princeton, NJ: Princeton UP, 2018.

———. "See Under Sebastian." *The Nabokovian* 24 (1990): 24–28.

———. "*Taina Naita*: Narrative Stance in Nabokov's *The Real Life of Sebastian Knight*." *Partial Answers: Journal of Literature and the History of Ideas* 6, no. 1 (January 2008): 57–80.

———. "Terminating the Sequence." In *Shades of Laura: Vladimir Nabokov's Last Novel* The Original of Laura, ed. Yuri Leving, 63–84. Montreal: McGill-Queens UP, 2013.

Bertram, John, and Yuri Leving. *Lolita: The Story of a Cover Girl: Vladimir Nabokov's Novel in Art and Design*. Blue Ash, OH: Print Books, 2013.

Best, Stephen, and Sharon Marcus. "Surface Reading: An Introduction." *Representations* 108, no. 1 (2009): 1–21.

Binyon, T. J. *Pushkin: A Biography*. London: Harper Collins, 2002.

Björklund, Jenny. "Queer Readings/Reading the Queer." *Lambda Nordica* 23, nos. 1–2 (2018): 7–15.

Blackwell, Stephen H. "Calendar Anomalies, Pushkin, and Aesthetic Love in Nabokov." *Slavonic and East European Review* 96, no. 3 (July 2018): 401–431.

Bowers, Fredson. "Editor's Foreword." In Vladimir Nabokov, *Lectures on Literature*. New York: Harcourt, Brace, Jovanovich, 1980, vii–xv.

Boyd, Brian. "The Last Word—Or Not? On Some Cards Named *Laura*." In *Shades of Laura: Vladimir Nabokov's Last Novel* The Original of Laura, ed. Yuri Leving, 243–257. Montreal: McGill-Queens UP, 2013.

———. "Literature, Pattern, *Lolita*: On Art, Literature, Science." In *Transitional Nabokov*, ed. Duncan White and Will Norman, 31–54. Bern, Switzerland: Peter Lang, 2009.

———. *Stalking Nabokov: Selected Essays*. New York: Columbia UP, 2011.

———. *Vladimir Nabokov: The American Years*. Princeton, NJ: Princeton UP, 1991.

———. *Vladimir Nabokov: The Russian Years*. Princeton, NJ: Princeton UP, 1990.

Boyd, Brian, and Yuri Leving. "Chronology of the Novel in Fragments: Composition, Publication, Reception." In *Shades of Laura: Nabokov's Last Novel* The Original of Laura, ed. Yuri Leving, 17–26. Montreal: McGill-Queens UP, 2013.

Boyer-Dry, Margot. "Welcome to the Bold and Blocky Instagram Era of Book Covers." *Vulture*, January 31, 2019. www.vulture.com/2019/01/dazzling-blocky-book-covers-designed-for-amazon-instagram.html.

Boym, Svetlana. *Common Places: Mythologies of Everyday Life in Russia*. Cambridge, MA: Harvard UP, 1994.

Bozovic, Marijeta. "The Transnational Vladimir Nabokov, Or, The Perils of Teaching Literature." In *Transnational Russian Studies*, ed. Andy Byford, Connor Doak, and Stephen Hutchings, 127–140. Liverpool, UK: Liverpool UP, 2019.

Bramley, Ellie Violet. "In the Instagram Age, You Actually Can Judge a Book by Its Cover." *The Guardian*, April 18, 2021. www.theguardian.com/books/2021/apr/18/in-the-instagram-age-you-actually-can-judge-a-book-by-its-cover.

Bruhm, Stephen. "Queer, Queer, Vladimir." *American Imago: Psychoanalysis and Culture* 53 (1996): 281–306.

Carlson, Scott. "The Net Generation Goes to College." *Chronicle of Higher Education* (October 7, 2005), www.chronicle.com/article/the-net-generation-goes-to-college/. Last accessed May 12, 2022.

Casey, Jim. "Digital Shakespeare Is Neither Good Nor Bad, But Teaching Makes It So." *Humanities* 8, no. 2 (2019): 1–19.

Cherchi Usai, Paolo. *Silent Film: A Guide to Study, Research, and Curatorship*. 3rd edition. London: British Film Institute, 2009.

"Chto takoe poshlost'?" *Radio Svoboda*, October 30, 2004. www.svoboda.org/a/24197194.html. Last accessed May 12, 2022.

Cole, Teju. "In Place of Thought." *The New Yorker*, August 27, 2013. www.newyorker.com/books/page-turner/in-place-of-thought. Last accessed May 12, 2022.

Connolly, Holly. "Is Social Media Influencing Book Cover Design?" *The Guardian*, August 28, 2018. www.theguardian.com/books/2018/aug/28/is-social-media-influencing-book-cover-design.

Connolly, Julian W. "The Major Russian Novels." In *The Cambridge Companion to Nabokov*, ed. Julian W. Connolly, 135–150. Cambridge: Cambridge UP, 2005.

Connolly, Julian W., ed. *Nabokov's "Invitation to a Beheading": A Critical Companion*. Evanston, IL: Northwestern UP, 1997.

Dal′, Vladimir. *Tolkovyi slovar′ zhivogo velikorusskogo iazyka*. 4 vols. Moscow: Russkii iazyk, 1990.

Davydov, Sergei. "Poshlost′." In *The Garland Companion to Vladimir Nabokov*, ed. Vladimir E. Alexandrov, 628–633. New York: Routledge, 1995.

De La Durantaye, Leland. "Kafka's Reality and Nabokov's Fantasy. On Dwarves, Saints, Beetles, Symbolism, and Genius." *Comparative Literature* 59, no. 4 (2007): 315–331.

———. *Style Is Matter: The Moral Art of Vladimir Nabokov*. Ithaca, NY: Cornell UP, 2010.

De Vries, Gerard. *Silent Love: The Annotation and Interpretation of* The Real Life of Sebastian Knight. Boston: Academic Studies Press, 2016.

Diment, Galya. "Masters and Servants: *Up*stairs and *Down*stairs in Nabokov." In *Nabokov Upside Down*, ed. Brian Boyd and Marijeta Bozovic, 131–142. Evanston, IL: Northwestern UP, 2017.

Diment, Galya, et al. "Publishing *Laura*." In *Shades of Laura: Nabokov's Last Novel* The Original of Laura, ed. Yuri Leving, 27–51. Montreal: McGill-Queens UP, 2013.

Dhooge, Ben, and Jürgen Pieters, eds. *Vladimir Nabokov's Lectures on Literature. Portraits of the Artist as a Reader and Teacher*. Leiden, Netherlands: Brill Rodopi, 2018.

Dolinin, Aleksandr. *Istinnaia zhizn′ pisatelia Sirina. Raboty o Nabokove*. St. Petersburg: Izdatel′stvo Akademicheskii Proekt, 2004.

Dolinin, Alexander. "Clio Laughs Last: Nabokov's Answer to Historicism." In *Nabokov and His Fiction: New Perspectives*, ed. Julian Connolly, 197–215. Cambridge: Cambridge UP, 1999.

———. "The Signs and Symbols in Nabokov's 'Signs and Symbols'." In *Anatomy of a Short Story: Nabokov's Puzzles, Codes, "Signs and Symbols,"* ed. Yuri Leving, 257–269. New York: Continuum, 2012.

Doyle, Martin. "Edna O'Brien: Lolita Author Nabokov Was 'Scathing of Women.'" *The Irish Times*, February 21, 2018. www.irishtimes.com/culture/books/edna-o-brien-lolita-author-nabokov-was-scathing-of-women-1.3399269.

Dragunoiu, Dana. *Vladimir Nabokov and the Poetics of Liberalism*. Evanston, IL: Northwestern UP, 2011.

Dwyer, Anne. "Why I Teach *Lolita*." www.insidehighered.com/views/2018/05/14/teaching-lolita-still-appropriate-opinion. Last accessed May 12, 2022.

———. "Why I Teach *Lolita*." In *Teaching Vladimir Nabokov in the #MeToo Era*, ed. Elena Rakhimova-Sommers, 31–41. Lanham, MD: Lexington Books, 2021.

Edelstein, Marilyn. "(How) Should a Feminist Teach *Lolita* in the Wake of #MeToo?" In *Teaching Vladimir Nabokov in the #MeToo Era*, ed. Elena Rakhimova-Sommers, 11–29. Lanham, MD: Lexington Books, 2021.

Eisner, Lotte. *The Haunted Screen: Expressionism in the German Cinema and the Influence of Max Reinhardt*. Translated by Roger Greaves. Berkeley: California UP, 1969.

Elsaesser, Thomas. *Weimar Cinema and After: Germany's Historical Imaginary*. New York: Routledge, 2000.

Emery, Jacob. "Guides to Berlin." *Comparative Literature* 54, no. 4 (2002): 291–306.

Feldstein, Steven. *The Rise of Digital Repression: How Technology Is Reshaping Power, Politics, and Resistance*. New York: Oxford UP, 2021.

Flaubert, Gustave. *The Dictionary of Accepted Ideas*. Translated by Jacques Barzun. New York: New Directions, 1968.

———. *The Letters of Gustave Flaubert 1830–1857*. Selected, edited, and translated by Francis Steegmuller. London: Faber & Faber, 1979.

———. *Lettres de Gustave Flaubert à George Sand*. Précédées d'une étude par Guy de Maupassant. Paris: G. Charpentier, 1884.

Foster, John Burt. *Nabokov's Art of Memory and European Modernism*. Princeton, NJ: Princeton UP, 1993.

———. "Poshlust, Culture Criticism, Adorno, and Malraux." In *Nabokov and His Fiction: New Perspectives*, ed. Julian W. Connolly, 216–235. London: Cambridge UP, 1999.

Frank, Thomas, and Matt Weiland, eds. *Commodify Your Dissent: Salvos from The Baffler*. New York: W. W. Norton, 1997.

———. *The Conquest of Cool: Business Culture, Counterculture, and the Rise of Hip Consumerism*. Chicago: U of Chicago P, 1998.

Freud, Sigmund. "The Uncanny." In *The Standard Edition of the Complete Psychological Works of Sigmund Freud*. Volume XVII (1917–1919): *An Infantile*

Neurosis and Other Works, ed. James Strachey, 217–256. London: Hogarth Press, 1955.

Fromberg, Susan. "The Unwritten Chapters in *The Real Life of Sebastian Knight*." *Modern Fiction Studies* 13, no. 4 (1967–1968): 427–442.

Gallop, Jane. *Around 1981: Academic Feminist Literary Theory*. New York: Routledge, 1992.

Garcia, Michael Nieto. "Nabokov's Index Puzzle: Life and Art Transcendent in *Speak, Memory*." *Nabokov Studies* 13, no. 1 (2014/2015): 167–191.

Genette, Gérard. *Paratexts: Thresholds of Interpretation*. Translated by Jane E. Lewin. New York: Cambridge UP, 1997.

Gilliatt, Penelope, "Vladimir Nabokov Interviewed by Penelope Gilliat." *Scraps from the Loft*, https://scrapsfromtheloft.com/2017/11/16/vladimir-nabokov-interviewed-by-penelope-gilliatt-1966/. Last accessed May 12, 2022.

Ginzburg, Lidiia. *Zapisnye knizhki, vospominaniia, esse*. St. Petersburg: Iskusstvo-SPb, 2002.

Gorky, Maxim. "Maxim Gorky on the Lumière Programme, 1896." Translated by Leda Swan. In *Kino: A History of the Russian and Soviet Film*, by Jay Leyda, 407–409. Princeton, NJ: Princeton UP, 1983.

Grossman, Lev. "The Gay Nabokov." *Salon*, May 17, 2000. www.salon.com/2000/05/17/nabokov_5/.

Gruner, Wolfgang. *Jewish Forced Labor under the Nazis: Economic Needs and Racial Aims (1938-1944)*. New York: Cambridge UP, 2008.

Halberstam, Jack. *The Queer Art of Failure*. Durham, NC: Duke UP, 2011.

Hanson, Ellis. "The Future's Eve: Reparative Reading after Sedgwick." *South Atlantic Quarterly* 110, no. 1 (2011): 101–119.

Hatteburg, Sarah J., and Kody Steffy. "Increasing Reading Compliance of Undergraduates: An Evaluation of Compliance Methods." *Teaching Sociology* 41, no. 4 (2013): 346–352.

Hoeft, Mary E. "Why University Students Don't Read: What Professors Can Do to Increase Compliance." *International Journal for the Scholarship of Teaching and Learning* 6, no. 2 (2012): 1–14

Hofstadter, Douglas. *Gödel, Escher, Bach: An Eternal Golden Braid*. New York: Basic Books, 1999.

Howard, Pamela J., Meg Gorzycki, Geoffrey Desa, and Diane D. Allen. "Academic Reading: Comparing Students' and Faculty Perceptions of Its Value, Practice, and Pedagogy." *Journal of College Reading and Learning* 48, no. 3 (2018): 189–209.

Huang, Suhua, Matthew Capps, Jeff Blacklock, and Mary Garza. "Reading Habits of College Students in the United States." *Reading Psychology* 35, no. 4 (2014): 437–467.

Iangirov, Rashit. "'Chuvstvo fil′ma.' Zametki o kinematograficheskom kontekste v literature russkogo zarubezh′ia 1920-1930-kh godov." In *Imperiia N. Nabokov i naslednikov. Sbornik statei*, ed. Iurii Leving and Evgenii Soshkin, 399–426. Moscow: Novoe literaturnoe obozrenie, 2006.

International Vladimir Nabokov Society. "The Nabokov Prose-Alike Centennial Contest." *The Nabokovian* 42 (1999): 32–37.

Jackson, Kevin. *Nosferatu: Eine Symphonie des Grauens*. London: British Film Institute, 2013.

James, Ryan, and Leon de Kock. "The Digital David and the Gutenberg Goliath: The Rise of the 'Enhanced' e-book." *English Academy Review* 30, no. 1 (2013): 107–123.

Jameson, Fredric. *The Political Unconscious: Narrative as a Socially Symbolic Act*. Ithaca, NY: Cornell UP, 2014.

Jarausch, Konrad H. "The Conundrum of Complicity: German Professionals and the Final Solution." In *The Law in Nazi Germany: Ideology, Opportunism, and Perversion of Justice*, ed. Alan E. Steinweis and Robert D. Rachlin, 15–36. New York: Berghahn Books, 2013.

Johnson, David K. *The Cold War Persecution of Gays and Lesbians in the Federal Government*. Chicago: U of Chicago P, 2004.

Johnson, Donald Barton. "A Guide to Nabokov's 'A Guide to Berlin.'" *Slavic and East European Journal* 23, no. 3 (1979): 353–361.

———. "Nabokov and the Sixties." In *Discourse and Ideology in Nabokov's Prose*, ed. David H. J. Larmour, 149–159. London and New York: Routledge, 2002.

Kaes, Anton. *Shell Shock Cinema: Weimar Culture and the Wounds of War*. Princeton, NJ: Princeton UP, 2009.

"Kak pered nei ni gnites′, gospoda, Vam ne sniskat′ priznan′ia ot Evropy." *Rossiiskaia gazeta*, March 19, 2022. https://rg.ru/2022/03/18/kak-perednej-ni-gnites-gospoda-vam-ne-sniskat-priznania-ot-evropy.html. Last accessed May 12, 2022.

Karlinsky, Simon, ed. *Dear Bunny, Dear Volodya: The Nabokov–Wilson Letters, 1940–1971*. Revised and expanded edition. Berkeley: U of California P, 2001.

Kierkegaard, Søren. *Repetition* and *Philosophical Crumbs*. Translated by M. G. Piety. London: Oxford, 2009.

Kokinova, Kate. "Lolita Reading *Lolita*: Rhetoric of Reader Participation." *Nabokov Studies* 14 (2016): 59–77.

Kopper, John M. "Correspondence." In *The Garland Companion to Vladimir Nabokov*, ed. Vladimir E. Alexandrov, 54–67. New York: Garland, 1995.

Kovačević, Nataša. *Narrating Post/Communism: Colonial Discourse and Europe's Borderline Civilization*. Milton, UK: Routledge, 2008.

Krainii, Anton [Zinaida Gippius]. "Sinema." *Zveno* 204, December 26, 1926. Reprinted and annotated in Rashit Iangirov, "Istoriia s 'sinema.'" *Literaturnoe obozrenie* 3–4 (1992): 101–105.

Kuzmanovich, Zoran. "Nabokov as Teacher." In *Approaches to Teaching Lolita*, ed. Zoran Kuzmanovich and Galya Diment, 8–9. New York: Modern Language Association of America, 2010.

———. "Suffer the Little Children." In *Nabokov at Cornell*, ed. Gavriel Shapiro, 49–57. Ithaca, NY: Cornell UP, 2003.

Kuznetsov, S. A., ed. *Bol'shoi tolkovyi slovar' russkogo iazyka*. St. Peterburg: Norint, 1998.

Laing, Olivia. *Funny Weather: Art in an Emergency*. New York: W. W. Norton, 2020.

Larmour, David H. J. "Introduction. Collusion and Collision." In *Discourse and Ideology in Nabokov's Prose*, ed. David H. J. Larmour, 1–11. London and New York: Routledge, 2002.

Lanchester, John. "Nabokov's Dreams." *London Review of Books* 40, no. 9 (May 2018): 18.

Leving, Yuri. "Introduction: Nabokov's 'Swan Song.'" In *Shades of Laura: Vladimir Nabokov's Last Novel* The Original of Laura, ed. Yuri Leving, 3–14. Montreal: McGill-Queens UP, 2013.

———. *Keys to "The Gift": A Guide to Vladimir Nabokov's Novel*. Boston: Academic Studies Press, 2011.

———. "Nabokov's Jewish Family." *Tablet*, last modified December 17, 2012, www.tabletmag.com/jewish-arts-and-culture/books/119287/nabokov-jewishfamily.

Leving, Yuri, ed. *Shades of Laura: Vladimir Nabokov's Last Novel* The Original of Laura. Montreal: McGill-Queens UP, 2013.

Livak, Leonid. "Jewishness as Literary Device in Nabokov's Fiction." In *Vladimir Nabokov in Context*, ed. David M. Bethea and Siggy Frank, 228–239. Cambridge and New York: Cambridge UP, 2018.

Lo Wang, Hansi. "Generation Z Is the Most Racially and Ethnically Diverse Yet." Last modified November 15, 2018. www.npr.org/2018/11/15/668106376/generation-z-is-the-most-racially-and-ethnically-diverse-yet.

Lokot, Tetyana. *Beyond the Protest Square: Digital Media and Augmented Dissent*. London and New York: Rowman and Littlefield, 2021.

Mason, Paul. *Why It's Kicking Off Everywhere: New Global Revolutions*. London and New York: Verso, 2012.

Maurin, Mario. "Annotated Nabokov." *The New Review*. November 15, 1980, 7.

Mayerson, Philipp. *Classical Mythology in Literature, Art, and Music*. Newburyport, MA: Focus, 2001.

Meyer, Priscilla. *Nabokov and Indeterminacy: The Case of* The Real Life of Sebastian Knight. Evanston, IL: Northwestern UP, 2018.

Michael, Robert. *A Concise History of American Anti-Semitism*. New York: Rowman and Littlefield, 2005.

Middendorf, Joan, and David Pace. "Decoding the Disciplines: A Model for Helping Students Learn Disciplinary Ways of Thinking." *New Directions for Teaching and Learning* 98 (2004): 1–12.

Mirsky, D. S. *A History of Russian Literature, From Its Beginnings to 1900*. Edited by Francis James Whitfield. Evanston, IL: Northwestern UP, 1999.

———. *A History of Russian Literature from the Earliest Times to the Death of Dostoyevsky (1881)*. London: A. A. Knopf, 1927.

Mitchell, David, and Sharon Snyder. "Narrative Prosthesis and the Materiality of Metaphor." In *The Disability Studies Reader*, ed. Lennard J. Davis, 222–235. New York: Routledge, 2006.

Mokhtari, Kouider, Carla A. Reichard, and Anne Gardner. "The Impact of Internet and Television Use on the Reading Habits and Practices of College Students." *Journal of Adolescent and Adult Literacy* 52, no. 7 (2009): 609–619.

Moses, Gavriel. *The Nickel Was for the Movies: Film in the Novel from Pirandello to Puig*. Berkeley: U of California P, 1995.

Nabokov, Dmitri, "Introduction." In Vladimir Nabokov, *The Original of* Laura. New York: Knopf, 2009, xi–xviii.

Nabokov, Vladimir. *The Annotated Lolita*. Edited, with preface, introduction and notes, by Alfred Appel, Jr. London and New York: Penguin Books, 1991.

———. *Bend Sinister*. New York: Vintage, 1990.

———. *Despair*. Translated by the Author. New York: G.P. Putnam's Sons, 1969.

———. *Despair*. Translated by the Author. New York: Vintage, 1989.

———. *Details of a Sunset and Other Stories*. Translated by the Author. New York: McGraw-Hill, 1976.

———. *The Gift*. Translated by Michael Scammell with the collaboration of the Author. New York: Vintage, 1991.

———. "Good Readers and Good Writers." In Vladimir Nabokov, *Lectures on Literature*, ed. Fredson Bowers, 1–6. New York: Harcourt Brace Jovanovich, 1980.

———. "Good Readers and Good Writers." In Vladimir Nabokov, *Lectures on Literature*, ed. Fredson Bowers, 1–6. San Diego: Harvest, 1982.

———. *Invitation to a Beheading*. Translated by Dmitri Nabokov with the collaboration of the Author. New York: Vintage, 1989.

———. *King, Queen, Knave*. Translated by Dmitri Nabokov. New York: Vintage, 1968.

———. *Lectures on Literature*. Edited by Fredson Bowers. San Diego: Harcourt Brace Jovanovich, 1980.

———. "L'Envoi." In *Lectures on Literature*, ed. Fredson Bowers, 381–382. San Diego: Harvest, 1982.

———. *Letters to Véra*. Edited by Brian Boyd and Olga Voronina. London: Penguin, 2014.

———. "A Letter That Never Reached Russia"; "The Return of Chorb"; "A Guide to Berlin"; "A Nursery Tale." *The Stories of Vladimir Nabokov*. Translated by Vladimir and Dmitri Nabokov. New York: Vintage, 2008, 137–141; 147–154; 155–160; 161–172.

———. *Lolita*. New York: Vintage, 1989.

———. *Lolita*. New York: Vintage, 1992.

———. *Mary*. Translated by Michael Glenny. New York: Vintage, 1970.

———. *Nikolai Gogol*. New York: New Directions, 1944.

———. *Nikolai Gogol*. New York: New Directions, 1961.

———. *Novels and Memoirs*. New York: Library of America, 1996.

———. "On a Book Entitled *Lolita*." In *The Annotated Lolita*, ed. Alfred Appel, Jr., 311–317. New York: Vintage, 1991.

———. "On Generalities"; "Anniversary"; "What Everyone Should Know." In *Think, Write, Speak: Uncollected Essays, Reviews, Interviews, and Letters to the Editor*, ed. Anastasia Tolstoy and Brian Boyd. New York: Knopf, 2019.

———. *The Original of Laura*. New York: Knopf, 2009.

———. *Pale Fire*. New York: Berkeley Books, 1982.

———. *Pale Fire*. New York: Vintage International, 1989.

———. "Philistines and Philistinism." In *Lectures on Russian Literature*, ed. Fredson Bowers, 309–314. San Diego: Harcourt Brace, 1981.

———. *Pnin*. New York: Vintage International, 1990.

———. *The Real Life of Sebastian Knight*. New York: Vintage International, 1992.

———. *A Russian Beauty and Other Stories*. Translated by the Author. New York: McGraw-Hill, 1973.

———. *Selected Letters: 1940–1977*. Ed. Dmitri Nabokov and Matthew J. Bruccoli. New York: Harcourt, 1989.

———. *Sobranie sochinenii russkogo perioda v piati tomakh*, vol. 1. St. Peterburg: Simpozium, 2004.

———. *Sobranie sochinenii russkogo perioda v piati tomakh*, vol. 4. St. Peterburg: Simpozium, 2000.

———. *Speak, Memory: An Autobiography Revisited*. New York: Vintage International, 1989.

———. *The Stories of Vladimir Nabokov*. Translated by Vladimir and Dmitri Nabokov. New York: Vintage International, 1997.

———. *The Stories of Vladimir Nabokov*. Translated by Vladimir and Dmitri Nabokov. New York: Vintage International, 2008.

———. *Strong Opinions*. New York: McGraw-Hill, 1973.

———. *Strong Opinions*. New York: Vintage, 1990.

———. *Think, Write, Speak: Uncollected Essays, Reviews, Interviews, and Letters to the Editor*. Ed. Brian Boyd and Anastasia Tolstoy. New York: Knopf, 2019.

———. *Vladimir Nabokov: Selected Letters, 1940–1977*. Edited by Dmitri Nabokov and Matthew J. Bruccoli. San Diego: Harcourt Brace Jovanovich, 1989.

Nabokov, Vladimir, and Edmund Wilson. *Dear Bunny, Dear Volodya: The Nabokov-Wilson Letters, 1940–1971*. Edited by Simon Karlinsky. Revised and Expanded Edition. Berkeley: U of California P, 2001.

Naiman, Eric. "Hermophobia (On Sexual Orientation and Reading Nabokov)." *Representations* 101, no. 1 (2008): 116–143.

———. "Nabokov and #MeToo: Consent, Close Reading, and the Sexualized Workplace." In *Teaching Nabokov's* Lolita *in the #MeToo Era*, ed. Elena Rakhimova-Sommers, 125–150. Lanham, MD: Lexington Books, 2021.

———. *Nabokov, Perversely*. Ithaca, NY: Cornell UP, 2010.

Nations, Daniel. "How Many iPads Have Been Sold? After an Early Spike, the Market for New iPads Stabilized," last modified March 3, 2021, www.lifewire.com/how-many-ipads-sold-1994296.

Nicholas, Arlene J., and John K. Lewis. "Learning Enhancement or Headache: Faculty and E-Textbooks." In *International Journal of Information Systems in the Service Sector* 5, no. 4 (2013): 63–71.

Norman, Will. *Nabokov, History, and the Texture of Time*. New York: Routledge, 2012.

Olesha, Iurii. *Izbrannie sochineniia*. Moscow: Gosudarstvennoe izdatel'stvo khudozhestvennoi literatury, 1956.

Pacatus, I. M. [Maksim Gor'kii]. "Beglye zametki." *Nizhegorodskii listok* (July 4, 1896): 3.

Parker, Luke. *Nabokov Noir: Cinematic Culture and the Art of Exile*. Ithaca, NY: Cornell UP, 2022.

Peterson, Walter F. *The Berlin Liberal Press in Exile: A History of the Parizer Tageblatt – Parizer Tageszeitung, 1933–1940*. Tübingen: Niemeyer, 1987.

Pieters, Jürgen. "Afterword: (Flipping) Nabokov in the Classroom." In *Vladimir Nabokov's Lectures on Literature: Portraits of the Artist as a Reader and Teacher*, ed. Ben Dhooge and Jürgen Pieters, 211–226. Leiden, Netherlands: Brill Rodopi, 2018.

Pitzer, Andrea. *The Secret History of Vladimir Nabokov*. New York: Pegasus Books, 2013.

Platonov, Andrei. "Vprok." *Krasnaia nov'* 3 (1931): 3–39.

Poe, Edgar Allan. "Twice-Told Tales, By Nathaniel Hawthorne: A Review." *The Works of Edgar Allan Poe*, ed. Edmund Clarence Stedman and George Edward Woodbury, 31–32. New York: Charles Scribner's Sons, 1927.

Pushkin, Aleksandr. *Eugene Onegin: A Novel in Verse*. Trans. Vladimir Nabokov. Princeton, NJ: Princeton UP, 1991.

Qinglong, Peng. "Digital Humanities Approach to Comparative Literature: Opportunities and Challenges." *Comparative Literature Studies* 57, no. 4 (2020): 595–610.

Rakhimova-Sommers, Elena, ed. *Nabokov's Women: The Silent Sisterhood of Textual Nomads*. Lanham, MD: Lexington Books, 2017.

———. *Teaching Nabokov's* Lolita *in the #MeToo Era*. Lanham, MD: Lexington Books, 2021.

Renaud, Terence. *New Lefts: The Making of a Radical Tradition*. Princeton, NJ: Princeton UP, 2021.

Ricoeur, Paul. *Freud and Philosophy: An Essay on Interpretation*. Translated by Denis Savage. New Haven: Yale UP, 1977.

Robinson, David. *Das Cabinet des Dr. Caligari*. 2nd edition. London: British Film Institute, 2013.

Ronen, Omry. "Viktor Shklovsky's Tracks in 'A Guide to Berlin.'" Translated by Susanne Fusso. In *The Joy of Recognition: Selected Essays of Omry Ronen*, ed. Barry P. Sherr and Michael Wachtel, 202–231. Ann Arbor: Michigan Slavic Publications, 2015.

Roper, Robert. *Nabokov in America: On the Road to Lolita*. New York: Bloomsbury, 2015.

Rorty, Richard. *Contingency, Irony, and Solidarity*. New York: Cambridge UP, 1989.

Rubinshtein, Lev. "'Sami-to ponimaiut?' Lev Rubinstein o poshlosti i shevelenii khvostami." *MBKh Media*, February 27, 2021; https://mbk-news.appspot.com/sences/sami-to-ponimayut/.

Russell, Kate Elizabeth. *My Dark Vanessa*. New York: William Morrow, 2020.

Schick, Ron. *Norman Rockwell: Behind the Camera*. New York: Little, Brown, and Company, 2009.

Schiff, Stephen. *Lolita: The Book of the Film*. New York: Applause Books, 1998.

———. *Véra (Mrs. Vladimir Nabokov)*. New York: Modern Library, 2000.

Schulman, Sarah. *Conflict Is Not Abuse: Overstating Harm, Community Responsibility, and the Duty of Repair*. Vancouver: Arsenal Pulp Press, 2017.

———. *The Gentrification of the Mind: Witness to a Lost Imagination*. Berkeley: U of California P, 2012.

Sedgwick, Eve Kosofsky. "Paranoid Reading and Reparative Reading, or, You're So Paranoid, You Probably Think This Essay Is About You." In *Touching Feeling: Affect, Pedagogy, Performativity*, 123–151. Durham, NC: Duke UP, 2003.

Shapiro, Gavriel. "The Beneficial Role of Jews in Vladimir Nabokov's Life and Career." *Nabokov Online Journal* 18 (2019): 1–19.

———. *Delicate Markers Subtexts in Vladimir Nabokov's Invitation to a Beheading*. Frankfurt am Main: Peter Lang, 1998.

Shrayer, Maxim D. "Jewish Questions in Nabokov's Art and Life." In *Nabokov and His Fiction: New Perspectives*, ed. Julian W. Connolly, 73–91. Cambridge: Cambridge UP, 1999.

———. *The World of Nabokov's Stories*. Austin: U of Texas P, 1999.

Shklovsky, Viktor. "Art as Device." In *Viktor Shklovsky: A Reader*, ed. and trans. Alexandra Berlina, 73–96. New York: Bloomsbury Academic, 2016.

Sloterdijk, Peter. *Critique of Cynical Reason*. Translated by Michael Eldred. Minneapolis: U of Minnesota P, 1987.

Spence, Paul. "The Academic Book and Its Digital Dilemmas." *Convergence* 24, no. 5 (2018): 458–476.

Starcher, Keith, and Dennis Proffitt. "Encouraging Students to Read: What Professors Are (and Aren't) Doing about It." *International Journal of Teaching and Learning in Higher Education* 23, no. 3 (2011): 396–407.

St. Clair-Thompson, Helen, Alison Graham, and Sara Marsham. "Exploring the Reading Practices of Undergraduate Students." *Education Inquiry* 9, no. 3 (2018): 284–298.

Street, Sarah, and Joshua Yumibe. *Chromatic Modernity: Color, Cinema, and Media of the 1920s.* New York: Columbia UP, 2019.

Streuman, Barbara. *Figurations of Exile in Hitchcock and Nabokov.* Edinburgh: Edinburgh UP, 2008.

Stuart, Dabney. "The Novelist's Composure: *Speak, Memory* as Fiction." *Modern Language Quarterly* 36, no. 2 (1975): 177–192.

Sweeney, Elizabeth Susan. "Academia." In *Nabokov in Context*, ed. David Bethea, 51–58. Cambridge: Cambridge UP, 2018.

———. "The Small Furious Devil: Memory in 'Scenes from the Life of a Double Monster.'" In *A Small Alpine Form: Studies in Nabokov's Short Fiction*, ed. Charles Nicol and Gennady Barabtarlo, 193–216. New York: Garland, 1993.

Tanselle, G. Thomas. *A Rationale of Textual Criticism.* Philadelphia: U of Pennsylvania P, 1992.

"Teaching Lolita Today." www.thenabokovian.org/comment/71. Last modified April 7, 2019.

Toker, Leona. "'The Dead Are Good Mixers': Nabokov's Versions of Individualism." In *Nabokov and His Fiction: New Perspectives*, ed. Julian Connolly, 92–108. Cambridge: Cambridge UP, 1999.

———. "Liberal Ironists and the 'Gaudily Painted Savage': On Richard Rorty's Reading of Vladimir Nabokov." *Nabokov Studies* 1 (1994): 195–206.

———. *Nabokov: The Mystery of Literary Structures.* Ithaca, NY: Cornell UP, 1989.

Tomasek, Terry. "Critical Reading: Using Reading Prompts to Promote Active Engagement with Text." *International Journal of Teaching and Learning in Higher Education* 21, no. 1 (2009): 127–132.

Tonkery, Dan. "The iPad and Its Possible Impact on Publishers and Libraries." *Searcher* 18, no. 8 (2010): 39–42.

Towles, Amor. *A Gentleman in Moscow.* New York: Viking, 2016.

Trzeciak, Joanna. "'Breaking the News' and 'Signs and Symbols': Silentology." In *Anatomy of a Short Story: Nabokov's Puzzles, Codes, "Signs and Symbols,"* ed. Yuri Leving, 216–223. New York: Continuum, 2012.

Updike, John. Introduction to *Lectures on Literature,* by Vladimir Nabokov, ed. F. Bowers, xvii–xxvii. San Diego: Harcourt Brace Jovanovich, 1980.

Vasmer, Max. *Russisches etymologisches Wörterbuch,* 3 vols. Heidelberg: C. Winters, 1953–1958.

Voronina, Olga. "Vladimir Nabokov's Correspondence with the New Yorker regarding 'Signs and Symbols,' 1946–8." In *Anatomy of a Short Story: Nabokov's Puzzles, Codes, "Signs and Symbols,"* ed. Yuri Leving, 42–60. New York: Continuum, 2012.

Walton, Jean. "Dissenting in an Age of Frenzied Heterosexualism: Kinbote's Transparent Closet in Nabokov's *Pale Fire." College Literature* 21, no. 2 (1994): 89–104.

Wetzsteon, Ross. "Nabokov as Teacher." In *Nabokov: Criticism, Reminiscences, Translations, and Tributes,* ed. Alfred Appel Jr. and Charles Newman, 240–246. Evanston, IL: Northwestern UP, 1970.

White, Duncan. *Nabokov and His Books: Between Late Modernism and the Literary Marketplace.* Oxford: Oxford UP, 2017.

Wiggam, Albert Edward. *Let's Explore Your Mind.* New York: Pocket Books, 1946.

Wilson, Jennifer. "Was 'Lolita' About Race? Vladimir Nabokov on Race in the United States," *Los Angeles Review of Books,* October 31, 2016.

Wood, Michael. *The Magician's Doubts: Nabokov and the Risks of Fiction.* Princeton, NJ: Princeton UP, 1994.

Wyllie, Barbara. *Nabokov at the Movies: Film Perspectives in Fiction.* Jefferson, NC: McFarland, 2003.

Wynn, Natalie. "Incels | ContraPoints." Accessed December 13, 2021. www.youtube.com/watch?v=fD2briZ6fB0.

Yumibe, Yoshua. *Moving Color: Early Film, Mass Culture, Modernism.* New Brunswick, NJ: Rutgers UP, 2012.

Zeitlin, Solomon. "The Names Hebrew, Jew, and Israel: A Historical Study." *Jewish Quarterly Review* 43, no. 4 (1953): 365–379.

Zimmer, Dieter E. "What Happened to Sergey Nabokov." January 2, 2017, http://www.d-e-zimmer.de/PDF/SergeyN.pdf.

Contributors

Galya Diment is the Byron W. and Alice L. Lockwood Professor in the Humanities at the University of Washington, Seattle, where she teaches in the Department of Slavic Languages and Literatures and is also an Affiliate Professor in Jewish Studies. She earned her PhD in Comparative Literature from the University of California, Berkeley. She is the author of *An Autobiographical Novel of Co-consciousness: Goncharov, Woolf, and Joyce* (1994), *Pniniad: Vladimir Nabokov and Marc Szeftel* (1997), and *A Russian Jew of Bloomsbury: The Life and Times of Samuel Koteliansky* (2011). She has also edited and co-edited five more books, including *MLA Approaches to Teaching Lolita* (2008), *Katherine Mansfield and Russia* (2017), and *H. G. Wells and All Things Russian* (2019) as well as published more than sixty articles, some of which appeared in *New York Magazine*, the *Times Literary Supplement*, and *London Magazine*.

Tim Harte is Provost and Professor of Russian at Bryn Mawr College. His academic research focuses on early twentieth-century Russian literature, film, and art. Harte is the author of *Faster, Higher, Stronger, Comrades! Sports, Art, and Ideology in Imperial Russian and Early Soviet Culture* (2020) and *Fast Forward: The Aesthetics and Ideology of Speed in Russian Avant-Garde Culture, 1910–1930* (2009) as well as over ten articles and book chapters, including several on Nabokov, and he is co-editor (with Marina Rojavin) on *Soviet Films of the 1970s and Early 1980s: Conformity and Non-Conformity Amidst Decay* (2021) and *Women in Soviet Film: The Thaw and Post-Thaw Periods* (2018).

Robyn Jensen is Assistant Teaching Professor in the Department of Slavic Languages and Literatures at University of California, Berkeley. She has published on Nabokov and is currently writing a book about Nabokov's engagement with photography and visual culture.

Sara Karpukhin, born and raised in eastern Siberia, currently lives in Madison, Wisconsin, where she teaches undergraduate courses as a Lecturer in Russian at the University of Wisconsin-Madison. Her doctoral dissertation was about Vladimir Nabokov and the classical tradition. In research and pedagogy, her interests include Nabokov, contemporary eastern European art, the uses of history and aesthetics, cultural trauma, clarifying boundaries of individual action and agency, and queering the canon. She also writes fiction and essays.

Yuri Leving is Professor in the Department of Slavic Languages and Literatures at Princeton University. Leving is the founding editor of the *Nabokov Online Journal* (since 2007). Leving has published over a hundred scholarly articles, many of them devoted to Vladimir Nabokov. Leving is the author of six monographs and editor of six volumes of articles, including *Train Station – Garage – Hangar (Vladimir Nabokov and Poetics of Russian Urbanism)* (2004), *Keys to The Gift: A Guide to Vladimir Nabokov's Novel* (2011), *Marketing Literature and Posthumous Legacies: The Symbolic Capital of Leonid Andreev and Vladimir Nabokov* (co-authored with Frederick H. White, 2013), *A Revolution of the Visible: Images on the Retina* (2018), *Shades of Laura: Vladimir Nabokov's Last Novel* The Original of Laura (2013), *Anatomy of a Short Story: Nabokov's Puzzles, Codes, "Signs and Symbols"* (2012); *The Goalkeeper: The Nabokov Almanac* (2010), *Lolita: The Story of a Cover Girl—Vladimir Nabokov's Novel in Art and Design* (co-edited with John Bertram, 2013) and *Nabokov in Motion: Modernity and Movement* (2022). He also served as a commentator on the first authorized Russian edition of *The Collected Works of Vladimir Nabokov* in five volumes.

Luke Parker is Visiting Assistant Professor of Russian at Amherst College. He works on literature, film, and visual culture in exile and is the author of *Nabokov Noir: Cinematic Culture and the Art of Exile* (2022).

Roman Utkin is Assistant Professor of Russian, East European, and Eurasian Studies and Feminist, Gender, and Sexuality Studies at Wesleyan University. He is the author of *Charlottengrad: Russia's Culture in Weimar Berlin* (forthcoming).

José Vergara is Assistant Professor of Russian on the Myra T. Cooley Lectureship at Bryn Mawr College. He specializes in prose of the long twentieth century with an emphasis on experimental works. His first book, *All Future Plunges to the Past: James Joyce in Russian Literature* (2021), examines the reception of Joyce's fiction among Russian writers, including Vladimir Nabokov. He has published on authors including Nabokov, Mikhail Shishkin, and Sasha Sokolov, among others, in a variety of journals, and his writing and interviews can also be found in the *Los Angeles Review of Books*, *Asymptote*, *Words without Borders*, *Music and Literature*, and *World Literature Today*.

Meghan Vicks is the author of *Narratives of Nothing in Twentieth-Century Literature* (2015) and numerous essays on modern and contemporary literature. She currently teaches in the Bay Area.

Olga Voronina, Associate Professor of Russian at Bard College, holds a PhD in Slavic Languages and Literatures from Harvard University and a MA from the Herzen Pedagogical University in St. Petersburg. A former Deputy Director of the Nabokov Museum in St. Petersburg, she has co-edited and co-translated, with Brian Boyd, Nabokov's *Letters to Véra* (2014) as well as published papers and articles on Soviet literature of the Cold War, the post-Soviet transformation of the Russian literary canon, and Nabokov's art and metaphysics. She is the editor of and a contributor to *The Brill Companion to Soviet Children's Literature and Film* (2019).

Lisa Ryoko Wakamiya is Associate Professor of Slavic and Courtesy Associate Professor of English at Florida State University. Her publications include studies of transnational literary migration, post-Soviet literature and film, translation, and the intersections between narrative and material culture.

Matthew Walker is Assistant Professor of Russian at Middlebury College and specializes in nineteenth-, twentieth-, and twenty-first-century Russian literature, with particular focus on Gogol, Nabokov, and the politics of contemporary Russian culture. His first book, *Gogol's Ghosts*, on the history of Nikolai Gogol in Russian literary criticism, is forthcoming.

www.ingramcontent.com/pod-product-compliance
Lightning Source LLC
Chambersburg PA
CBHW080912170426
43201CB00017B/2300